Fréderike Geerdink

THE BOYS ARE DEAD

The Roboski Massacre and the Kurdish Question in Turkey

Gomidas Institute
London

Cover photo by Namık Durukan. Design by Anoush Melkonian.

This publication was made possible in part by a subsidy from the Fonds Bijzondere Journalistieke Projecten, Amsterdam (*www.fondsbjp.nl*).

Translation from Dutch and editing: Anna Asbury, Vivien Glass and Brendan Monaghan

ISBN 978-1-909382-19-0

Gomidas Institute
42 Blythe Rd.
London W14 0HA
United Kingdom
www.gomidas.org
info@gomidas.org

May our hearts shrivel
if we forget Roboski

Introduction to the English Translation

This book was first published in the Netherlands, early 2014. I remember that up until the last moment, I made changes to keep the text up to date. What steps did the survivors and the families of those who died in the massacre take to get justice, and how did attempts to get recognition for their loss and pain fail?

But they were all minor changes within a wider truth that never seemed to change: the Turkish state did not take responsibility for the political murders it committed. Not only the full truth about Roboski massacre remained covered up, but also all other state murders, from the suppression of the Seikh Said uprising to the Dersim massacres in 1937-1938 and the political murders in the 1990s. Of course, these were unsolved murders only to a certain extent : the fact known to many was that the perpetrator was the state.

Right before the publication of this English translation, the ceasefire and peace process between the state and the PKK went to smithereens. It had lasted for two and a half years. The ceasefire was meant to give way to democratic reforms, which would again have paved the way for the final disarmament of the PKK and a truly peaceful future for Turkey. A future which would also have, as the last chapter of this book explains, finally brought answers to those who had lost loved ones at the hands of the state.

The current end of the peace process is a disappointment for the Kurds. On the other hand, history has taught them that their struggle is not a straight line towards justice. The road to peace – which is more than the silence of the weapons – is a bumpy one. There are times of progress, inevitably followed by times of decline. The Kurds have come to consider periods of decline, like the one they are experiencing now, as a part of their ongoing struggle, a part of the way up. Eventually, they will get there.

When you look at developments with such a perspective, you also see that the recent break in the ceasefire and the end of the peace process do not represent change. The constant in this story is, after all, the struggle. And the struggle continues, until the Kurds reach their goal: self determination.

August 2015, Diyarbakir

CONTENTS

Chapter One

28 December 2011, 21:39 - 22:24

You can clearly hear the hum of the drones overhead. There is nothing unusual about that in the mountains on the border between Turkey and Iraq; the men – most are just boys, in fact – who are crossing the border into Iraq to pick up smuggled goods, don't bat an eyelid. The nearby army posts have not sent warning of any planned military activities, and so off they go.

The mules are prepared, and thirty-eight men and boys from the villages of Ortasu and Gülyazı begin to make their way up through Ortasu, keeping well off the main road. The road soon becomes a narrow path, the snow making it increasingly impassable. It's about six kilometres to the border, and they know the way like the backs of their hands, but it will take them a good two hours in these conditions.

They cross the border at post number fifteen: a simple stone with the words TÜRKIYE on one side and IRAQ on the other. A couple of kilometres further on, a lorry is waiting for them, filled to the brim with petrol and sugar. The jerry cans and sacks are strapped to the mules, and then the smugglers turn around and head back to the border on foot.

It's almost half past nine in the evening when they reach the border. The group has split into two, and when the first group crosses back into Turkey, they discover to their surprise that the army has closed off all three paths back to the village. It's not unusual for two paths to be blocked, but the pass is never cut off completely. They start walking back towards the border.

Shots are fired. They don't know why, and carry on walking – everyone in the area knows what they are doing there, so they are not unduly worried about their safety. Shortly afterwards, Turkish Air Force F-16s appear. The first group of smugglers, about eighteen of them, are hit by a bomb. Less than five minutes later, another bomb falls; followed twenty minutes later by another, and one last bomb at half past ten.

Not everyone is immediately killed; eight boys are severely injured. Seven of them die before they can be taken back to the village; one of them, seventeen-year-old Hasan Ürek, spends many months in hospital, but eventually recovers. Another three also survive.

* * *

Back in Ortasu, thirty-six-year-old Lezgin Encü is watching television. He doesn't hear the F-16s, until children start knocking on the door, shouting, 'Planes!' He runs outside and sees them. Shortly afterwards he witnesses bombs falling and feels the ground tremble beneath his feet. 'Our people!' he thinks. 'Our people are being bombed!'

He and some of the other men from the village pile into a few cars and drive as close as they can to the scene of the disaster. The last stretch has to be negotiated on foot. They see soldiers, and shout in panic, 'You're bombing our people!' 'No worries,' they answer, 'we're just scaring them off, that's all.' The bombing resumes a little later.

By now, men have been rounded up in Ortasu and Gülyazı. 'Blankets, bring blankets – as many as you have!' It's about a kilometre from where they had to leave the cars to the site of the bombings. The men climb up a hill. Lezgin Encü says you could see it well from there: fire and smoke. And you could smell it. Gunpowder.

They trudge on further through the snow. When they reach the border, they see what they already know: it wasn't a warning, it was a targeted bombing. All but eight of the smugglers are dead. The wounded are wrapped in blankets and each carried back to the cars by four or five men; seven of them die before getting there. Salih Ürek, just twenty-three, dies in Lezgin Encü's arms.

Once the wounded have been tended, the bodies are also wrapped in blankets, as far as possible. Some of the bodies have been torn apart and it isn't easy to work out which parts belonged to which body. Nor is it always simple to tell whether a particular piece of bone and scorched flesh is from a human being or from one of the pack animals.

* * *

Turkish MP Ertugrul Kürkçü has watched seven hours of video footage. The images are from unmanned Israeli-made Heron drones, used by the Turkish army. These aircraft are permitted to fly up to five kilometres into Iraqi air space and to use thermal cameras.

A month and a half after the bombings, on 15 February 2012, Kürkçü watches the footage with the other members of a specially established subcommittee of the parliamentary human rights commission. All four parties in Turkey's parliament are represented in the eight-member strong commission, and they all see the same thing: civilians smuggling.

The caravan slowly moves from Turkey into Iraq. On the other side, no more than a kilometre from the border, the lorries are waiting with their loads of petrol and sugar. The contraband is fastened onto the mules, and the group heads straight back.

It's as clear as day that they aren't rebels from the Kurdish guerrilla group, the PKK – not only because of what they are doing, but also because of the size of the group, and their total lack of discipline. It is, all things considered, a disorderly bunch. The group doesn't work as a unit; some of them are walking hundreds of metres ahead of others. There are almost forty of them, while rebels never move in groups of more than eight to ten people; and although rebels do use mules, they would never use dozens of them in a cross-border mission.

One of the commission members is crying, even before the images of the bombing have started. It affects him deeply to see the smugglers walking straight towards their deaths. And then the sound of the F-16s. 'What would rebels do?' Kürkçü asks. 'They would immediately spread out and run for cover.' The smugglers do the exact opposite, running to each other, forming a tight group and holding on to each other. 'They were afraid,' said Kürkçü. 'They were just kids.'

Chapter Two

The Village

Seven days after the massacre, I'm sitting on the floor of a house in Gülyazı. The smell of sweaty feet pervades the over-heated room. I'm surrounded by relatives of the dead, all wanting to tell their own stories. Everybody is talking at the same time, all of them wanting my attention. One of the women lost a son in the tragedy; her other son had lost a foot from stepping on a landmine – how would they survive now that their main breadwinner was dead? Someone else points out a young boy of about twelve whose elder brother was killed and who was already fatherless; from now on he would have to smuggle to provide an income for his family.

I notice a teenage girl and a younger boy sitting quietly by the fire; she has tears in her eyes. 'Who are you?' I ask. Her name is Semire, she's seventeen, and the boy next to her is her eleven-year-old brother, Seyvan. They have lost their brother Bedran in the bombing. At just twelve, he was one of the two youngest victims. 'Bedran should have been back from the trip at about eleven o'clock,' Semire gently tells me. 'We'd prepared a meal for him, but afterwards I fell asleep. When I woke up the next morning, I heard people crying – Bedran was gone.'

* * *

I see the news on my phone on 29 December 2011, the morning after the bloodbath. Before getting out of bed, I check my mobile – as I do every morning – for the past few hours' tweets. I follow many Kurds and Kurdish media, and the stream of tweets soon makes the news clear to me: it looks like the army has bombed a group of Kurdish villagers who were smuggling on the Turkish-Iraqi border. More than thirty people have been killed.

Jumping out of bed, I turn on the television and flip through the television news channels, NTV, CNN Türk and Habertürk. I see weather forecasts, economic news and something about football. This surprises me, but I realise I've switched on halfway through a broadcast and will probably have to wait: the most important news is recapped on the hour and half hour. I don't bother showering – unable to miss a second of the news – I make coffee and carry on flipping from one channel to the next in my T-shirt and jogging bottoms.

In the meantime, I start tweeting about the news myself. Since I'm not yet sure exactly what happened, I'm careful what I write. Photos start coming in on my Twitter feed from the Kurdish press agency Dicle Haber Ajansı (DIHA for short). I see a row of bodies wrapped in blankets, feet in sturdy shoes sticking out from underneath. People tying bodies to mules, so they can be taken to the tarmac road, where a car is waiting and bodies are being piled into it. Men crying with their hands over their eyes. I forward the images to my Twitter followers and let them know that the Turkish channels have not yet said anything about the tragedy.

The news on CNN Türk is just starting. I'm on the edge of my seat – how are they going to break the news. To my consternation, however, they simply don't. The main item is the Turkish National Security Council's response to a law passed by the French parliament a week earlier, making it a criminal offence to deny the Armenian Genocide of 1915. Then there's an item about whether President Abdullah Gül will leave politics at the end of his term of office. And then? Football – more specifically the bribery scandal engrossing Turkey at the time. It's no different on the other channels.

I deplore the Turkish media on Twitter: more than thirty civilians have died and this isn't news? How is it possible? If a Turkish soldier is killed in fighting, it's all over the news, but thirty-odd Kurdish villagers isn't a newsworthy item?

Then I suddenly receive a private message on Twitter – from a journalist at one of the major Turkish television channels. She writes: 'My dear, we fought the whole morning to bring out at least one short news item about this but Ankara said 'no'! It's out of our hands. I'm so sorry.'

She immediately sends another message: 'Believe me.... We are in tears here.... This is turning into a masquerade.....'

And then another: 'They just called us and said: "Unless this story is confirmed by an official, you are not permitted to report on this. Full stop."'

Prime minister Erdoğan* – that's who she means by 'Ankara' – has had his officials call the major television networks to tell them what they may and may not broadcast. I'm flabbergasted, but not surprised. Since coming to

* Prime Minister Erdogan was elected President on 10 August 2014

Turkey in 2006 as a freelance correspondent, with human rights as one of my specialisations, I've explored the country's press freedom – or rather, lack of it. In the months before the bloodbath, the government strengthened its grip on the press.

Earlier that year, on 20 October, editors in chief and media owners had already been summoned by the prime minister. The meeting followed a PKK attack in Hakkâri province on the night of 19 October, in which twenty-four servicemen had been killed and twenty-two injured. After discussions between the prime minister and the press, various press agencies, including the semi-official Anadolu Agency, which is used by practically all the media, declared they would adhere to official publication bans. When reporting on news related to 'terrorism and incidents of violence,' they would 'take public order into account.' They also promised 'to refrain from reporting news that could instil fear, chaos, hostility, panic and intimidation,' and that 'no publication whatsoever shall contain propaganda for an illegal organisation.'

It was not only press agencies that acceded to these demands, but also major newspapers and television stations, such as CNN Türk – which is owned by media tycoon Aydin Doğan's Doğan Media Group. The rationale is simple: Turkish media tycoons almost always have other business interests, in the building industry, the energy market and mining, to name just a few sectors. If you don't want to damage those business interests, or forego potential government contracts, you deploy your media strategically. Complying with Erdoğan's wishes is also good for sales figures, since the average Turkish newspaper reader is not interested in critical journalism that pursues the truth; they prefer not to have their Turkish nationalist world image upset. A few days after attending the meeting with Erdoğan, Yasemin Çongar, assistant editor-in-chief of *Taraf*, a newspaper fiercely critical of the army, wrote that she was taken aback to see media owners make more proposals than Erdoğan himself to 'standardise' the press.

In an interview a year and a half later, Çongar said: 'It began with a speech by Erdoğan in which he talked about what he regarded as the thin dividing line between propaganda and journalism. The rest of the meeting was private and "off the record," but now I'm able to talk about it. Aydin Doğan suggested establishing a group of publishers and chief editors, who would draw up rules on how to break sensitive news. A government representative was also to be included in the group, but Erdoğan did not think it necessary. I don't know whether the group was ever set up. Someone else, however, proposed three main rules: don't invite anyone who doesn't regard the PKK as a terrorist organisation, don't talk to the PKK or visit their camps on the Iraqi border as this would be propaganda for the PKK, and limit "breaking news" about violence related to the struggle against the PKK to fifteen seconds.' Çongar also said that the meeting included discussions about stopping visits to 'certain places' and talks with 'certain people.' Çongar added: 'As no one said a word, I eventually decided to speak up and said I was one of those people that visited "certain places" and talked to "certain people," and would definitely continue to do so.'

Incidentally, the meeting didn't change existing practice; the unwritten rules were simply reconfirmed, and the audience with Erdoğan gave it extra weight.

Fellow chief editors complimented Çongar on her protest afterwards. 'But during the meeting itself,' Çongar commented, 'everyone kept their mouths shut, afraid of the publishers and owners of their newspapers, who were also present. *Taraf*'s owner was there too, but *Taraf* is independent and not part of a large company, so I have greater freedom.'

However, that eventually came to an end too. In December 2012, both chief editor and prominent columnist Ahmet Altan and Yasemin Çongar resigned from *Taraf*. Altan said he wanted to devote more time to writing novels; Çongar was silent at the time, but a couple of months later she said, 'The pressure was too much for me. Ahmet could no longer write what he wanted to, and I had no freedom in compiling the front page. For example, *Taraf*'s owner brought me ready-made articles that hadn't been written by journalists, and I refused to publish them. But at the same time I understood him: he had invested a lot of his own money in the newspaper, the banks were refusing to lend to him, and he was losing advertisers – all due to government pressure. Ahmet and I didn't want to bend to the pressure and resigned.'

There's no doubt about it: the journalists are always the ones left holding the baby, as it were. The journalist who sent me a private message on Twitter was only prepared to talk to me if I promised her total anonymity, so I haven't even used her initials. 'The phone calls,' she says, 'were either from Erdoğan's officials or from deputy prime minister Arınç's department, which deals with media issues. They constantly keep an eye on all the major channels. The chief editors were warned on the morning after the bombing in Uludere not to show any images, provide any figures or use the red banners that normally announce breaking news. Neither were we allowed to report the news on the website or on the news ribbon at the bottom of the television screen.'

In practice, my colleague told me, Twitter is the only way of breaking news to the outside world in this kind of situation. Not that she did so herself: 'If, like me, you use your own name on Twitter, you have to be careful. I work for a major television station.' If she broke the rules, she'd be out of a job.

At the end of the morning, at 11:45, the editors of the major television channels are given permission to report on the tragedy. They broadcast an eight-point statement from the military leadership on the bombing.

The first point in the statement is a reminder that the air attack is in line with permission given by the Turkish parliament on 17 October 2007 to carry out operations on Iraqi territory, permission that was granted for one year and renewed each subsequent year. The army then states that the 'leaders of the terrorist organisation' were planning a retaliatory attack for earlier losses and strengthening their troops in the Sinat-Haftanin region in Iraqi Kurdistan. Information from various sources and a technical analysis apparently showed that the terrorist organisation was planning an attack on a police station and an army base near the border.

The army also states that in earlier attacks carried out by the separatist terrorist organisation, the terrorists smuggled the heavy weapons, ammunition and explosives on mules across the border from Iraq. Since they were receiving more and more information about an activity being planned by the separatist terrorist organisation, observations had been intensified, and on 28 December 2011 at 18:39, a group was identified approaching the Turkish border from Iraq. The army then states that the area was used regularly by terrorists, and it was for this reason that the decision was made to fire on the group. The army defines the place where the bombing took place, the Sinat-Haftanin region, as an area where the separatist terrorist organisation had base camps and which was not inhabited by civilians. Finally, the army states that an administrative and legal investigation into the incident is still under way.

On the Way to the Village: Who Are These Smugglers?

I spend the last few days of the year glued to the television, on Twitter, and perusing the newspapers. The images of the funeral on 30 December affect me deeply. A great mass of people is moving through the rugged, snow-flecked mountain landscape towards the burial ground, a ribbon of thirty-four coffins draped with the Kurdish colours red, green and yellow, visible in the crowd. Nineteen of the dead are under the age of eighteen; twenty-six are from the Encü family.

It touches me deeply, but at the same time I understand so little. Who are these smugglers? What were they doing there on the Iraqi border, even though it's well-known that the PKK has base camps there? Why would they take that risk? And young lads of twelve or thirteen, do they really get sent out smuggling? If so, why?

There's another thing I don't understand; many of the victims come from families of village guards, armed villagers who pass on information to the army, who are supposed to protect their village against the PKK and who can be called up to join the fighting. All this for a fixed monthly salary and a Kalashnikov from the state. If they were working as village guards – and thus receiving an income – why would they smuggle? As far as I know, the village guards are despised by many other Kurds.

Yet another question keeps going through my mind. Was this bombing accidental? If the Kurdish media is to be believed, the smugglers were in close contact with the local army posts, and they always turned a blind eye to smuggling. In fact, the army posts were said to always warn the villagers about any planned anti-PKK activities, so smuggling could be postponed for a couple of days in the interests of safety. Was that true? Had that not happened this time? Why not?

Within a couple of days, media coverage becomes completely polarised, as is always the case in Turkey. The Kurdish media loudly declare that the bloodbath in Uludere was not an accident but a deliberate murder of Kurdish civilians. I'm appalled by the overblown rhetoric; how could they possibly reach such conclusions after just a couple of days?

In the meantime, Erdoğan has the 'standardised press' just where he wants it. The entire affair is framed as an accident, and what's more, as an accident that the villagers have more or less brought upon themselves: what were they doing in PKK territory anyway? Some Turkish newspapers tell their readers that the victims were not smugglers at all, but PKK supporters, transporting its weapons. In other words, you reap what you sow.

About five days pass, and I can't stand it any longer. What am I doing in Istanbul when 1700 kilometres away – whichever way you look at it – the Turkish state has committed the biggest massacre of Kurds for decades? I pack my suitcase and call my assistant Beyda: 'Are you coming with me to Uludere?' We meet the next morning at 5:25 am, on the first flight to Diyarbakır.

* * *

I've never been to Şırnak, the province in which Ortasu and Gülyazı are located. Şırnak and Hakkâri are Turkey's two most southeasterly provinces. Şırnak borders Syria and Iraq; Hakkâri is adjacent to Iraq and Iran. To the west of Şırnak is the province of Mardin, to the north of which is Diyarbakır province. Almost all Turkish provinces are named after the provincial capital.

Diyarbakır is by far the largest city in the Kurdish southeast of Turkey, with approximately one million inhabitants; the entire province has a population of around half a million. It is the cultural and political heart of the Kurdish region, although nothing suggests this as you approach it by air. There is a single runway; the aeroplane always parks at the same spot, after which you have to walk across the concrete to the tiny arrivals hall with a single rattling baggage conveyor belt.

Civil aviation is a minor activity here; the airport is primarily a military base. It is from here, the home base of the Eighth Air Wing of the Second Air Force Command, that Turkey fights the PKK. F-16s depart from here every day, soaring noisily above the city, often on their way to bomb PKK camps in northern Iraq. It's grating enough for visitors, let alone for the city dwellers, many of whom have relatives in the PKK.

The airport is right next to the city. Go one street further and you're in the middle of Baglar, a large working class neighbourhood. Come rain or shine, the streets are always bustling. Hawkers push handcarts along loaded with goods, tea is hauled around, shops display their wares out on the pavement, and shoe shine boys accost passers by whose shoes look like they could use a lick of polish. Diyarbakır is also full of smells – the aroma of roasted chestnuts, fresh bread from bakeries and street ovens, the smell of smouldering iron from the smithies, fried *kenara*, fruit, tobacco and the fires women make on the streets for grilling vegetables. It often smells of tear gas.

As soon as we arrive, Beyda and I get the bus to Şırnak, a little over 200 kilometres further east as the crow flies. The journey takes us through Mardin, a beautiful ancient hilltop town, predominantly inhabited by Christians and Arabs for centuries. The historic centre, with its many stone steps and incredible views over the plains of Mardin, is only really accessible on foot. As we drive away from Mardin, I sit twisted awkwardly in my seat, so as to enjoy the view of the city for as long as possible.

We turn left out of Mardin and drive along the Syrian border, which at the time is still a haven of peace in an already turbulent Arabic world. Signs on fences warn of landmines. According to the Turkish Committee on Mine Clearance, which is affiliated with the Ministry of National Defence, there are almost 614,000 landmines along the Syrian border. Some of these were planted between 1956 and 1959, during the Cold War, when tensions were high between Syria (supported by the Soviet Union) and Turkey as a member of NATO. Most of them, however, were planted after 1984, the year in which the PKK began its armed conflict. No more landmines have been laid since 1999, when the international Mine Ban Treaty came into force, although Turkey only officially became a party to the treaty in 2003.

For the PKK, this has never been a practical border through which to enter Turkey. The area is flat – you can't keep a low profile here, as you can in the mountains on the Iraqi border. When the PKK, and its leader Abdullah Öcalan, fled to Syria following the military coup in Turkey in 1980, they did forge links with the Syrian government; but from 1984, when the armed conflict began in earnest, almost all attacks were carried out from Iraq.

Our first stop in the province of Şırnak was Cizre. On arrival, it looks just like any other ordinary town. It's cold, there's muddy snow on the ground and the streets are characterised by men in dark robes, some sporting purple or black and white checked headscarves. The bus station is tiny; you can buy chicken or beef rolls, crisps and biscuits, but that's it. We have a ten-minute break. Some of the men go outside for a cigarette, and tea, of course, as the Kurds are wont to do if they have even a minute to spare. The station toilets are clean enough.

Just as you're getting snug in your seat, and the monotonous sound of the wheels is sending you to sleep, there is the most spectacular view of one of the two lifelines of Mesopotamia: the Tigris River. For a short stretch, the road runs parallel to the wide river, with its backdrop of bare, rocky mountains. It is breathtakingly beautiful, particularly thanks to the river's austerity. Broad and majestic, it flows unstoppably and undisturbed by man; no tea gardens, no amusement, no boats, no souvenirs; nothing but the great river itself.

We finish the 285 kilometre route in five hours. Şırnak bus station is little more than a car park, where two young men are waiting for us when we arrive. They are friends of Beyda – that is to say, she is friends with the sister of one of them, which makes her a friend of the family who will put us up for the night. I'm starting to realise that you cannot afford Kurdish people any greater pleasure than to be a guest in their home. 'Are you only staying for one night? You will stay with us on your way back, won't you? Are you hungry? Here, have some tea.'

When I'm lodging somewhere, you can do me no greater pleasure than giving me a traditional Kurdish bed. Every Kurdish home has several of them, piled up in one of the rooms and covered with a large sheet. They are brought out for everyone each evening – no one has their own bed or bedroom. First there is a really heavy mattress, about a centimetre thick and made of raw cotton stuffed with wool. This is usually – but not always – covered with a sheet, and then a duvet, which is as heavy as lead and almost impossible to lift with one hand. It's also filled with wool, and instead of raw cotton, it's covered with a soft, glossy material in bright colours. You sleep like a baby, under a duvet weighing around ten kilos.

Smuggling With the Army's Knowledge

The next morning, a minibus brings us to Gülyazı. Beyda and I are joined by Aziz. We met by chance the day before, in Şırnak – he's a friend of the family we're staying with, and has come to visit them in the evening. A correspondent for the Kurdish press agency Dicle, he's one of the journalists who have been reporting from Gülyazı and Ortasu over the last few days. He says he can easily bring us into contact with people there.

The road to the two villages is winding and the landscape desolate. There are army posts everywhere, along the roadside but also higher up in the hills and mountains. There are two military police checkpoints on our route. We discuss whether we need a 'strategy,' in case we are questioned, but I'm not in favour of it. My residence permit, which they will want to see if we're stopped, bears the word BASIN (press) in capital letters, so there is no point whatsoever in claiming I'm a 'traveller' or even a 'tourist.' And yes, we are stopped twice. We smile, answer questions truthfully about where we are going (the road we are on has very few destinations anyway), and are waved on. It doesn't surprise me; in the years that I have been working in Turkey, no one has ever obstructed my work as an officially accredited journalist.*

The further we drive, the more impressive the mountains become; steep, craggy and with little vegetation. Large areas of land are fenced off: military terrain, entry prohibited. Occasionally we come across a shepherd with a herd of sheep. I am told the herds used to be much larger, but since the fences were erected and many mountain pastures (*yaylas*) were declared off limits, so much less land is available for grazing that people can barely make a living from sheep herding.

On the other side of the road, a stream, the Ortasu, runs parallel to the road, sometimes so deep in the valley that you lose sight of it. As we round a bend, an enormous concrete wall looms up in front of us: it's a dam under construction. The heavy trucks and machinery needed for the work have damaged the road to such an extent that our *dolmuş* (shared taxi) can only proceed by jolting and lurching along at a snail's pace. This dam, like others being built in the area, doesn't provide the locals with work. The companies that build these enormous installations are based in other parts of Turkey, and bring their own employees to do the work.

About an hour and a half later, just one bend in the road away from the village of Ortasu, Aziz asks the driver to drop us off; we have arrived in Gülyazı. Fifty metres behind us is a petrol station and ahead, to the left, is an enormous white tent. On the left there is an internet café and two small shops. The Ortasu rises in the mountains further up from here, and flows through the village of Gülyazı and under the road, before taking a wide bend and continuing through the countryside. Single storey houses, their roofs protected from the snow and rain with blue tarpaulins, are perched on the banks of the stream, set against the mountain backdrop.

We turn left behind the white tent – which turns out to be an open-sided sports hall – onto the only tarmac road leading to the village. The road has been poorly maintained and is full of potholes, and our shoes are like giant suction pads on the mixture of mud and snow. The road bends to the left near the mosque, and I'm shocked to suddenly see a fence with an enormous plastic banner hanging from it, bearing the faces of the victims of the bombing. The faces of thirty-four men and boys stare at us. The words on the banner read: 'Erdoğan's thirty-three bullets. Dersim, Zilan,

* This changed early 2015, when the state started to prosecute me for making propaganda for a terrorist organisation.' I was aquitted on 13 April 2015 but the prosecutor appeals my acquittal.

Ağrı, today Qilaban. Erdoğan, murderer.' Thirty-three bullets is a reference to the killing of thirty-three Kurdish smugglers on the Iranian border by an army commander in 1943, which has gone down as an infamous massacre in Kurdish history. There were Kurdish rebellions in Dersim, Zilan and Ağrı in the 1920s and 1930s, which were brutally crushed by the Turkish army, resulting in many deaths. Qilaban is the Kurdish name for Uludere.

We don't have much time. It's ten o'clock and we want to get a minibus back before it gets dark at the end of the afternoon. I actually rather dislike this kind of hurried journalism – particularly when it involves something as terrible as this – but I have other work waiting for me. This was an unscheduled trip, and Aziz also has to get back by the next day for his other job, in the municipality of Şırnak. Nevertheless, I want to write two reports in the couple of hours we have: one for the Dutch news agency ANP on something newsworthy that will hopefully come my way, and one for the Dutch weekly youth newspaper *7Days* on youngsters who smuggle.

I'm taking in the faces of the predominantly young victims on the banner, when Aziz appears with some men he has gathered together. 'Who do you want to speak to? It's your call,' one of them says. They seem to be used to journalists who need to write at least one story in limited time. 'The relatives,' I say, 'child smugglers. A survivor of the bloodbath, if possible.' 'Who do you want first?' They are apparently all available on demand. 'It doesn't matter,' I decide. So I get all of them at once; in a hot, packed house, where, like everyone else, I leave my shoes at the front door.

Smuggling, Servet Encü (thirty-five) tells me, has been going on in the region ever since the border was drawn between Iraq and Turkey, in 1926. It's one of the few ways of scraping together a living here. Smuggling petrol is particularly lucrative, because the fuel tax is sky high in Turkey, but not in Iraq. Sugar and cigarettes are another popular source of trade. 'And there is hardly any other work to be found here,' he says. The others nod in agreement.

The villagers tell me what I've already read in some media: smuggling takes place with the army's knowledge. The local army commanders know full well that there are few other sources of income and turn a blind eye to illegal trade. Servet Encü: 'We keep in touch with the army posts. They tell us when activities are planned against the PKK, so we can postpone the smuggling for a couple of days. It's been this way for years.

This time we didn't receive any warnings that something might happen, so we went.'

He tells me they heard drones flying over the area, 'But there are always drones; it doesn't mean anything.'

During my travels through southeastern Turkey, I often witness proof of the semi-legality of smuggling. The day before in Cizre, for example, our bus had driven to a deserted car park, where there were warehouses with iron shutters. The bus stopped close to one of the warehouses, a couple of men came out, the shutters rattled open and a small fuel pump was rolled outside. The pump's hose led to a tank inside the warehouse, and hey presto, the bus was refuelled with illegal petrol. Everyone knows where to find these places, and no one does anything about it.

The upshot is that petrol stations often don't sell petrol, simply because there is no demand. A few months later when I was in Şırnak and my rental car was almost out of petrol, I only found fuel at the third petrol station I tried. The first petrol station was primarily a grocer and car wash. 'Fill her up,' I said with a smile to the attendant, after parking my car alongside the pump. 'Sorry, we don't sell petrol,' was his answer. Fortunately, at the second station, which apparently only served as a carwash and carpet cleaner, they were able to tell me where to find a petrol station in Şırnak that actually sold fuel.

I certainly find survivor Servet Encü's story convincing. The area is so overrun by soldiers that it would be impossible for the villagers to smuggle without the army knowing about it. There are gendarmerie posts scattered all over the mountains, and drones circle constantly above both Turkish and Iraqi territory: American ones over the mountains in Iraq and Turkish drones on the Turkish side of the border. The Americans share the information gathered by their drones with Turkey, and images are constantly scanned and assessed by Turkish army experts.

If a group of as many as twenty to fifty smugglers, together with at least as many mules, takes the same route from Turkey to Iraq and later back again at about the same time year in year out, this simply cannot have gone unnoticed. Which means Servet Encü is right: the smugglers are always recognised, and left in peace.

I feel a bit uncomfortable asking Servet if it's true he's a village guard. No, he says, he's never been a guard. 'But plenty of others here are,' he adds. 'Did you see any factories on the way here? No. There's nothing here, absolutely nothing – you're either a village guard or a smuggler; there's no other work here.' Villagers with government weapons are paid 700 lira (less than 250 euros) a month by the government, in return for their support in the struggle against the PKK.

The system of village guards in Turkey dates back almost a century. It was set up in the early days of the Turkish Republic, which was founded in 1923, to help guard the newly established long borders. It was abolished in the 1960s, as it was deemed undemocratic.

After the first PKK attacks in August 1984, the system was soon re-established, and by late 1985 there were already around 13,000 village guards. Some of them were forced to become guards; those who refused were either forced to leave the village or murdered. Some Kurds voluntarily took up arms for the state – primarily those who belonged to the elite and enjoyed significant power in traditional feudal Kurdish society. To them, opposing the communist, fiercely anti-feudal PKK was a way of securing their own power. The number of village guards increased to between 50,000 and 90,000 during the 1990s.

As I understand it, village guards are despised by other Kurdish people for their loyalty to the state, and often feared too. And yet the images I saw on television of the mourners and the funerals in Gülyazı, and my encounters with people here, seem to demonstrate a great sense of unity and solidarity. So how do things stand? Is the village united – or was it divided, and has it come together at a time of such tragedy? Servet Encü: 'It makes no difference who is or isn't a village guard, and no one is judged for doing so. It's just a way of earning money. What else can we do?'

How Villagers Became Village Guards

It isn't until months later that I hear the real story about how the people of Ortasu and Gülyazı became village guards, and then I understand Servet's story better. Until the 1990s, Ortasu and Gülyazı were apparently small villages, little more than hamlets. A large proportion of those who now live here lived in Zevîya at the time – Tarlabaşi in Turkish – a tiny village even closer to the Iraqi border.

One day in April 1993, soldiers arrived in Zevîya. Kadriye Encü, now 55 years old, remembers it clearly: 'It was early in the morning. They pointed their guns at us and told us we had to become village guards. We refused, just like we had done before. That's why we had to leave. We barely had time to grab any of our things.'

Kadriye and her husband went outside with their children, taking a single mattress and blanket with them; that was all. As they left Zevîya on foot, together with the other villagers, the soldiers set fire to the village. Kadriye: 'When we saw the flames, it was as if we ourselves were set alight. The fire burnt inside us.'

Only later did they see and hear that the army had cleared many other villages in the same way. Kadriye: 'I think Zevîya was one of the first villages in the area they set fire to. We had been under pressure from the army for years because they suspected us of helping the PKK.'

Kadriye recalls occasionally coming across fighters when they took their livestock to graze in high pastures. She calls the PKK fighters *heval*, and sometimes uses the word *karker*: *heval* is Kurdish for friend; *karker* means worker – and is a reference to the meaning of the acronym PKK: *Partiya Karkeren Kurdistan*, or the Kurdistan Workers Party. 'The *heval*,' she says, 'explained to us who they were and what they were doing. We didn't really understand much.'

She laughs as she tells us that she was afraid the first few times she saw PKK fighters. 'I thought that Azrael, the angel of death, had come to get us. But the *heval* spoke Kurdish, they were our people, so we felt safe with them nearby.'

From her story, and those of other villagers originally from Zevîya, it is clear that they were always stuck between the PKK and the Turkish army. 'The PKK would come to us at night for food,' Kadriye said, 'and the army during the day. We gave both of them bread. The PKK was angry that we gave bread to the army, and the army put us under pressure not to help the PKK. What could we do? We couldn't send someone away hungry, could we? If it was our last bread, we would still give it away – even to the army, and even though they treated us badly.'

This bad treatment has been going on for years. Kadriye and some of the other women remember how the army often came to search their homes early in the morning. Everyone would have to gather in the village square and wait until the soldiers had turned their houses upside down. Kadriye: 'They took anything they thought we might use to help the PKK. That's how we lost our radios and sewing machines.'

Several villagers told us, independently of each other, about a mortar attack on Zevîya sometime before the village was cleared. It lasted the whole night, the villagers hiding in caves near the village cemetery. Nobody died, only some cattle. The next day, the soldiers arrived with spades, surprised to find the villagers alive; they had come to bury the dead. It was not only the PKK and the army who came to the villagers for food and other help, but also the Peshmerga, Kurdish soldiers from northern Iraq. They were fleeing from Saddam Hussein and wanted shelter, which the villagers provided. Kadriye summarises the situation: 'We helped everyone, but nobody helped us.'

The Turkish army began clearing villages at the end of the 1980s. This was legal because a state of emergency had been declared in the region, giving the district governor the authority to evacuate villages without informing their inhabitants beforehand.

Kurdish villagers were not the primary target of the evacuation and burning of the villages, but rather the PKK. The guerrilla group, set up in 1978, staged its first attack in 1984. The villages in the southeast were of vital importance to the organisation: villagers provided fighters – be it voluntarily or under pressure – with food and sometimes clothing, and were also an important source of information. Razing the villages to the ground and driving away their inhabitants was a heavy blow to the PKK.

According to American journalist Aliza Marcus, who wrote the book *Blood and Belief* about the history of the PKK, the areas between the cities and the mountains were virtually uninhabited during the latter half of the 1990s, thanks to the forced evacuations. Even new recruits who wanted to join the PKK found it difficult or even impossible to reach PKK camps in the mountains. According to international human rights organisations Amnesty International and Human Rights Watch, a total of almost 3,000 villages and hamlets were destroyed. It's impossible to say exactly how many people were forced to leave their homes, but estimates by both Turkish and international human rights organisations range from 275,000 to two million.

Many thousands of villagers were left homeless, most of whom migrated to the large cities, either in or outside Kurdish areas. Cities like Diyarbakır and Batman grew explosively, and all of the provincial capitals in the southeast were inundated with refugees from the villages. Some of them had to live in tents for extended periods, even during the freezing winter months.

Migration to other parts of Turkey also increased greatly during those years; people moved as a result of the violence, and the increasingly deplorable economic situation in the southeast. Cities like İzmir in the west, and Mersin and Adana in the south, now have tens of thousands – and Istanbul even has millions – of Kurdish inhabitants.

There was not much press freedom in those days either: on the army's orders, Turkish media kept absolutely silent about what was happening in the southeast of the country. Turks didn't know anything about the destruction of thousands of villages, and regarded the Kurdish immigrants not as refugees but as economic migrants. Urban life resulted in massive poverty for many of these people. Firstly, there was hardly any work for all of them; and secondly, the cost of living was much higher. In the villages people often made a living from small-scale farming and from their animals; in addition, they didn't have to pay rent because they built their own homes. In the city, they had to buy groceries and pay rent.

It was different for the refugees from Zevîya. A small number fled straight over the border, settling in the Iraqi border town of Zakho. Villagers who witnessed the event said that the army arrested seven heads of families from the remaining group of around 400 people. They were used for blackmail: if the villagers wanted their leaders back, every family would have to provide one village guard. The villagers agreed in order to save their men from Turkish prisons. Henceforth, they were village guards.

Their new contract with the state deprived them of the freedom to determine their own future. Moving to an urban centre to find other work was no longer an option since they now worked for the army. In the first year after the village was evacuated, they lived in simple, rickety houses made of wood and sticks, near Ortasu and right next to the stream. The army then moved all the remaining villagers to an unoccupied gendarmerie outpost, where they ended up spending a year. 'There were hardly any windows,' Kadriye says. 'And there weren't enough rooms for everyone. We were squeezed in together – sometimes there were three families in a single room.'

Their final destination, two years after Zevîya was burnt to the ground, was Gülyazı. The part of the village where they now live – the part I was shown on my first visit – right beside the main road, did not exist before the 1990s. Kadriye Encü was thirty-six when she rescued her children from the flames that destroyed Zevîya in 1993. Her son Hamza was just a toddler at the time; she lost him in the bombing of Uludere.

Zevîya, the Ruined Village

One morning in the spring of 2013, I get into a car with two older men wearing traditional green robes and black and white checked scarves wrapped around their heads, and two younger members of the Encü family, and travel with them from Gülyazı to Zevîya. I want Kadriye to come with us, but that turns out to be impossible: every morning she goes to a nearby field with a large group of women, where goats are herded and milked every day by their owners. Many of the men go to Zevîya every morning, so it made sense to go with them.

We first drive through Ortasu, turn left, passing the place the villagers had lived during that first year after Zevîya was evacuated. After a while, in the middle of nowhere, one of the men gets out: this is his land. Women from Gülyazı are picking herbs in the fields and along the road verges, gathering them in large, loosely woven traditional rucksacks worn loosely over the shoulders.

After some five kilometres, the tarmac road forks, and we park the car. Twenty-one-year-old Faruk Encü points at the road that heads left, disappearing into the mountains. 'That road goes to Zakho, but there are mines further on and an army post, so you can't go there.'

We take the road to the right, which soon becomes a dirt track. After a couple of hundred metres, I look behind me and can't see the other older man any longer. He has disappeared in the long grass, making his way to his land. Suddenly, on the left side of the road, we see the ruin of a house. Part of the façade is still standing, as is part of the wall on the left. 'This was my family's house,' says Faruk. We clamber through the ruins and he explains what we are looking at.

There's an arch, which was the upper aspect of the front entrance. It is only partially visible because the rubble is piled at least a metre high. Above this, two equidistant holes in the wall mark where the supporting beams were originally. Another family lived on the upper floor. There is a huge walnut tree in front of the house, which provided so many nuts that they sometimes had enough to sell part of the harvest.

The heart of the village was a little further along. There are several dozen blue beehives among the ruins of the first house we see. They are still in use, providing Gülyazı with honey. To the left of the house, I notice a man on a patch of land; he's wearing traditional clothes and a black and white checked scarf around his head. It is fifty-seven-year-old Sefik Encü. He tells us that he comes here every day, often covering the distance between Gülyazı and Zevîya on foot. He is on his way to plant some tomato plants a little higher up.

We scramble after him. The land where he grows his vegetables is right next to where he used to live. Today he's planting tomatoes; later in the week it will be aubergines and peppers. 'Just hang on a sec,' Sefik says, 'I'm going to get water.' I expect him to return with a bucket of water, but they do things differently there. I see him digging his spade into the earth at a couple of strategic spots, and lo and behold, the village brook now also branches off to his plot. A few shovel loads and the water is now flowing right between the strips of land where he is about to plant his tomatoes.

He passes the spade to Faruk, who makes another branch for some lower-lying land, with a couple of well-aimed plunges. Using a stick he's sharpened, Sefik then pricks a couple of rows of holes in the ground. He puts the plants in the holes, fills them in, and that's that. In two months they will bear fruit.

'We never used to have to buy any of our food,' Sefik Encü tells us. 'We grew grapes, nuts, tomatoes and aubergines here, and took them to Zakho, just over the border. We exchanged our goods for sugar, tea and rice.'

They only really needed money to buy clothing and household items, which they earned by selling meat and wool, as well as smuggled goods. The proceeds were also spent in Zakho, which is where they bought their clothing and household goods.

In a way, they did pay tax on the goods that crossed the border illegally, Stefik says. 'If we were coming home with a fifty kilo sack of sugar, we would sometimes have to hand over some of it to the soldiers, let's say twenty kilos. It was not officially tax, but nevertheless.'

Everyone in Gülyazı objects to the word 'smuggling'; that's not how they see it. Smuggling requires a border, and although they know that there is one officially, things are different in their perception. Survivor Servet Encü: 'There is a border stone at the spot where we were bombed. Border stone number fifteen. On one side is the word 'Turkey,' on the other, 'Iraq.' That stone wasn't there when I first started smuggling, not yet. The people we trade with are family. Officially, they live on the other side of the border, but to us it's our own land, land we've lived on for centuries. It's all Kurdistan.'

The Map of Kurdistan

Kurdistan. Few words evoke such powerful emotions in Turkey. Time and again, Turkish people have challenged me to pick up a map and show them Kurdistan. 'You won't be able to,' they add triumphantly, 'because Kurdistan doesn't exist!'

When President Abdullah Gül uttered the word in March 2009, Turkey was up in arms. The K-word! Out of the president's mouth! Gül himself was undeterred. He had said the word to journalists during a visit to Iraq, the first visit by a Turkish president in thirty-three years. The semi-independent north of Iraq is officially known as the 'Kurdistan Autonomous Region,' and the president had referred to it accordingly.

So what exactly is 'Kurdistan'? Is it a myth that exists only in the Kurdish imagination? No, certainly not. It is known that even Atatürk used the term prior to the foundation of the republic. In Ottoman times, 'Kurdistan' was a common name for Kurdish areas – which, with the exception of the Iranian part, were all within the empire's boundary. In the middle of the nineteenth century, it was the official name of the province now called Diyarbakır.

There are maps of this officially non-existent Kurdistan. Although not everyone uses the same criteria to determine boundaries, maps are usually based on the ethnicity of the population. The most logical criterion is to select areas with a Kurdish majority. You could add another 100,000 square kilometres if you include areas where Kurds represent at least thirty percent of the population. This would mean that Turkish cities with very mixed populations, such as Sivas, Malatya and Gaziantep, are part of Kurdistan. Advocates of the thirty percent criterion have one major advantage: their Kurdistan has maritime access, in the southern province of Hatay. The smaller and more commonly accepted Kurdistan has no beach and no port.

However, there is water. Countless mountain streams wind their way through the landscape, stemming from or flowing into the Euphrates and particularly into the Tigris, as it slowly meanders through the Kurdish lowlands and mountain valleys. It is this water that makes the landscape dreamlike, so full of life. Without all that shimmering water, Kurdistan would simply be gruelling, rugged, dry, rocky and raw.

Kurdistan covers around 410,000 square kilometres, which is about eleven times the size of the Netherlands. The largest part is in Turkey, covering approximately 195,000 square kilometres, which is about a quarter of Turkey. The Iranian part of Kurdistan is around 125,000 square kilometres in size, which amounts to a thirteenth of the country. Iraqi Kurdistan is about 72,000 square kilometres, a sixth of the country (larger, in fact, than the official territory of the semi-autonomous Kurdistan Region of Iraq, which covers 40,000 square kilometres, a tenth of the country). The smallest part of Kurdistan is in Syria; at 18,000 square kilometres, it covers almost a tenth of the country.

The area is populated by around thirty million Kurds: approximately seventeen million in Turkey, just over four million in Iraq, over five and a half million in Iran, and approximately one million in Syria. Almost half a million Kurds live in Armenia and Azerbaijan, and almost a million in Europe, primarily in Germany.

By no means all Kurds live in originally Kurdish areas, particularly in Turkey. In fact, the city with the highest Kurdish population is not Diyarbakır, but Istanbul. Other cities in western and southern Turkey are also home to tens of thousands of Kurds, including İzmir, Adana and Mersin. It is also important to note that Kurds are not the only inhabitants of Kurdistan: there are also Assyrians, Arabs, Armenians. Let it also be noted that not all Kurds are Muslims: there are Yezidi Kurds too. Yet all these geographical details, statistics and dimensions say so little about the feel of Kurdistan. I think the best way of expressing that feeling is with contrasts. Kurdistan is rugged yet gentle, heavy yet light, imbued with pain but also with solace, proud yet modest, dusty yet sparkling with sequins.

That sparkle is provided by the women, and the traditional dresses they wear – some every day, others on special occasions. These ankle-length dresses have long sleeves and high necklines, but the bust and waistline are accentuated above the wide flowing skirts. The fabric is glossy and brightly coloured – pink, green, blue, red – with thousands of silver-coloured sequins. I never tire of looking at these costumes and the women wearing them. Their eyes filled with self-confidence and their upright posture – that's pride. Their smiles, without a trace of arrogance, show their modesty.

The Treaty of Sèvres and the Kemalist Revolution

An imaginary 'Kurdistan' with clearly-marked borders appeared on a map in 1920. It was part of the Treaty of Sèvres, to be precise, a treaty which sought to establish peace between the Ottoman Empire and the winners of the First World War. In the treaty, the area which is now Turkey was largely divided between Italy, France and Great Britain, which had already occupied Ottoman territory since the end of the war in 1918. What was left over for Turkey was a single patch of land in central and northern Anatolia. Thrace (to the west of Istanbul) and part of the west coast went to Greece, while the east fell partly into Armenian hands. The area around Istanbul was placed under international supervision. The Allies planned a Kurdistan in the southeast of Turkey, although no decisions were taken regarding the exact borders.

Did that Kurdistan take root in the minds of the Kurds themselves at the time? I ask Howard Eissenstat, lecturer in the history of the Middle East at St Lawrence University, Canton, in the US. 'Yes,' he says, 'but only among a small group of intellectuals, primarily in Istanbul, and not among the people.' Eissenstat continues: 'I define nationalism as a popular movement which claims that nations have the right to a state. This was already a phenomenon in Europe, one that crossed to the Middle East in the 1920s. Prior to this, in the mid nineteenth century, Kurdish intellectuals began to emphasise their identity as Kurds, just like the intellectuals of other nations. At the end of the nineteenth century, the elite class also began to consider the possibility of their own country, although it was not yet a people's movement.'

That reminds me of an angry email I once received from a Turkish nationalist who believed the Kurds had forfeited their right to their own state by failing to fight for it. He wrote, 'At least the Turkish people fought for their country. The Kurds didn't, and now it's too late. It's their own fault.'

It doesn't surprise me that Eissenstat considers this something of an oversimplification. He outlines the situation in which the Kurds found themselves when the Ottoman Empire fell. 'The final years of the Ottoman Empire,' he said, 'were chaotic. The main rivals in the area where the Kurds lived were the Christian Armenians. They claimed part of the same territory as the Kurds.'

That is clearly shown on the map illustrating the agreements laid down in the Treaty of Sèvres. A significant part of the land that is now considered Kurdish territory, such as the current provinces of Bitlis, Mus, Ağri and Van, is shown as part of Armenia. Eissenstat: 'Remaining within the Islamic Ottoman Empire would give the Kurds a greater chance of maintaining some authority with regard to their territory. Can you imagine what would have happened had they not supported the nationalists? The Ottomans still had an army, as did Russia, which supported the

Armenians. There may have been around twenty million Kurds in those days, but they had no political or military power. So they chose the best option available at the time: they joined forces with the Kemalists.'

During the First World War, the Kurds fought with dedication. The Ottoman Empire promoted the struggle as a holy Islamic war, and the religious Kurds required little persuasion from their religious leaders. They had great respect for both the Sultan and the caliphate; furthermore, relations between Kurdish tribal leaders, sheikhs (religious leaders) and the Sultanate in Istanbul were generally good. It also made sense for the Kurds to join the fighting in the War of Independence, headed by General Mustafa Kemal, between 1919 and 1923. The war was intended to expel the foreign powers from Anatolia and thus annul the Treaty of Sèvres. In doing so, the Kurds may have given up the land that had been promised to them in the treaty, but as we know, having their own country was not their main priority. Defending the Ottoman caliphate was important, as was maintaining the relative freedom enjoyed by the Kurds on their own territory.

Eissenstat points out that Turkish nationalism, which was to become the norm in the republic, played no part in the rhetoric of Mustafa Kemal's followers, the Kemalists, at the time. In those days, the identity it concerned was that of the 'Ottoman Muslim.' Eissenstat: 'There was little talk of Turkish nationalism during the War of Independence. At meetings in western Anatolia, the terms 'Turk' and 'Muslim' were used synonymously and regarded as interchangeable, but the Kemalists in eastern Anatolia were more cautious, as was the case at the Erzurum Congress.'

During that important congress, which was held in 1919 under the auspices of Mustafa Kemal (who in 1934 was honoured as the founding father of the Turkish Republic with the name Atatürk, meaning 'Father of the Turks'), representatives from six eastern provinces, all occupied at the time by First World War Allies, announced that they wanted to remain part of the Ottoman Empire, rather than becoming territories of France, Great Britain and Italy. Representatives from the Kurdish provinces of Bitlis, Van and Erzurum also attended. One of the most important decisions of the congress was that the country would be unified and indivisible.

The Kurds assumed they were fighting on an equal footing with the Kemalists, that they would join forces in the War of Independence, and later form a new country together, based on the familiar and trusted

Ottoman-Islamic values and practices. They regarded this as an unwritten contract with the Kemalists. Eissenstat: 'The Kurds could not have anticipated that the Kemalists would fail to honour that 'contract' once the War of Independence was over, that they would even take away the Kurds' power in their own territory, banning their language and culture.'

Eissenstat does not think that the Kemalists had a blueprint for the future state of Turkey, 'but they knew more or less how they wanted it to be. Their course was determined by their conviction that they represented civilisation, unlike the people from the east of the country, in other words the Kurds. They would centralise power, taking it away from the peoples of the Ottoman Empire in their own territories. Turkish would become the national language, and the people in the east would become part of that greater entity.'

After the War of Independence came the Kemalist Revolution, which aimed to turn Turkey into a modern, Western-oriented country. The Republic of Turkey was founded in 1923; secularisation began, and from then on the country was to be governed strictly and centrally from the new capital city of Ankara. This also marked the end of the relative freedom which the Kurds, and peoples within the Ottoman Empire, had enjoyed in handling their own affairs.

Moreover, turning Turkey into the unitary state Mustafa Kemal wanted meant eliminating the old 'Ottoman Muslim' identity. Under the new nationalism, everyone was a Turk, even those who were not – end of story. Mustafa Kemal preached the lofty virtues of Turkish civilisation, dismissing the power of the sheikhs, as part of the Kurdish elite: 'the Turkish Republic cannot be a country of sheikhs, dervishes, disciples and deranged people.' Instead he stated that 'the best, the truest order is the order of civilisation.'

The following famous words of his also stem from the early days of the republic: 'Ne mutlu Türküm diyene,' or, 'How happy is the one who says, "I am a Turk."'

Pride in the new Turkish identity went hand in hand with the repression of everything not Turkish, and the Kurds, as the largest non-Turkish group, were an obvious target. The use of the Kurdish language in education was prohibited and religious schools were closed down. Since there was little other education available in the Kurdish region, this meant that education immediately became inaccessible to the Kurds, and that the new generation of Kurds who did go to school were drilled to become young Turks from their very first day. The Kurdish language was also forbidden in courts of law, which meant that Kurds could no longer defend themselves.

From then on, any new government officials in Kurdish areas were Turkish, apart from low-level civil servants, who were strictly screened; anyone suspected of the slightest Kurdish nationalist sympathies was out on his ear. The Kurdish candidacy for the 1923 parliamentary elections was manipulated. The term 'Kurdistan' was removed from all books and government communication, and a move began to replace Kurdish geographical names with Turkish ones.

The Uprising of Sheikh Said

Within a couple of years, there was little left of the original reasons for the Kurds fighting the War of Independence together with the Kemalists. The anti-Kurdish measures were bad enough, but it was the abolition of the caliphate in 1924 and the advent of secularisation that delivered the final blow to the ideological bond between the Kurds and the Turks. At any rate, these events turned the first Kurdish revolt against the new Kemalist regime, in 1925, into something of a people's revolution.

That revolution was led by Sheikh Said, a powerful religious leader. Although he had been sentenced to death a few months after the start of the revolution for wanting to establish an independent Kurdistan, his objective was not to provide the Kurds with a country of their own. He was an extremely religious man, who considered the abolition of the caliphate as a direct attack on Islam, and he swore he would oppose the secularisation of Turkey.

The original plans for the revolt were indeed about creating an independent Kurdistan. However, it was a group of Kurdish intellectuals, including Kurdish army officials, rather than Sheikh Said, who contrived the revolt. They had united in the secret Azadi movement (Azadi is Kurdish for 'freedom') in order to rebel against the anti-Kurdish measures of Mustafa Kemal's new government. They called on assistance from several powerful sheikhs to make a large-scale people's revolution possible. After all, the sheikhs had the power and authority they lacked over the ordinary people.

The government in Ankara, however, got wind of the Azadi plans. Most of its military leaders were arrested, and many other members of the movement subsequently backed down. The sheikhs remained the most important leaders and were highly motivated. They had not been fighting for an independent Kurdistan anyway, but rather to 'save the faith.' It was for this reason that Sheikh Said and his people were able to encourage huge numbers of Kurds to join the revolt: the Kurds had always held the caliphate in high esteem and regarded the Sultan as the successor to the prophet Mohammed.

The first Kurdish revolt had begun. The fact that it was very much a religiously motivated revolt for the sheikhs and the other rebels – most of them peasants – is clear not only from the inflammatory speeches held by the sheikhs before it began, but also from the symbols used during the rebellion. People waved copies of the Koran, carried Islamic flags and shouted religious slogans.

Although the revolt began favourably in 1925, it was all over very quickly: in late March 1925, the Turkish army suppressed the rebellion, using both ground troops and airstrikes. Apparently many Kurdish rebels were terrified; they had never even heard of planes, let alone seen them. Sheikh Said was arrested in mid April and publicly hanged in late June 1925, together with other leaders of the revolt.

Eissenstat believes that Sheikh Said and his fellow rebels had never expected the new Turkish state to intervene so drastically. In the days of the Ottoman Empire, when the Kurdish territory was governed by local tribal leaders and feudal lords, violence was often a stepping stone to new political relations or alliances based on mutual respect. Eissenstat: 'But those days were gone for good.' The new course became clear, not only from the way the revolt had been so mercilessly suppressed, but also from the measures that were subsequently taken to nip any further rebellion in the bud. All the religious Sufi orders which Sheikh Said and the other rebel leaders belonged to, were banished, along with any expression of Kurdish culture. The increasingly dictatorial first president of Turkey, Mustafa Kemal, seized on the Sheikh Said Rebellion to rouse support for secularisation and Turkish nationalism.

And so it was that within five or six years, the Kurds lost not only a potential state of their own, but also the right to live as Kurds on their home territory.

That political status quo, however, is by no means proof that Kurdistan does not exist. For the people that live there, Kurdistan has been a reality for generations. If you follow the Kurdish question from a distance, hearing mostly political news and reports of violence, 'Kurdistan' seems to be no more than an emotionally charged idea about which there is constant political conflict, a continually sensitive subject. But anyone travelling through Kurdistan will soon see this is not the case.

Take, for instance, the people of Gülyazı and Ortasu. They suffer greatly under the repressive politics of the Turkish state; they demand justice and long for peace and quiet, but in the meantime they spend their days caring for their families, not fighting for activist causes. Kurdistan is an entirely natural part of their everyday lives. It is where they trade their goods, visit family, and where they used to shop for groceries, on the other side of the mountain, a place that just happens to be called Iraq. Over the years, their country has been divided between four states, but that does nothing to alter the fact that the Kurds still live there. Nor does the fact that their villages and towns now have Turkish names mean that they are no longer inhabited by Kurds. And the fact that the summer meadows, high up in the mountains, are no longer accessible does not stop the Kurds' history from being inextricably linked with those fields.

For Kurds, like those in Gülyazı and Ortasu, 'Kurdistan' is not a statement, nothing political, but a simple reality. Their hopes do not concern the official demarcation of borders for their country. Of course, if you pursue the question, their eyes will light up and no Kurd would deny dreaming of having their own country one day, but for them, an independent state is not what it is all about. What is important to them is gaining recognition for the fact that Kurdistan exists and has done for centuries, and that they, their language and their culture are an integral part of it.

Goodbye to the Village

On that first day in Gülyazı, I also visit the cemetery. A group of us travels there in a minibus. You can walk, but the road is steep, and it's winter, so conditions are not exactly conducive to walking far. At lunchtime I send my news snippet to the ANP press agency in The Hague: the relatives of the bombing victims are refusing the compensation offered by the government. My report (slightly altered from the original text):

> *RELATIVES OF KURDS REFUSE COMPENSATION*
>
> *GÜLYAZI – The families of the thirty-four men and boys killed last week in a bombing by the Turkish army will not consider accepting compensation from the government. On Tuesday, prime minister Erdoğan informed the families of the men who came under fire while*

smuggling on the Iraqi border that they would receive compensation within a few days. Zahide Encü, mother of fifteen-year-old Aslan, who was killed in the attack: 'First they blast my son to pieces, then they offer me money? We don't want money; we want to know what happened.'

The village of Gülyazı, where twenty-five of the thirty-four dead lived, is still in mourning. The other nine are from Ortasu, a stone's throw away, all in the district of Uludere. The Turkish Ministry of the Interior is offering 20,000 lira, approximately 8,000 euros, for each villager killed. Survivor Servet Encü (thirty-five): 'The government knows that the people here are poor. That's why they think they can make things right with a bag of cash. But that's not how it works. I would rather eat grass than accept money from the government.'

Zahide Encü (forty-five) has six children, two of them sons. Eight years ago, the oldest, now twenty-six, stepped on a landmine while out gathering firewood and can no longer contribute to the family income; the youngest, Aslan, is now dead. 'What are we going to live on? I don't know. No, I did not for a second consider accepting Erdoğan's money. I trust that God will help us.'

The villagers say that they have no faith in an investigation by anyone in Turkey. They think that an investigation should be carried out by an EU human rights commission. But many fear that the Turkish government would not allow an independent investigation.

What exactly happened last week, we will never know. For the time being, the Turkish government maintains that it was an 'accident' and promises an in-depth investigation, but the villagers don't believe a word of it. Survivor Servet Encü: 'Everyone knew about the smuggling, even the police and security services. The village head even received telephone calls from the army when air or ground activities were planned in the area where smuggling took place, and then we wouldn't go. The last month had been so quiet on the routes that we started going with larger groups, and took more donkeys with us. And then, suddenly, all the return routes had been closed and we were bombed.'

A family can earn a monthly income of 600 to 700 lira from smuggling. In a village, that provides just enough to live on. There is barely any other work: large parts of the province are prohibited military areas, or full of landmines, which makes it impossible to keep sheep. There are no factories. Children help to earn the family income 'as soon as they can walk,' that's why children from the age of thirteen or fourteen go smuggling with the rest.

Ironically enough, the age at which children begin to smuggle is decreasing. Eight-year-old Sinan is going for the first time next week, when the period of mourning is over, in the place of his brother Sivan (thirteen), who was killed. It's two hours to the border and two hours back. Can he manage that? Sinan: 'I'm allowed to ride a donkey on the way there.'

(News agency ANP, 4 January 2012)

Seventeen-year-old Semire and her younger brother Seyvan come with us to the burial ground. Their story affects me deeply, particularly as they were so quiet earlier in the day, while others could hardly wait to share their stories with me. Semire and Seyvan just sat there. When I asked them something, their answers came in whispers, and before Semire had finished speaking, the adults took over the conversation.

At the burial ground, Semire comes and walks by my side. I feel a strong urge to hold her close, she seems so vulnerable, but I'm not sure if that's the done thing here, so I hold back. I stroke her arm, lay my hand against her cheek and look at her. At the burial ground, Semire sits quietly by her brother's grave. She has brought along some surahs from the Koran which provide solace for the bereaved, and murmurs them quietly into the distance.

Thirty-four mounds of earth on a hillside. The sun shines on the snow-covered mountains around us; with my feet between the graves, I look towards the place where these people met their deaths. Each grave is marked with a stone bearing the name of the deceased in dripping wet black paint.

Each grave is demarcated with grey concrete and adorned with plastic flowers in white and bright yellow, pink, red and orange. Scarves in the Kurdish national colours of green, red and yellow are wound around many of the stones. On some graves, like that of Bilal Encü (fifteen), there is a note: 'He did it for a computer.'

That's how ordinary smuggling is. Bilal was saving up to buy a computer. Later, I hear other similar stories. Sixteen-year-old Cemal Encü went smuggling so he could pay off his debts to the school canteen, debts adding up to sixteen lira (seven euros). Less common is the story of

Serhat Encü (seventeen), who went smuggling to save up for a headstone for his mother's grave, two years after her death. A smuggling trip, I was told, is worth between fifty and eighty lira, between twenty and thirty-five euros. Ten to fifteen trips and you have enough for a computer. A pair of shoes or a winter coat take less time. Those are the 'extras' here. Some people smuggle for 'treats' like this, others simply to earn enough to survive. At the cemetery, I spoke to nineteen-year-old Özer Ürek, who grew up in Gülyazı before starting a degree course in tourism in Antalya, southern Turkey. 'I did a lot of smuggling too, especially between the ages of thirteen and sixteen,' he told me. 'I had less time after that, as I was studying to pass my university entrance exam. Since I've been at university, I've been going smuggling with the rest when I'm back in the village to pay my tuition fees. I have to; my parents couldn't possibly afford it otherwise.'

He still gets nervous about the trips. 'You can be shot at by the soldiers,' he says. 'They know that smuggling goes on, and they tolerate it because they know we'd have no income otherwise, but they sometimes shoot anyway. Luckily, nothing has ever happened to me.'

Servet Encü tells me that they went with a relatively small group on the night of the attacks. 'There were very few problems with the soldiers in the previous months, so we went smuggling more often and took more people along. Sometimes there were fifty or sixty of us, and just as many mules.' It becomes increasingly clear to me how commonplace smuggling is for the youngsters in this part of Turkey. Kids in the Netherlands do a paper round; in Turkey they go smuggling. The work is tougher and more dangerous, and it's illegal, but there are no other jobs.

These children also grow up much faster: their childhood is over from the age of about twelve. From then on, they contribute to family life, the boys financially, the girls by helping with domestic chores. It has been that way for centuries, and traditions here are strong. It also means that adults grow old faster. Deeply lined faces and stiff bodies often make people look ten years older than I reckon they really are. Generations move on more quickly: the father of a twenty-year-old might still be in his thirties, and a grandmother might be in her forties.

Later, at Servet Encü's house, I write my story about child smugglers for the Dutch weekly youth newspaper *7Days*. My mobile internet connection gives up and another laptop – with a good connection – is quickly brought for me from another house. The room here is also hot and packed, primarily with women who have come over specially from the neighbouring province of Hakkâri to offer the villagers their condolences. The bombing affects not only the families and villagers directly involved, but the entire Kurdish community. 'Are you hungry?' my hostess asks as I type. 'Here, have a cup of tea....' Moments later there is a plate of food beside me: rice with chickpeas and chicken.

I feel like a typical headline-chasing journalist as we announce around half past four that we have to leave if we want to be back in Şırnak that evening – like one of those journalists who travels to remote corners of the world for a couple of quick stories, usually about elections or some disaster, not bothering to get to know the places they visit, and not letting their lack of knowledge stop them publishing a story. These journalists learn the facts, but not in any real depth, so that the headline-chasing stories they produce barely scratch the surface. I consult Beyda about returning for a little longer later in the year. She sounds out Servet Encü and asks if he knows someone I could perhaps stay with in the village, adding that we don't need an answer straight away; we can call later. But Servet doesn't hesitate for a moment: I can stay at his house, anytime, just say the word and I'll be welcome. We exchange telephone numbers and Beyda, Aziz and I bid farewell to the many people there. The men shake hands with us firmly, and the women kiss us on both cheeks and hug us tightly. They warn us that there will be no more buses to Şırnak from the village that day, but we assume it won't be long before something comes along the main road. We put our shoes back on again and trudge through the muddy snow in that direction.

Little did I know at the time that I would return to this place and these people time and again; that the bombing would haunt me until I figured out what exactly happened that night, and why; that the event would drag me irrevocably into Kurdish history, searching for parallels, delving deeper into its background. I did not know how this quest would force me to reflect on myself and my profession: why am I doing this, and what is my position as a journalist? Nor did I realise that this story would be suitable for a book, because the Uludere bombing encapsulates the Kurdish question in a single square kilometre.

I'm not sure exactly how long the journey back to Şırnak took. Since no *dolmuş* appeared, we decided to hitch a lift. It was already dark and the first truck that came along stopped. It took some persuasion before the three men in the cabin decided to take us with them. We had to convince them that, no, we really didn't mind sitting in the back of the trailer. We had hats and scarves and warm coats with us. We really wanted to get back to Şırnak that evening, and it wasn't that far anyway, was it? A smile, a nod of the head and up we climbed into the back of the truck.

We huddled together in the corner of the trailer, shared out the scarves, hats and gloves to keep the three of us as warm as possible, and resigned ourselves to the biting wind and bumpy road. We rattled through the night for two or three hours, the wind rushing past our faces. The mountains were pitch black silhouettes, and in the distance, snow-capped peaks stood out against a crystal-clear, star-studded night sky. Lights twinkled here and there – army posts.

I wanted to ask Aziz which direction Iraq was from here, and Syria too, but I kept quiet. It didn't matter. We were in the heart of Kurdistan.

Chapter Three

The People

'Penç,' says a middle-aged woman sitting on the floor next to me, holding up her hand with her fingers splayed. Drying her tears with the tip of her white headscarf, she is rocking back and forth. *Penç* is Kurdish for 'five' – children, she means. Osman Kaplan, thirty-four, had five children when he died in the Uludere bombing.

I don't yet know exactly who this tall and slender-bodied woman with light brown eyes is. It doesn't matter all that much right now; she is suffering intensely and I hold her hand. Osman's twenty-eight-year-old widow, Pakize, is sitting next to her. She looks numb as she pours tea.

It's late April 2012, and I'm back in Gülyazı. For the last few months I was in touch with Servet Encü, a survivor who was willing to put me up for a few weeks during my visit to the village. About three weeks before my arrival, however, I lose contact with him: I can't get hold of his phone. I soon find out why: the human rights organisation Mazlumder reports that he has fled with his family to Iraqi Kurdistan.

The reason seems to be that he felt his head was on the block: he spoke too openly about the bombing, and the authorities were leaning on him to keep mum. I'm too far away to verify the reason for his departure, but I have no doubt that he has indeed fled. Why else would his phone not work for days on end? Besides, Mazlumder is a reliable organisation, which immediately went to the village the morning after the bombing to investigate the facts, and which has many contacts amongst the local population.

For a moment I consider not going back to Gülyazı. Surely I can't just show up and expect someone to take me in – for a few weeks at that? I could call someone else in the village, but then what? Invite myself to stay with a family over the phone? It all feels a little too direct.

Frankly, I'm also having doubts about the purpose of my visit. Why do I want to go there? What am I hoping to discover? What's the point? This book isn't yet on my agenda, and I won't be able to sell a background story about this tragedy to a Dutch magazine – it's all happening too far away for Dutch readers to be concerned. Am I just going to satisfy my own curiosity? Is that a good enough reason to pry into the villagers' private lives?

Return to Gülyazı

I go back anyway. I simply can't get the bombing off my mind; the journalist in me is drawn to Gülyazı. Everyone in Turkish politics is desperate to give their take on the incident, but relatives and other villagers are seldom heard. I might not be able to sell articles about it, but I can blog about it on my website, which has a decent number of visitors. At the time some of my blogs are translated for a Turkish website, which might give me the opportunity to redress the biased coverage just a little.

My first visit, just after the bombing, proved just how much this is needed. One of the newspaper stories that caught my eye before I went to Gülyazı for the first time was about an attack by villagers on the governor of Uludere, Naif Yavuz. The governor, appointed by the Justice and Development Party (AKP) government – and a party man himself – had come to express his sympathy to the relatives, but was almost lynched by a group of villagers.

There's a video of the incident on the internet, and it looks quite violent. It shows a road with a steep embankment sloping down to a riverbank next to it. The governor is walking on the verge, trying to protect himself from jeering men pushing and trying to hit him. Cornered, Yavuz has no choice but to run down through the mud towards the stream. A few furious men go after him – and then the film stops before he is somehow rescued. Apparently he was later taken to hospital by ambulance, with injuries to his head and face.

Turkish newspapers scream bloody murder, pointing the finger squarely at one man: Hasip Kaplan, MP for the pro-Kurdish BDP. His warning to AKP politicians not to go to Gülyazı and Ortasu is interpreted as inciting the near-lynching. The state-controlled press organisation Anadolu Agency visits the governor in hospital and distributes an interview with him, which is printed in many Turkish newspapers. Yavuz claims it wasn't villagers who attacked him, but 'agitators' who were brought to the village especially for the lynching.

Add to this Kaplan's warning, and as far as the Turkish media are concerned the story is done and dusted. The governor came to offer his sympathy to relatives, Hasip Kaplan called for a lynching – albeit indirectly – and the Kurdish movement dispatched some thugs to the village.

The incident is touched on during my first visit to Gülyazı. We're on the main road when a young man from the village, pointing at the ground sloping towards the stream, asks, 'Did you see that video of the governor?' I recall the film, and recognise the place. 'Yes, I've seen it,' I reply. 'Was it here? Were you there?' He says he was there, and recounts what happened. 'Look! That's where the governor came from, and that's where he ran to.'

'I've read an interview with the governor,' I say, 'in which he says the people who attacked him came from outside the village.' My conversation partner throws his hands in the air and exclaims: 'People from elsewhere? Definitely not! It was us – I was there too! What do you think? That man has never been here before, he knows nothing about us, never does anything for the village. Then he rocks up a few days after the massacre – which was committed by his party – to make a good impression! Shove off!'

Who should I believe – him, or the governor? Why would this boy admit to participating in the violence if he didn't? I discuss it with other villagers, and ask why the governor would falsely claim that the people weren't locals. The villagers are in complete agreement: if he had publicly pilloried the residents of his district, he could have kissed goodbye to any future visits to the village.

I ask a few boys how the governor actually escaped. Having seen the place, I know that he really was cornered. 'Hasip Kaplan,' replies the boy who admitted being there and who wants to remain anonymous. I hadn't realised Kaplan was present. 'Kaplan was standing over there' – he points to a spot that wasn't visible in the film – 'with a megaphone. He told us to stop.' BDP politicians are highly respected here, especially veterans like Kaplan, who is one of the MPs for Şırnak, the province Uludere is part of.

Several months later Faruk Encü, a boy in his teens, tells me: 'I had a bottle of petrol and was about to light it and throw it at the governor. When I pulled my lighter out of my pocket, Hasip Kaplan grabbed my wrist. Thanks to him I didn't throw that bottle. Of course it was very stupid to want to do something like that, but I was grief-stricken and had lost control of myself.'

Two days after the attack on Yavuz, the incident is back in several newspapers: six boys from Gülyazı have been arrested, accused of manhandling the governor. Five of them are from the Encü family (Faruk is one of them) who have lost three of their cousins in the bombing. So much for external agitators. Nobody mentions that Hasip Kaplan saved the governor.

My Stay with Pakize, Widow and Mother

I go back to Gülyazı to continue my blog, but also because I want to know more about the background of the village and the bombing. I hear and read so much in the media that I'm unable to judge for myself, and it's driving me to distraction – so I go back, on my own this time. The only person who knows of my arrival is Irfan, a tall, well-dressed businessman in his forties and the local BDP politician. 'Call me when you get here,' he says. 'I'll have someone pick you up.'

It's the end of April, and the valleys I pass on the way have burst into an abundance of green. The rivers and streams are swollen with meltwater from the mountains. When I get out of the *dolmuş* in Gülyazı, and the sound of the van has died away, all I can hear is the gentle gurgling of the Ortasu. A few children are playing in the square between two shops. I call Irfan, and a little later someone picks me up.

We drive down the road behind the gymnasium into the village and turn left after the mosque, heading upwards. We soon leave the village behind, passing the cemetery, which isn't visible from the road but is indicated by a sign. The road winds uphill, towards the other half of Gülyazı. The view is breathtaking, the valley below green with spring foliage, and above us the mountains – which are also green now, with patches of snow here and there on their flanks.

It's the first time I notice the army post on the other side of the valley, directly opposite the village on the mountainside. A noisy helicopter is just taking off from the helipad, heading for the Iraqi border.

Buildings start appearing again – first houses, then a little square with an internet café and a shop. We turn onto a strip road and continue uphill until we reach a group of houses. We park the car and follow a trail to the right, where Irfan is waiting for us in front of his brand new house. 'Welcome! Are you hungry? Here, have some tea.'

An hour later, I realise we've got our wires crossed. I'm sitting on the floor in the living room, in the company of Irfan and three middle-aged gentlemen. They are talking about politics – or rather about history. In rapid Turkish with a Kurdish accent, which is extremely difficult for me to follow, I'm given a crash course on Kurdish political history while enjoying the lunch served by Irfan's wife. 'You're most welcome,' Irfan says, 'stay as long as you like.'

Help! He is under the impression I have invited myself to stay at his home – that I want to observe everyday life from one of the most luxurious houses in the village, and speak to high-ranking gentlemen. In my mind I crack up laughing, while making a desperate and completely futile attempt to follow the discussion. Every so often I utter meaningless expressions in keeping with what I think the men are saying. 'Gosh, I didn't know that.' 'Really?' 'How interesting.' 'You're absolutely right.'

After yet more tea and once the men have left, I explain to Irfan that I haven't come to stay with his family, that I was actually supposed to be staying with Servet Encü, but he was no longer around. And that I was hoping he, as a politician who knows the local community well, would be able to help me find another place to stay. 'I would like to see how the bombing has changed the lives of those involved,' I explain. 'Ordinary people here in the village.'

He thinks about it for a few minutes, makes a phone call and then we leave. On the right of the square with the internet café and the shop, we climb a narrow, slippery path between several houses. Villagers hanging laundry or drinking tea on their roofs watch us inquisitively. Chickens are scurrying around, and I spot a goat on one of the roofs. The path bends to the right, ending at a house that turns out to be our destination.

A man is working outside the house, and welcomes us. I'd say he's in his late thirties; he has blond hair and is wearing green fatigues – I later learn that they are usually only worn by village guards. We walk up onto the concrete patio in front of his house. Producing a couple of plastic chairs, he introduces himself as Mehmet. A small troop of children is buzzing around us, staring at me and smiling shyly. A woman comes out of the house. 'Have you eaten yet?' She serves us tea.

I let Irfan do the talking. He explains who I am, that I have been to the village before and what I am here for. Mehmet turns out to have lost his younger brother, Osman Kaplan, in the bombing. He was thirty-four when he died, leaving behind his wife Pakize, who is twenty-eight, and five children. She lives two doors away. Mehmet points down a narrow alley next to his house. There is a house on the left, and Pakize's house is at the other end of the alley. Mehmet decides I can stay with her, and we head straight there. Lugging my suitcase behind me, I feel a little uncomfortable, as the men have made this decision without consulting

Pakize. Does she feel like having a guest? Isn't it too soon after the loss of her husband, just four months ago? But Pakize doesn't bat an eyelid when her brother-in-law and Irfan arrive with their foreign guest. She bids me welcome with a shy, or rather modest, smile. Drawing the white curtains at the entrance to her house aside, she lets me in. I have to stoop a bit to avoid bumping my head on the door frame.

There are several household appliances in the hallway – a large refrigerator next to a stove, and a washing machine draped in a shiny light purple cloth. The living room is on the left, through a battered wooden door covered in flaky blue paint. A simple metal coat rack is fixed on top of it. The teapot is simmering on the wood-burning stove, and flat cushions are arranged along the walls on the floor, as well as sturdy, round cushions for backrests. There is a rug in the middle of the room and a TV in a cabinet in the corner, but it is broken. The only socket in the room doesn't work: it has blown and is charred.

The kitchen, toilet and shower aren't in the house: they are in the alley we just walked up between the houses, where I saw three wooden doors. The large metal water tank behind the first door is the kind you often see in Turkey, with a tap and a socket: almost everyone has hot water here. There's a piece of soap and a metal bowl next to the tank, and a water pipe connected to the cold water. To shower, you mix water from the tank and the hose in the bowl, and drench yourself.

The squat toilet is behind the adjacent door, with a piece of yellow hose connected to a tap for cleaning and flushing. The room next door has a hot water tank and a cold water hose: the kitchen. Two families share these amenities.

All three rooms have rough concrete floors and walls; a couple of nails in the wall function as hooks. A light bulb dangles in each room from a makeshift fitting. There are toothbrushes and a comb on top of the water tank in the kitchen. They don't have a mirror, nor a connection to a municipal water supply: the taps are connected to a system which transports water from a spring above the village. It's clean enough to drink – at least they do so there; and so do I, hoping for the best.

A blond boy comes in, and gives me a cheeky look. I say 'Hoi!,' Dutch for 'Hi!' Laughing, he scampers off. That was five-year-old Mahmut, Pakize and Oman's youngest child. I meet the other children that afternoon. Özkan, eleven, is the eldest: a dark-blond boy with a thoughtful air. Esra, ten, has long dark hair in a ponytail and an intelligent expression. Sinem, nine, also sporting long curly hair in a ponytail, has a gentle, slightly shy appearance. Hülya, seven, has a shock of completely tangled, wild hair and mischievous eyes.

That same afternoon I nickname little Mahmut 'monkey,' because of his cheeky little face, cropped hair, and the way he bounces all around the house and its environs, climbing everything. Not having any toys, he swings back and forth from the living room door; outside he climbs trees and people, and tries to clamber up the wooden poles supporting the terrace canopy. Grabbing hold of him as he tears past, I look at him and say: 'Hey, monkey.' Turning around, he replies: 'Mon-kay.' I'm sold.

There's a photo of Osman in the cabinet under the television, next to a bunch of pink and yellow plastic flowers. Looking up into the lens with a shovel in his hand, he has short, light-blond, curly hair, and a narrow, friendly face. He's working next to the stream, where the family is growing vegetables. Click.

Parliamentary Inquiry

The Turkish parliament sets up a parliamentary commission to investigate the incident soon after the bombing, on 11 January 2012. The commission is a subgroup of the standing parliamentary human rights investigative commission, consisting of eight members: İhsan Şener (the chairman), Mehmet Kerim Yıldız, Hamza Dağ, Abdurrahim Akdağ and Gülşen Orhan (all from the ruling AKP), Levent Gök (from the main opposition party, the CHP), Ertuğrul Kürkçü (from the pro-Kurdish BDP) and Atila Kaya (from the ultranationalist MHP).

Five members from the ruling party and three from the opposition – that doesn't bode well: the commission decides on procedure by majority vote, and only a simple majority is required for adoption of the final report.

In addition, several crucial documents are classified, barring the commission from seeing them, and the most senior military and political decision-makers are not obliged to speak to the commission.

All of this creates the impression the commission is there more to insulate Prime Minister Erdoğan and the army leadership than to get to the bottom of the incident. There is a real concern that the AKP's predominance in the 'Uludere commission,' on top of it being chaired by a party man, will make sure this happens.

Which questions exactly have been raised by the bombing? A joint report by the independent human rights organisations Mazlumder and İHD gives a good indication. They immediately visited and investigated the scene of the incident, one day after it had taken place. In their report, released on 3 January 2012, they pose a series of questions in order to establish the causes of the incident.

Why weren't the villagers informed about an impending operation against the PKK, as they had been on previous occasions? Did the drones reveal information about the goods being carried by the group of men, and whether they were civilians or not? Why was medical aid not given immediately after the bombing, as several witnesses have stated, to minimise the loss of life?

The human rights organisations argue that all civil and military officials in positions of responsibility should be suspended from active service until the investigation is complete, in order to enable effective investigation of the incident. They are of the view that the investigation should be carried out by the parliamentary human rights investigative commission. Those found guilty should subsequently be brought to justice.

İHD and Mazlumder argue that the government should take political responsibility: the Minister of Interior Affairs should resign, and the Chief of General Staff and the leadership of the army units involved (in the army and air force) should be fired. They call on the state to recognise it as a massacre, offer its sincere apologies, and pay the relatives of the bombing victims compensation.

But villagers have just rejected compensation because of the way in which it was offered: the families regard it as hush money rather than compensation. Such incidents might in principle be settled with a sum of money, but only on condition that the offender shows remorse for what has happened and apologises. Only then is it possible to discuss money. This condition has not been met.

It is important for residents of Gülyazı and Ortasu to shed light on how the bombing could have happened, in order to rule out recurrence. They also want to know who ultimately gave the order.

The Uludere commission has not set itself a specific target. Its remit is 'to examine the claim that the right to life of thirty-four civilians has been violated.' Commission members visit the village and talk to survivors and relatives, as well as visiting army posts in the area, where they speak to local commanders and attempt to gain access to official information; a futile endeavour, since all the crucial documents have been classified confidential.

In the middle of February a hermetically sealed session is organised, during which the commission is shown images shot by drones flying above the border on the evening of the incident. Turkey's drones are allowed to fly up to five kilometres across the border. One of the members of the commission, Ertuğrul Kürkçü, wanted to see images from American drones flying above Iraqi territory, but this request was rejected by majority vote. The reason given is that foreign powers may submit manipulated images which could result in misinformation.

Ertuğrul Kürkçü later says that watching the drone recordings was a harrowing experience for him. 'You can clearly see it's not a troop of soldiers,' he recounts. 'It's a ragtag band of people, there's no military discipline; it's a caravan.'

The images were shot with a thermal camera, which doesn't render details, but you can see reasonably well what's going on: people are clearly distinguishable from animals, and the outline of the goods on the animals is discernible. Kürkçü: 'Several experts were present to help members of the commission interpret the material; but they were completely unnecessary, as the images were clear enough.'

At the very least, the information provided by the drones undermines the official account that the massacre was an accident.

For one thing, the large group of people, with at least as many pack animals, travelled first from Turkey to Iraq and then took the same route back. This is not exactly a logical manoeuvre for a group of rebels, as the army must have known after almost thirty years of waging war against the PKK.

In Iraq, goods were loaded from a truck onto dozens of mules. Kürkçü: 'The cargo was white – meaning it was cold – and wasn't shaped like weapons but like rectangular packages.' The PKK might sometimes transport arms on pack animals, but not by the dozen. Moreover the transfer wouldn't have taken place on a high plateau, easily visible to reconnaissance aeroplanes.

Kürkçü will never forget the video footage shot after the first bombing; and even though I've never seen it, it's seared in my mind's eye. 'If it was a group of rebels, they would have scattered and looked for cover to limit the loss of men. This group did the opposite: instead of hiding they huddled together, holding on to each other. They were afraid. Most of them were children.'

İhsan Şener, chairman of the commission, announces in early April 2012 that the report will be wrapped up before the end of the month. 'We're just waiting for a report from the Ministry of Interior Affairs,' he tells the Turkish press. Deputy Prime Minister Bülent Arınç doesn't even wait for the report's conclusions, declaring on 1 March that there 'was no foul play' in Uludere.

The 1930s: Dersim Massacre

But what if it was intentional? The information I have managed to gather so far, makes the government's claim it was an accident less and less credible. I realise I find the idea too disturbing to admit, partly because I can't imagine why the state would gratuitously murder a group of civilians. What could the reason be?

When I put the question to people in Gülyazı, they usually reply: 'Kürt olduğumuz için' – 'Because we're Kurds.'

That doesn't exactly explain the events of that night, but I understand why they answer 'because we're Kurds.' Not only people in Gülyazı, but many Kurds elsewhere in the region also give this as the sole explanation for the bombing when I pose this question. When I delve more deeply – Why that night? Why that place? Why the smugglers? – the response is a shrug of the shoulders. Or that the details of the circumstances must, of course, be brought to light, but the victims' Kurdish identity is the core issue. They know the state only too well.

The text on the banner I saw during my first visit to Gülyazı speaks volumes: it refers to 'Dersim 1938.' It was the largest-scale destruction of Kurds in Turkish history – as well as being the last time traditional Kurdish tribal and religious leaders opposed the Turkish state.

'Just listen to the songs,' says Yektan Türkyılmaz, an anthropologist and associate professor at Duke University in Durham, United States. He sent me some links to old songs from Dersim. 'We took our weapons, we handed them in, and surrendered. (...) They rounded us up, and they put us in a line. They slaughtered us, and left our corpses, our bodies, behind in the sun. (...) Why are our lives in Kirmanciye worth so little?' Kirmanciye is a local name for the area.

'I don't need archives to know what happened in Dersim,' Türkyılmaz says. 'What happened is this: people did everything they could to prevent the massacres, but there was no escape.' Not that he relies solely on old songs: Türkyılmaz speaks Turkish, Kurdish and Armenian, and can read Ottoman and French. He has done a great deal of archival research on how Anatolia became Turkish in the final years of the Ottoman Empire and the first decades of the republic, up to 1938 – the year in which the Dersim operations came to an end. He unequivocally calls the Dersim massacres genocide. The songs are a plain, raw telling of that story.

The official Turkish account is that the Dersim region needed to be instilled with 'civilisation.' Turkish civilisation, that is – according to Kemalist principles this was lacking in Dersim, as the region had long been run by traditional leaders, chiefs and so-called 'Pirs,' wise men who took a neutral position between the tribes.

It is true that Dersim had not submitted to central authority, nor had it for centuries. The Kurdish regions, including Dersim, had been a part of the Ottoman Empire since the sixteenth century, but most of them had special autonomous status. Their autonomy went far beyond the limited freedom that other peoples of the empire enjoyed in relation to the Sunni Muslim majority: the Kurds governed themselves, paid no taxes, and their sons didn't serve in the Ottoman army. This arrangement also suited the sultan, as it would have been too troublesome to keep a lid on the myriad tribes and clans, with all their contradictory, ever-shifting loyalties.

The relationship between the state and the Kurdish regions began to change around the middle of the nineteenth century. The Ottoman Empire lost more and more territory, and in an effort to halt the decline the decision was made to centralise power. The Sultan wanted to put an end to the relative freedom of non-Muslims – who, for example, had always been able to use their own legal systems – as well as fully subjugating the Kurdish regions to central authority.

Military campaigns in the Kurdish regions started in about 1830, and gradually one region after another was violently subjugated. The Hakkâri region was the last to fall, between 1850 and 1860. This policy failed in Dersim and a few other, smaller regions, however, perhaps because there were too many different tribes to take on, the region was relatively densely populated and spread over numerous villages, and the terrain was inhospitable – which would have made military action very complicated, certainly in those days. But maybe some regions were simply lower down the list of priorities: Dersim was centrally located, not on the fragile borders of the empire like Hakkâri.

There were several military operations aimed at bringing Dersim to heel between that period and the founding of the Turkish Republic in 1923, but none of them were successful. After 1923 other areas in the east and southeast were first in line: there was almost continuous warfare, flaring up intermittently in various places, until well into the 1940s. Many of the uprisings and 'civilisation offensives' – like those in Koçgiri, Hazro, Zilan, and Ararat – are virtually unknown; some have never even been investigated. The army's military superiority was always vast, and the Kurds invariably got the worst of it.

Dersim was one of the last sizeable regions where power was still in the hands of Kurdish clans, where no tax was paid to the state, and where boys refused military service. In this context Yektan Türkyılmaz remarks that Dersim may be geographically rather inaccessible, but they knew very well what was happening elsewhere in the country – and what had happened to the Armenians. They were only too aware it was now their turn.'

The Surrender of Seyid Riza

According to documents published by the newspaper *Radikal* in late November 2011 that were secret at the time, preparations for a military operation began in 1933. The documents are about an action plan drawn up by the Supreme Command of the Gendarmerie, and include proposals to remedy Dersim's 'lack of submission.' After this a legal framework was gradually constructed enabling intervention in Dersim.

The first step was the 1934 Resettlement Law, which applied to the whole of Turkey. It aimed to ensure that Kurds – meticulously described as 'people whose assimilation into Turkish culture is desirable' – were dispersed across the country. People who already had Turkish culture, would be resettled in areas where there were too few of them. In other words, Turks had to move to Kurdish areas, and Kurds had to leave their native areas. In addition, some regions were designated as unsuitable for habitation, and the local population was forcibly expelled.

The law also nullified all the property rights of tribal and religious leaders. After being dispossessed, these leaders were the first to be forced to leave their native areas – a clear signal that this policy also aimed to break the ties between leaders and their communities, impeding them from using their power to incite their people to rebel against the republic. Finally, the law forbade all associations and groups, including for instance guilds and cultural clubs, in which the majority of members did not speak Turkish.

The Tunceli Law followed a year later, which depicted the region as 'a sick area needing an operation.' Dersim was renamed Tunceli and martial law was declared. The military governor was given the power to arrest people and expel them. There was a build-up of troops in the region, and roads and bridges were built to transport all the soldiers. In 1936 Atatürk declared in Parliament that Dersim was 'Turkey's biggest domestic problem.'

Yektan Türkyılmaz: 'The main clan leaders like Seyid Riza did everything they could to avert disaster, even handing in their weapons and surrendering. It was all in vain; their fate was sealed.'

The army intervened. Villages were evacuated and razed. Men, women and children, young and old – no one was safe from the army's bloodlust. The methods of instilling Dersim with 'civilisation' ranged from shooting and stabbing people, to drowning and burning them alive, bombing them from the air and even smoking them out of caves. Incidentally, the first female combat pilot in the world also took part in the bombings: Sabiha Gökçen, Atatürk's adopted daughter. Istanbul's second airport is named after her – I can't help thinking about Dersim when I'm at that airport and see old photos of her and Atatürk.

In September 1937, seven Kurdish leaders surrendered, including Seyid Riza. He was sentenced to death and hanged on 15 November 1937, and the other leaders also paid with their lives for their surrender. A clean break, just in time for Atatürk's visit to the province on 17 November to inspect the progress of the 'civilisation offensive.'

After the winter – during which the area was virtually inaccessible – the military operation continued unabated. Even clans that were loyal to the state or had surrendered weren't spared. Men, women, children and elderly people were again massacred in their dozens, and sometimes in their hundreds. The army proudly reported the number of 'bandits' that had been 'destroyed.'

It is estimated that between 20,000 to 30,000 people were killed in Dersim, out of a total population of around 65,000 to 70,000 at the time. Survivors were forcibly resettled in other parts of Turkey.

Türkyılmaz's response to the popular argument that the Dersim operations were the result of a rebellion is, 'There was no rebellion. On the contrary, the leaders did everything they could to obey the state, to save lives. They knew the republic didn't negotiate. When the violence began they did their utmost to resist, fighting for their lives, but they didn't stand a chance and soon realised this.' To the Kurds, Seyid Riza is the hero of Dersim. A legendary rebel leader, honoured with a statue in the city of Dersim. Yet Seyid Riza wasn't a rebel leader, he was a resistance leader.

The newspaper *Radikal* delved into the Turkish parliamentary archives to see how those in power responded to the operation.

On 1 November 1938, nine days before Mustafa Kemal Atatürk's death, Prime Minister Celâl Bayar read a speech to parliament on behalf of Atatürk, who was too ill to attend: 'The outbreaks of mass brigandry in Tunceli, which have continued for many years and have occasionally assumed extreme proportions have, as a consequence of efforts within a specific programme, within a short space of time, been liquidated and consigned to history such that events of this nature will never be repeated in that area.' The minutes record shouts of bravo and applause in parliament.

In September 1937, after the first operations in Dersim, Prime Minister İsmet İnönü talked in parliament about the six tribes that he thought were involved in opposition to 'development and rehabilitation' by the republic: 'Today, however many members there are of these six tribes, these, along with their chiefs, have been entirely deprived of the opportunity to act.'

The parliamentarians regularly interrupted the speech with applause. İnönü continued: 'The members of the army and the Republic's gendarmerie that took up arms against the rebels, even though their weaponry was most effective and they displayed no reluctance to resort to arms, acted with extreme compassion to save and protect every single life.'

Dersim would remain inaccessible and under military rule until 1947. All of Turkey east of Malatya remained off-limits to foreigners until 1960.

Kurdish Lessons

I spend my first afternoon in Gülyazı with Hülya, Sinem and Esra. Özkan has gone to the internet café, and Mahmut is playing outside. All three girls go to school, but because there are too many children and not enough teachers and classrooms – as in many parts of Turkey, including my Istanbul neighbourhood, Üsküdar – they only go to school in the morning. You could call it doing shifts.

They show me their school books. It's Hülya's first year at school and she's learning to read. Sitting close to me, she opens her book, and using her finger to follow the words, reads me four whole stories. She doesn't seem to pay any attention to the content, nor is she concerned about intonation – as long as the words come out properly. It goes well, and when she falters, I give her a helping hand.

Esra, already in her fourth year, is doing her English homework. She does her exercises half sitting on the ground, and I help her or explain things when necessary. When she realises I know a lot of English words she asks for a sheet from my notepad. Drawing a vertical line, she asks: 'What is...,' looks around, 'door in English?' She writes the Turkish word for door left of the line, passes me the pen and paper, and I write 'door' on the right.

We make a whole list of everyday things – skirt, trousers, hair, school, girl, boy, tomato, cucumber, pepper, aubergine, salt, broom, carpet, cushion, window, ear, nose, mouth, face. It dawns on me that this is an excellent opportunity to expand my limited Kurdish vocabulary – and to do a little test: how do the Kurdish words they use correspond to what I've learnt in Istanbul?

Kurdish is Kurdish, you might think; but it's not that simple. There are no less than four Kurdish dialects: Kurmanji, Sorani, Zazaki and Gurani. In Turkey, and in a large part of Iraq, the vast majority of Kurds speak Kurmanji. A small minority, particularly in the northern provinces of Bingöl, Dersim/Tunceli and Elâzığ, speak Zazaki. Sorani is spoken in Iraq. Gurani is a small dialect, and is spoken in the southernmost part of Kurdistan, largely by Iranian Kurds.

But it gets even more complicated. Kurmanji has developed differently in each region. The differences are not huge, the main one being accent, but the words may also vary a little ('four' is ça*r* in Diyarbakır; in the neighbouring province, Batman, they say çor), and in some cases they are completely different.

The Kurmanji – which for convenience I'll just call Kurdish, like everyone here – I learnt in Istanbul is 'academic Kurdish.' That is Kurdish in its purest possible form, purged of the tremendous influence Turkish has had on the language in the past century. The problem is that Turkey's assimilation policy is causing academic Kurdish to disappear from everyday life. It is therefore unclear how far it will get you in the villages and towns of the southeast. To both learn the original language and be able to converse with ordinary Kurds, it is therefore a good idea to study the academic variant, to recognise regional differences, and to identify assimilated Turkish rules and words. Easier said than done!

My teacher was Abdurrahman ('Apo'), a grey-haired man in his fifties, with cheerful eyes and a moustache, and always in jeans and trainers. During the first lesson he puts my mind at ease: Dutch and Kurdish are both Indo-European languages, whereas Turkish is not, so Kurdish will be easier for me to learn than Turkish.

Still, I prepare for the worst. Learning a language can drive an impatient person like me to distraction, as I discovered in the seven years I've spent learning Turkish. To make matters worse, the lessons will be in Turkish, and I am the only foreigner in the group of six.

The others are young Kurds whose parents or grandparents migrated from southeast Turkey to Istanbul, and who never properly learnt their mother tongue in the metropolis. In recent years there has been a resurgence of Kurdish consciousness, and they feel the need to master their long-forbidden mother tongue.

Classes are every Saturday afternoon, on the seventh floor of an old building without a lift near the centrally-located Taksim Square, at the edge of the old and impoverished neighbourhood Tarlabaşi, which has had a large Kurdish population since the 1990s. Apo, a retired geography teacher who has worked for state schools all his life, organises the lessons himself. It is his contribution to the preservation of his language. He has been granted free use of the room by a Kurdish charity. The beginners' course costs next to nothing: the equivalent of 125 euros for twelve three-hour classes.

After the first three months, I promptly sign up again for exactly the same course – during the lessons, I've been closer to tears than to laughter, and I don't feel at all ready for the second level. On top of that, I'm planning to go to Gülyazı after the first four lessons, and won't be able to complete the course. Apo thinks this is excellent, as of course it is: I can start putting what I'm learning into practice.

The Word for 'Salt'

'Tomato,' I say to Esra. We've torn another page out of my notepad and drawn a vertical line down the middle. I'm curious how she will write

Kurdish words. Before going to school, she only spoke Kurdish, but has never learnt to write the language. Turkish is drummed into children from day one at school – and Kurdish is prohibited. As a result, children like Esra are never introduced to the letters used in their own language and not in Turkish: *x*, *w*, *q*, î, ê, and û.

Esra ponders for a moment, and writes *bocosehrik*. Well, there's a good start, it bears utterly no resemblance to the word I learnt, *firingî*. Cucumber is next. She writes *gihor*. The correct spelling is *xiyar*, pronounced *xee-yar*: in Kurdish the *x* is pronounced like the *ch* in 'loch.' She has changed the *a* into an *o*, which many Kurds do – Kurdistan is often called *Kurdiston*.

Things become even more interesting with 'salt.' Esra hesitates for a long time, not knowing what to do, eventually writing ğug with a shrug. I ask, 'How do you pronounce that?' She says the word I know: *xwê* – which is impossible to write in the only language she can write.

Next, I decide to choose a straightforward word every Kurd knows and is easy to write: *roj*. It means both 'day' and 'sun.' The sun is depicted on the Kurdish flag, and RojTV is a well-known Kurdish TV station that broadcasts from a backwater near Brussels, and is watched throughout Kurdistan. So I ask, 'What is "sun" in Kurdish?'

To my astonishment Hülya shouts, with her finger in the air as if she were at school: '*Güneş*, like in Turkish!' Esra and Sinem nod in agreement. Appalled, I cry: 'No, no, *roj*!' Three little faces stare at me in surprise. *Roj*? Never heard of it. 'RojTV,' I ask, 'you know that, don't you?' Yes, they do. 'Well, that's the sun!' I decide what's needed here is some rote learning, and shout '*Güneş*?' They shout back '*Roj*!' and all four of us put our fists in the air. We do it ten times. They roar with laughter, and I look at them with feigned severity: 'Remember!'

I don't speak much with Pakize that first day. She never went to school and therefore never learnt Turkish, and the smattering of words and little phrases I know in Kurdish doesn't get us far.

After a meal of rice, bread, cucumber yoghurt and chicken, several people drop by who want to meet me. The atmosphere is downcast; Pakize pours tea and I hold the hand of the middle-aged woman next to me, as she rocks back and forth, occasionally drying her tears with the tip of her white headscarf.

She too only speaks Kurdish, but she has her daughter Hatice with her who can also speak Turkish and helps us understand each other. The older woman is called Belkiz. She must be pushing fifty but doesn't know her exact age. It turns out that she was largely responsible for raising Osman, Mehmet and their three brothers – she took care of them after they father died, when Osman was five years old. Osman's mother married Pakize's father after she was widowed. She was Pakize's father's second wife, whom he married because his first wife only bore him daughters. He and Osman's mother had another six children. For all those years, care of the Kaplan boys was entrusted to their aunt, Belkiz. Even though Belkiz did not bear Osman, she feels every bit his mother.

The children's elated mood of the afternoon has disappeared. Esra and Sinem are doing their homework; Hülya and Mahmut are sitting with us, with tired, vacant faces. Özkan, who went to the internet café after dinner, comes home in the early evening.

When the children are about to drop off, Pakize collects a few mattresses from the other room, lays them in a row and puts the children to bed. The blankets – not the heavy kind, but ordinary ones – are laid right across the whole brood; two are enough. Pakize puts her own mattress next to theirs later in the evening, as well as a third blanket. She has made a bed for me in the other room, to the right of the hallway-cum-kitchen at the entrance. A simple, thin mattress, a sheet, and a blanket. I'm exhausted and soon fall asleep.

What is a Kurd?

Bilgin Ayata laughs when I ask her what a Kurd really is. A sociologist at the Free University of Berlin, she has been researching (amongst other things) Kurds and national identity since the 1990s. 'What is a Kurd? I don't have a conclusive definition,' she replies, adding, 'except perhaps that a Kurd is someone who defines themselves as a Kurd.'

Her response shows exactly where Ayata stands in regard to 'peoples' and 'nations': in her opinion these are always artificial constructions. 'Until the 1980s, peoples were described as groups sharing a language, territory, culture, history and ancestors. This kind of definition developed hand in hand with rising nationalism.' In other words, if you are of the opinion that a people has the right to its own country, you cannot avoid demarcating peoples and defining them. Nationalism increased the relevance of the concept of 'ethnic identity.'

Ayata contends that this definition has always been problematic for Kurds. Just take language: as a result of Turkey's assimilation policy, there are now thousands of Kurds that know Turkish better than their mother tongue – does this mean they are not Kurds? The definition is inadequate.

Turkish identity is an excellent example of how nations are constructed. It is unclear to what extent modern Turkey's founding father, Mustafa Kemal, had a strictly Turkish state in mind when he started the war of independence in 1919. Yet the decision a few years later to call the country *Türkiye Cumhuriyeti* (the Republic of Turkey) speaks volumes. It put other ethnic groups firmly in their place.

To make the country strong, ethnic unity had to be forged where there was none. This lack of unity is still palpable today – just ask a Turk about their ancestors. I often do, and always get surprising answers. An acquaintance of mine has both Albanian and Egyptian ancestors; I know a Turk with Bulgarian, Greek and Jewish blood; there are Turks with roots in Georgia, Syria, Lebanon and so on.

Minorities in the Treaty of Lausanne

In the Ottoman Empire, your ethnicity did not ultimately matter to the state; it was religion that was crucial in determining your rights and obligations. Ottoman Muslims were administrators and city-dwellers, while Kurds were neither one nor the other: almost all Kurds lived in the countryside at the time, and weren't incorporated into Ottoman administration. Atatürk drew on this legacy when 'forming' Turkish identity, whilst severing the relationship with Islam. This left the Kurds on the sidelines.

In 1923, after the Turkish War of Independence, the Treaty of Sèvres was replaced by the Treaty of Lausanne, which granted rights to non-Muslim minorities. In practice, this meant Greeks, Armenians and Jews (who were not explicitly mentioned in the treaty) were entitled, amongst other things, to organise their own education and teach their children their own language.

Western powers – who were party to the negotiations – insisted on these clauses, bearing in mind what the Armenians had endured in the Ottoman Empire's final days. They also advocated granting rights to ethnic and linguistic minorities, but this was successfully resisted by Turkish nationalist negotiators, who envisioned the unity of the country's Muslim population as the backbone of the new state.

As a result, Muslim minorities – including Kurds, but also Arabs and Alevis – were not granted recognition, nor any special rights to protect their culture, language and religious rituals. Turkey still applies exemption clauses to parts of international treaties that grant protection to ethnic and linguistic groups, referring to the validity of the Treaty of Lausanne.

All of this is useful to know if you ever get into a discussion about minorities with a Turk. I wasn't aware of these niceties when I first arrived in Turkey, and ended up in an incomprehensible discussion with a Turkish friend. We eventually realised we weren't using the same definition of 'minority.' Like everyone in Turkey, he had been taught the details of the Treaty of Lausanne over and over again at school. He was adamant that everyone who is Muslim was, by definition, not part of a minority. Christians and Jews were minorities.

This friend turned out to be a real fanatic, even claiming that granting minority rights to Muslim groups would encourage inequality. According to him, all citizens of the republic were equal before the law, and special laws for special groups would undermine this. He considered concepts like 'ethnic minority' to be Western imports, which were not applicable to Turkey. Indeed, if it hadn't been for the Western powers – which according to him and many other Turks were still out to weaken and divide Turkey – the Kurds would never have come up with the idea of opposing the unitary state.

In this way, non-Muslim (and non-Sunni) groups were excluded from the new Turkish identity, which was considered a badge of honour. The Armenian Genocide was a harbinger of this: Kurdish and Turkish Muslims worked together to expel and murder Armenian Christian 'traitors' in eastern Anatolia.

Writing this, I'm inevitably reminded of an interview I did years ago in Istanbul with a lawyer called Fethiye Çetin, who had written a book about her grandmother Heranush. The latter had only survived the Armenian Genocide of 1915 because she had been pulled out of her mother's arms by an Ottoman army corporal when they were on a forced march, i.e. a death march, to Syria.

The corporal and his wife took Heranush in as their daughter, called her Seher, and brought her up as a Muslim. Her parents went looking for their daughter after the First World War – her mother had survived the march, her father had been in the United States at the time of the genocide – but although they tracked her down, the family could not be reunited. Heranush/Seher was married by then, and her new family refused her permission to visit her parents in Syria.

Heranush kept her Armenian identity secret all her life – until she was over ninety, her health was deteriorating, and she was nearing the end. She finally confided in her granddaughter Fethiye, and asked her to do her best to get in contact with her family in the United States. Fethiye was bewildered – family in the United States? In the many long conversations that followed with her grandmother, the true identity of the woman everyone knew as Seher came to light.

I asked Fethiye during the interview why her grandmother only started talking about her past at such a late stage. She replied, 'I asked her, but she never gave a clear answer. Perhaps it has to do with the enormous taboo that still exists on the subject. Just after the war, around 1920, everyone knew what had happened and who the girls and boys were with Turkish names and Armenian roots, but then it was hushed up.'

Çetin argues that this is related to the emergence of modern Turkey: 'The Ottoman Empire was not a unitary state based on one nation, but that's what Atatürk wanted to make Turkey into. But there was no such thing as a Turkish identity. It had to be created, and that was done by elevating Turkishness to the greatest good. The result was a taboo on not being Turkish – being Armenian was something to be ashamed of.'

Fethiye actually did manage to track down her grandmother's family. By that stage Heranush was too weak to travel to the United States, and she died without ever seeing her family again.

In this context it is interesting to note the furore surrounding comments President Gül made in December 2008. A large group of Turkish intellectuals published a petition on the internet offering their apologies for what they called 'the Great Catastrophe the Armenians were subjected to in 1915' in the final days of the Ottoman Empire, and expressing their empathy with the Armenians' pain. The petition ignited a fierce debate, not least about whether its authors should be regarded as traitors.

When asked by the Turkish press for his view, President Gül refused to comment, simply saying that freedom of expression was alive and well in Turkey. A parliamentarian from the opposition CHP party (founded by Atatürk and still very loyal to his ideas) responded to this by suggesting that Gül must have Armenian blood or he would have rejected the petition out of hand.

It would have been wonderful if the president's response had been that it doesn't matter what blood runs through your veins, or even that it is quite possible that the Gül family has some Armenian ancestry, as millions of Armenians once lived in the Ottoman Empire, or something along those lines. Instead he chose to assert the pure Turkishness of the Gül lineage. He swore all of his ancestors had been Muslims and Turks.

The affair was extremely painful for the Armenian community in Turkey. It was not the first time they had been reminded that there is no greater shame than having Armenian blood.

'We are Kurds!'

In Turkey you learn from a young age to be proud of your Turkish blood. The 'student oath,' which every schoolchild has to recite in front of the school's obligatory Atatürk statue at the start of each school day, was introduced in 1933.

I see this also goes for Esra, Sinem and Hülya Kaplan, whom I walk to school one morning. In their blue and white uniforms they recite:

'I am a Turk, honest and hard-working. My principles are to protect the younger, to respect the elder, to love my homeland and my nation more than myself. My ideal is to rise, to progress. May my life be dedicated to the Turkish existence. Oh Great Atatürk, who created our life today; I swear to always walk on the path that you have paved, in the country you established, with the purposes you have set. How happy is the one who says I am a Turk.'

(The last two sentences were added in the 1970s. Prime Minister Erdoğan abruptly abolished the obligation to recite the oath in the autumn of 2013.)

Atatürk's 'Address to the Youth' is displayed at Gülyazı's primary school, as it is everywhere where children congregate. In it, he urges young people to make every effort to protect the independence of the republic, described as 'the only foundation of your existence and of your future,' against malevolent people both at home and abroad.

This is where the Turkish expression, 'a Turk's only friend is a Turk,' comes from. Foreign powers are basically intent on weakening Turkey, or even carving it up, as the Western powers did after the First World War. Moreover, non-Turks (such as Armenians and Greeks) in the country should be treated with suspicion, as according to Turkish nationalist doctrine they can never be completely loyal to the homeland. Everyone who fits into the doctrinal definition of Turkishness – that is to say, everyone except the Christians – has to be loyal. Anyone claiming another identity is a 'traitor' or a 'separatist.'

That's not how I found Kurds to be. If I had to describe Kurds in Turkey in a few words, I would choose humble, proud, religious and politically aware. The latter is especially noticeable in everyday life.

I remember once wanting to take a photo of a group of ten-year-old boys in Diyarbakır. As soon as they saw the lens, they pulled up their shirts to cover half their face, making themselves unrecognisable, raised their index and middle fingers to make a V sign in the air, and shouted (in Turkish, not Kurdish) 'Biz Kürdüz!,' 'We are Kurds!' The political struggle for full recognition of their existence is ubiquitous, and even boys like this – and girls for that matter – are quite able to explain what it is all about.

It's one of the reasons I like to be in the area so much. I'm not good at trivial conversation, I can't do chitchat – and in Kurdistan, you never have to. The conversation is always about politics; relatives, fellow villagers or friends who have joined the PKK, have died in the struggle or have been imprisoned for political reasons; memories of villages that no longer exist because they were razed to the ground; the latest developments in the capital Ankara and within the Kurdish party, the BDP; the next PKK funeral; a newly-discovered mass grave; the latest adolescent to be killed by the police; developments in a political trial; Abdullah Öcalan's most recent remarks; people who have been arrested or released; and how Kurds in Iraq, Iran and Syria are faring.

This, too, is part of a constructed identity, according to the German academic Bilgin Ayata – or, more specifically, a politicised identity. The Kurds are a prime example of this. A politicised identity derives from a 'collective identity,' which is a group whose members share more or less the same beliefs, feelings and a common fate – workers, women, Christians, Muslims, Americans, Dutch people.

A collective identity can become politicised if, in the words of the *Wiley-Blackwell Encyclopedia of Social and Political Movements*, a consciousness of 'shared grievances' emerges that are blamed on an external enemy. This offers the politicised group a framework through which it can regard other social and political groups as either allies or opponents. The more politicised members of a collective identity become, the more willing they are to take collective action in order, for instance, to encourage the government or the general public into taking action or to choose sides.

Any identity can become politicised, and apart from Kurds, it has also happened to some extent to homosexuals, African Americans and women who took to calling themselves feminists.

The Kurdistan Revolutionaries and the PKK

Kurdish identity started to become politicised when the PKK was established, and when the Turkey-PKK conflict broke out in 1984. On my travels I've often heard poignant stories about how this awakening took place. I'll never forget my long interviews with Yakut Yılmaz, a newspaper delivery boy from Diyarbakır. From the early 90s, he spent fifteen years delivering the initially prohibited newspaper *Özgür Gündem* (Free Agenda) and the only Kurdish-language newspaper in Turkey, *Azadiya Welat* (Freedom of the Country). For the first couple of years, he was joined by his elder brother Nihat, who soon 'went to the mountains' to join the PKK.

The two newspapers were alone in reporting on Kurdish issues, and faced enormous repression in those years. A total of 76 newspaper employees – both journalists and delivery boys – were murdered. *Özgür Gündem*'s Istanbul office was bombed in 1994 – by the state, as leaked documents swiftly proved. Both newspapers have had endless publication bans, and have been repeatedly silenced with high fines.

For delivery boys like Yakut – who was barely out of adolescence at the time – this resulted over the years in dozens of arrests, beatings on the street and in police stations, and numerous raids – in which the police turned his whole house upside down, often finding piles of banned newspapers. Yakut told me about his mother Mevlude: 'She didn't understand what was happening – how come they kept attracting the police's attention? She knew nothing about politics or about the repression of the Kurdish people, even though she was one of its victims. Not speaking Turkish and being illiterate, she couldn't read *Özgür Gündem* and *Azadiya Welat*.'

Mevlude's sons explained to their mother what the papers they delivered said. They made her realise that much of the misery she had experienced in her life, like being forced to leave their village Külboğa, also in Diyarbakır province, in the early 1990s, was due to anti-Kurdish state policy. She had been in the dark, like many others in her generation.

I spoke to Mevlude too. She said, 'At first I had wanted them to quit those newspapers; it was too dangerous. However, once they explained to me what they were doing and why, I let them get on with it. They were with our own people – that reassured me and had to be good. And I understood they were doing it for our own people.'

She supported her sons as best she could, nursing their wounds every time they were assaulted and tortured. When they went on their delivery rounds in the mornings, she threw water after them to shield them from misfortune.

Özgür Gündem and *Azadiya Welat* would never have existed without the PKK. Originating from the more loosely organised Kurdistan Revolutionaries, the PKK was founded in 1978. What made it different is that it did not restrict itself to its training and base camps in Lebanon, Syria and Iraq, but also sent its members into the Kurdish community. They recruited new fighters and explained the tactics of their armed struggle to the population, as well as its purpose: an independent Kurdistan established along communist lines.

Opposition to the Kurdistan Revolutionaries and the PKK – both headed by Abdullah Öcalan – was not tolerated. The theory was that revolution was served by having only one party in control; others would get in the way. In the early years, before the first attack on the Turkish state in 1984, the Kurdistan Revolutionaries and the PKK targeted rival Kurdish revolutionary groups and rich Kurdish landowners. Öcalan and his followers used weapons and violence against them.

In the 1960s and 70s Turkey was teeming with political groups, and the left was particularly well-represented. Kurdish nationalists initially expected support from socialist groups for the Kurds' struggle for recognition of their cultural and political rights. Left wing groups decided not to get involved in the issue, however, partly because they believed both Turks and Kurds would automatically be liberated when the socialist revolution was achieved.

Kurds started creating their own (mostly illegal) organisations. Most advocated a socialist Kurdish revolution, but the Kurdistan Revolutionaries and the PKK were the only ones who actually took up arms. This was a crucial aspect of their appeal, according to interviews the American journalist Aliza Marcus conducted with Kurds that joined Öcalan's group in those years, and from which she quoted in her book about the history of the PKK, *Blood and Belief*.

PKK member Ramazan Ülek, a student who joined Öcalan in 1977 recounted, 'In my village [...] everyone had a relative who had been beaten by the soldiers and the PKK was a stand against that. The PKK was also against the *aghas* [wealthy landowners] who would steal everything, even gold off a woman's neck. After years of being repressed, suddenly there was something and everyone ran to the PKK.'

The group permeated every level of Kurdish society, to the point of taking control: anyone wanting to express the Kurdish consciousness they had rediscovered in, say, political action or journalism, could only do so with the PKK's implicit consent. All the groups that emerged in the period adhered to the PKK's ideology, whether they were newspapers, political groups, cultural associations or youth clubs.

The 1980s: a Military Reality

The Turkish state didn't stand idly by in the face of these developments. Official doctrine still denied the existence of the Kurds, and therefore of the Kurdish question. According to this logic, the PKK was not a consequence of the oppression of Kurds, but rather a terrorism problem threatening the Turkish people's unity and endangering the country's territorial integrity. Military force was the only possible response to PKK violence.

This approach was not at all out of place in the political – or more specifically the military – reality of the 80s and 90s. The Turkish army staged a coup d'état in September 1980, ushering in a very repressive period. About 650,000 people were arrested and tried by military courts – most were left-wingers and Kurds, but right-wingers were not spared either. Turkish prisons gained notoriety the world over for their severe torture, which claimed the lives of 300 people; fifty death sentences were pronounced and carried out; political parties and trade unions, as well as thousands of associations, were banned. Martial law was declared over the whole country.

Official military rule did not last long: a new constitution was adopted in 1982, elections were held in 1983, and civilian rule was officially re-established at the end of the year. The civilian government, led by Prime Minister Turgut Özal, was under full military control, however. The new constitution greatly expanded the powers of the National Security Council (or *Milli Güvenlik Kurulu* in Turkish, abbreviated to MGK) – which had been established after Turkey's first military coup in 1961 – and obliged the government to heed its 'recommendations.'

The National Security Council's monthly meetings were chaired by the president – between 1983 and 1989 that was General Kenan Evren, the leader of the coup. The Secretary General of the National Security Council was the commander-in-chief of the Armed Forces, and the commanders of the Army, Air Force, Navy and the Gendarmerie each held a seat on the council. The government was represented by the prime minister and the ministers of Foreign Affairs, Interior Affairs and Defence.

The official civilian-military balance did not, however, amount to much in practice: the armed forces set the agenda and formulated the statements that were subsequently approved and sent to the government. To boot, all of these statements, including reports with background information, were prepared by the National Security Council Secretariat, staffed by 400 serving or retired military personnel and headed by the National Security Council secretary general, who was also the commander-in-chief of the Armed Forces. The government representatives were toothless.

Incidentally, the National Security Council was responsible for the bombing of *Özgür Gündem*'s offices in 1994: Prime Minister Tansu Çiller signed the order three days before the attack.

The National Security Council was not the only organisation to hold sway over politics – there were two new institutions created by the 1982 Constitution: YÖK (Council of Higher Education) and RTÜK (Radio and Television Supreme Council). Put bluntly, they were there to ensure that academic life and all radio and television broadcasts were in line with the basic tenets of the state: subservience to the secular state and the indivisibility of the country as founded by Atatürk. The army was given a prominent place on both councils.

The Kurdish population was not spared in any way during the fight against the PKK. Within a decade, almost every Kurdish family had first-hand experience of the conflict between the PKK and the state: villages were forcibly evacuated and destroyed; prisoners tortured; Kurdish politicians, intellectuals and ordinary citizens disappeared; and young relatives who joined the PKK often paid for that choice with their lives.

The artificial Turkish identity, and the uncompromising way in which the state clung to it, ironically contributed to the construction and politicisation of the very identity it was trying to destroy: Kurdishness.

A broad popular nationalist movement – which had not existed when the treaties of Sèvres and Lausanne were signed, had not been represented by Sheikh Said and had been absent from Dersim in the 1930s – now suddenly sprang into existence within a few years.

Ever since, it has been possible to say, 'A Kurd is someone who defines themselves as a Kurd.' Yet this definition does not do justice to history. What about women like the newspaper delivery boy Yakut's mother, Mevlude, who did not define herself as Kurdish for a large part of her life? What about the rich landowners and tribal elders, who identified themselves more with the elite than with their ethnic background? What about the small group of intellectual, urban Kurds in the Ottoman Empire, who saw themselves as 'Ottoman citizens,' regarding 'Kurd' more as a synonym for 'backward peasant'? Were none of them Kurds because they did not call themselves that?

'Yes they were; but not Kurds in the political sense, but rather as a social and cultural reality,' says Cengiz Güneş, lecturer at the Open University in the United Kingdom. Nowadays, he too would describe a Kurd as someone who calls themselves a Kurd; this definition applies when a people sharing a social and cultural context is united – a process which has taken place in the last thirty years.

But is there really unity? Aren't Kurds just an amalgam of innumerable tribes and clans, with different languages, religions and traditions who have often enough in history been at each others' throats? I note that I frequently hear claims that it is no wonder Kurds do not have a state, for how can you see a 'nation' or a 'people' in so much heterogeneity?

Güneş flips this logic around: 'It's not the case that Kurds don't have a state because they lack unity. On the contrary: it's because Kurds don't have a state that they were never able to unify. Many nations, in Europe too, weren't unified until they had their own state – take Turkey for instance, or Italy. You need to have your own state in order to build institutions, organise education, establish one or more official languages and standardise them, and so on. Kurds have never had that opportunity.'

In the past thirty odd years, more Kurds than ever have said the same as those boys I photographed in Diyarbakır: 'We are Kurds!' Some, like them, by making a V sign in the air, others by taking up arms or putting pen to paper in journalism or literature, taking the floor in parliament or defending their fellow Kurds in the courtroom. Who knows which identity they will cherish if the Kurdish question is ever resolved, and they can express their Kurdishness freely in all aspects of life. Shouting

'We are Kurds!' would no longer be a revolutionary or political act, and the Kurdish identity might perhaps once again become a natural and self-evident given, not requiring explicit mention to secure its survival. Just as it was for a long time.

A Suburban Neighbourhood in Hengelo

I've been asked countless times in recent years why I'm so involved with Kurds. The answer is that the subject enables me to write about something I've always found important: human rights. Yet at the same time, this explanation is far too simple. Over the years, Turkey has fundamentally changed the way I think about myself and what I consider important.

It is true that human rights have always been important to me. To be more precise, from the moment, aged about twelve, when I read an Amnesty pamphlet about torture. Its contents were of course not intended for twelve-year-olds – a bag over your head, electric shocks to the genitals, beatings on the soles of the feet, being hung from the arms and legs, and spending nights in a dark cell, hearing nothing other than the screams of other prisoners being tortured. All of this could happen, I read to my amazement, just because you didn't agree with the government.

I remember taking the pamphlet to school and showing it to some classmates. 'You have to read this! Look what's happening!' My school friends weren't very interested, and I, too, was more preoccupied with music and clothes than with tyrannical prisons at that age. But I remember that pamphlet and my consternation – rereading those scenes time and time again out of sheer disbelief – as the moment I became aware of the barbarities people inflict on each other.

Not that my parents kept me and my sisters in ignorance about the fact that the world was bigger than our suburban neighbourhood in the small Dutch town of Hengelo. Even our neighbourhood had reasons to discuss war: six of the fathers in our row of eight houses worked for Hollandse Signaalapparaten, a Dutch arms manufacturer, which was also the biggest employer in the adjacent row of houses. My father was proud to earn his living with the railways – still a respectable job in those days.

We sponsored a Foster Parents Plan child, Melody from the Philippines, and wrote letters to her. I still have to laugh recalling the time I told Melody about the new carpet in my bedroom. My mother told me that Melody probably wouldn't understand what it meant. We went through the pictures we had of the girl and her family, and sure enough, there were no signs of bedrooms or carpets in her slum in Manila.

My sister Marike had a subscription to the development magazine *Klap*, and I received the children's version, *Samsam*. On Saturday mornings Marike, my other sister Hanneke and I occasionally wrote letters to the children's page of a national newspaper. Hanneke, who couldn't yet write, once made a drawing of a village in a poor country and Marike wrote Hanneke's words next to it: 'Children in poor countries also have a right to food, drink and curtains.' The drawing was published in the newspaper.

So it wasn't very surprising that I came across that Amnesty pamphlet – nor that it shocked me deeply, given that my world, although well-informed, had hitherto been utterly peaceful.

I think my childhood played another important role in the way I became captivated by the Kurdish question. It has everything to do with identity, and the fact that I grew up in a family in which I was allowed to be myself. My parents didn't toe the line; nor did they expect their three daughters to. Not that they were such misfits, but they were not – and did not try to be – like other parents. My father was one of the few people in the street who didn't work for *Hollandse Signaalapparaten*, and my mother was the only working mother in the vicinity, having gone back to work when Hanneke was six and I was nine.

They weren't outrageously exceptional, but still, choosing one's own path, standing behind one's choices, and not caring what other people thought: mum and dad taught by example. That was also true of small things, like the time a button came off one of my father's shirts. The joke at work was that Henk's wife was so busy working that she didn't even have time to sew a button back on. When my mother wanted to do it one evening, my father stopped her, saying, 'Just leave it a little bit longer; I'll wear it one more time to the office without a button tomorrow morning.' He did, and this shut them up.

Encouraged by my father, I did something similar myself. My mother made me a jumper dress when I was about ten. It went all the way down to the middle of the thigh and you wore tights underneath it – the height of fashion in 1980. I thought it was gorgeous and proudly wore it to school, where I was promptly laughed at by my classmates. At lunchtime I wanted to change into other clothes, but dad, who happened to be at home, asked me an essential question: 'Do *you* like it?' 'Yes, I do.' 'In that case,' he said, 'don't worry about what other people think. The best thing you can do is just to go back to school as you are. Get on a table, spin around and shout, "Come on all of you, have another look and a good laugh!" Bet you no one will laugh then!'

So I decided to go back to school in my jumper dress. I didn't have the nerve to stand on a table, but it wasn't necessary – no one made fun of me anymore.

A Dutch Woman Abroad

These are some of the most valuable lessons I have learnt in life, and since people often ask about my interest in the Kurds, I've often found myself thinking about these things again. Just saying, 'I think human rights are important,' sounds so hollow, so meaningless. Who doesn't? It's how I would have put it back in 2004, when my plan to work as a journalist in Turkey was first taking shape. I didn't yet know Turkey; and, not insignificantly, I didn't yet know myself as a Dutch woman abroad. Nor did I yet know how frustrating it was not to be able to live according to that lesson from my youth which is so deeply ingrained in me: always be yourself.

I had many a sleepless night during my first years living in Turkey and getting to know the country. I was completely baffled: the leader of the Social Democratic Party was spewing rabidly nationalist diatribes, Turks who called themselves democrats advocated unseating Prime Minister Erdoğan with a coup, in Turkish secularism state and religion were inseparable, and feminists defended the view that women with headscarves should be barred from the labour market.

Whenever a conversation went beyond small-talk, the person I was talking to turned out to be a nationalist to some degree. This was not just disagreeable, but also confusing: all these nationalists were also just incredibly pleasant, welcoming, helpful, polite, often intelligent and sometimes even charming people. It was not in keeping with my one-dimensional Dutch image of nationalists as anomalies, as shadowy, aggressive people, recognisable from afar. In the Netherlands I didn't even know any nationalists; in Turkey just about everyone seemed to be one!

But hardest of all were the major issues in Turkey ; and it was these subjects in particular that drew my attention as a journalist interested in human rights and women's issues. With hindsight, I realise they were ultimately about identity, about being who you are: the endless discussions about headscarves, the freedom of religion, and the like. A large section of the Turkish population harbours a deep fear of Islamists, especially since 2002, when the AKP won the first of a series of landslide election victories, enabling them to rule on their own.

Almost all of the AKP's founders and leaders hail from parties that were banned for being openly Islamist. Atatürk's followers particularly mistrust the AKP, suspecting the party of having a hidden agenda. As a result of this fear they regard any measure that increases religious freedom as a step towards an Islamic state and as an attack on Atatürk's secular principles. In my view this fear is lethal to individual liberties – for example, the right to study is violated when women wearing headscarves are forbidden from entering university campuses.

But if you want to get to know a country, you can't carry on relying on your own truths; you have to dare to question them. I did, which resulted in all those sleepless nights trying to square the circle. A good strategy was to sell an article on the subject perturbing me, and then to confront it head on.

I sold a story to the leading Dutch feminist magazine *Opzij* about Turkish feminists and the headscarf issue, and had a long interview with a feminist who was a faithful disciple of Atatürk. She explained to me that women with headscarves had to be prevented from acquiring official positions to protect all women in Turkey. She said, 'Islamists want to give women with headscarves more rights so that those women can gain positions within government and business. They are infiltrating everywhere, in order to be able to take over the state. If that happens, all women in this country will lose their freedoms.'

In short, individual rights are a luxury Turkey cannot afford. Yet when I spoke to the women in question, I failed to detect any such devious plan – they just wanted to study and get a degree without having to go to Europe, the United States or Malaysia. They wanted to use their knowledge to benefit their country, and not be forced to stay at home or work abroad.

An Ankara acquaintance of mine who wears headscarves studied at ODTÜ, one of the best universities in Turkey. She once told me about her dream of having a career at a Turkish university. It was unattainable: students with headscarves may now be tolerated, but an academic career is impossible for them. I asked her what she thought her future held in store. She said, 'If I can't work at a university after my studies, I'll get married and have kids. It's good for children to have a mother who studied. Perhaps it'll be different for my daughters.'

Of course they wouldn't have told me about their devious plan if it existed, but I can't accept that millions of people in the country have been taking part in a vast charade for years whilst secretly conspiring to introduce Sharia law one day. For a start, this would undermine their own freedom to practise their faith as they want to. They have nothing to gain from Islamising Turkey.

It is interesting to note that the people who warn about the dangers of women with headscarves – like the feminist I interviewed and other Turks I've discussed the matter with – are themselves Muslims. A Turk once tried to convince me of the Islamist threat by claiming that Islam, unlike Christianity, covers all aspects of life, including law and politics. 'But,' I argued, 'surely that doesn't mean every Muslim wants Islam to rule the country? You're a Muslim yourself, and that isn't what you want, is it?'

His argument that the tightly-worn headscarf, concealing every last hair, was an expression of that desire didn't ring true to me. I know plenty of women who wear headscarves and they all make different choices in life, based on their individual faith; in other words, they don't all share exactly the same beliefs. In fact, the only woman in Turkey who ever refused to shake my hand because I am not a Muslim – and you have to be quite orthodox to do that – wasn't even wearing a headscarf.

Exactly the same mechanism is at play in the Kurdish question. Our Western values – giving peoples the right to their own language and culture, or even to self-determination – are all very laudable, but Turkey cannot afford to live by them, on the contrary: Atatürk's legacy dictates that Turkey has to oppose them. The Western countries now urging Turkey to respect the rights of peoples are, after all, the exact same countries that wanted to pull Turkey apart after the First World War. Brought up on a nationalist diet of Kemalism and the fight against foreign invaders, many Turks believe this is still the intention of Western powers. Unity has to be preserved – at any cost.

Identity is Multi-Faceted

The state forbidding its citizens to be themselves was not something I'd ever experienced in the Netherlands. At least as importantly, in my family and in the Netherlands I'd never experienced what it is like when you are not able to be yourself, when no one knows the real you. I learnt how it felt in Turkey.

Not that I know everything about myself, but I know which identities I value: I'm a journalist, I'm Dutch, I come from the Dutch region of Twente, I'm a woman, daughter, sister, friend, I'm my own boss, and an emigrant. I want to be able to freely express the whole mix – from the identities I choose to the people and the country that have shaped who I am – in an ever-changing balance.

Since moving to Turkey I've lost this ability.

No one in this country has known me longer than I've lived there. Nobody knows the town and country I grew up in; no one knows my parents or the family that formed me; and the language in which I write, think, and can express myself best is unfamiliar to most people here.

In the Netherlands people do know me. Yet even though my parents, sisters and all my friends have come to visit me, know how I live, and have strolled around in Istanbul, nobody in the Netherlands really knows what my life here is like. Nobody knows what it's like to live here and work as a journalist, no one who is important to me knows Turkey as I do, and most of them have never lived in another country. I don't necessarily feel a sense of distance from them - I actually feel more connected to some people than I did when I left the Netherlands - but there is an important part of me they will never know nor understand.

At a conference in Diyarbakır a while ago, I bumped into a Dutch friend who has lived in Turkey much longer than me. He remarked, 'You're really starting to settle in this country, aren't you?' I thought it was a nice compliment, and it was true: I would like to delve deeper into Turkey, and take root here. But while working as a journalist here and immersing myself in the country has been a fantastic experience, it can be infinitely frustrating at times. I cannot share this experience – neither with family and friends in the Netherlands nor friends and colleagues here. Not just because nobody in Turkey knows me well enough, but also because of the language barrier. I can manage in English, but I have more and more friends and acquaintances who only speak Turkish, or Kurdish and Turkish. An everyday one-to-one conversation is usually fine, but they don't often develop into truly personal conversations. Group discussions invariably leave me feeling lost – I'm unable to follow them, and never get the jokes or references to all sorts of things in Turkish and Kurdish society and history that I'm not familiar with. I feel reduced to a quiet, insecure woman who sits there with nothing to say; one thing I'm definitely not!

It has shown me how deeply it affects you when you cannot be yourself, when you're not recognised. In my case it is a self-elected and voluntary state of being – even though I didn't realise what I was getting myself into when I came here in 2006. But just imagine you weren't *allowed* to express a significant part of who you are, that part of your identity was denied and suppressed by force to such an extent that you forgot who you were.

This is not only intolerable for an individual, but for a people too. Living here has taught me that the core of the political and legal concept 'human rights' is all about being able to express yourself freely and to live according to your identity. It is essential for every human being, regardless of how you interpret identities such as female or male, believer or non-believer, Dutchman, Turk or Kurd, townsman or villager, or whatever you bring together in yourself.

When this dawned on me, everything fell into place. Turkey does not give me sleepless nights any longer; I understand and can explain most mindsets here, but I've also learnt at a much deeper level that 'human rights' are not some Western luxury. The notion that Turkey cannot afford to give priority to human rights is nonsense.

Incidentally, Turks themselves are a wonderful example of the multiplicity of identity. Far from being only Turks, they are often proud of the region they come from, some of them identify fanatically with a major football club, others make the sign of the ultranationalist Grey Wolves in the air with their fingers when they see comrades, or wave the Turkish Communist Party flag at demonstrations to show who they are and what they stand for. Diversity: it's simply a part of all of us.

I would never have been able to specialise in the Kurdish question without everything I've learnt about Turkey and the personal development I underwent. I wouldn't have been able to go beyond a superficial level, nor counter the inevitable criticism that I see things through Western eyes. Now I can.

No one can reproach me for being Dutch or European, because that's who I am and there's nothing I can or want to do about it. My Western perspective is part of me, but I'm now familiar with many others and have learnt to view this country and its issues from different points of view. My final conclusion is that human rights matter; but nowadays I prefer to call them identity.

The question of why I'm involved with Kurds and not with homosexuals, Alevis, Roma, or one of the other groups in Turkey that is denied the freedom to be themselves is easier to answer. It's a professional choice I have made as a journalist. The Kurdish question is Turkey's most pressing problem: the struggle between the state and the PKK has claimed at least 40,000 lives, causes much division between the ethnic groups that share this country, and affects Turkey's relationship with neighbouring countries with Kurdish populations.

Moreover, the Kurdish question is not primarily about Kurds, but about identity. If this problem really is solved, everyone will at the very least officially have the freedom to be themselves, whether they are Kurds, Turks, Armenians, gays, heterosexuals, Roma, Muslims, Christians, atheists or anything else. Writing about the Kurdish question is, by extension, also writing about all the other groups that make Turkey what it is.

At the *Yayla* with the Women

The upper part of Gülyazı, where Pakize lives, is the 'old part.' The new part is populated by migrants who left their original villages in the 1990s after they were burned down by the army. Pakize was born and raised here, as was her late husband Osman. I was pottering about near Pakize's house when in the distance I saw her neighbours Çiğdem, Belkiz and Leyla approaching with several children and a donkey. They told me they had been to the *yayla*, a pasture above the village, where they had been milking goats. The donkey was laden with large white plastic bottles, filled to the brim with milk. 'Why don't you join us next time?' Çiğdem asks. 'When will that be?' I return. The women laugh: 'Every day, of course! We leave at about eight o'clock.'

Wear your trainers, they insist, not your flip-flops: it's not a long walk, but the path is rough enough in places. Pakize goes with us the next morning; she only has three goats, and sometimes gets other women to milk them for her. On other days she milks someone else's goats – Çiğdem's, for example, who is pregnant with her third child, and will soon be out of the running for some time.

The next morning we walk out of the village on a sandy track, which also leads to the cemetery where the bombing victims are buried. I know the track because Pakize's daughters took me to their father's grave the first afternoon I was there. We reach a fork in the track, one path leads down to the cemetery, and we take the other one up to the *yayla*.

Our group includes five women, Çiğdem's son and daughter, who are still too young to go to school and are sitting on the donkey, and Pakize's youngest child, Mahmut. He keeps running ahead of the group, letting it pass him as he climbs a tree, then catching up again. Another group of women walk some distance ahead of us. I hear pack animals slowly approaching from behind, and turning around see three women on mules. They are wearing colourful Kurdish dresses; their animals have coarse red, blue and orange cotton saddlebags and matching harnesses with coloured tassels. It's such a powerful image that I can't keep my eyes off them.

As they pass, I see Pakize and the other women standing next to the track, palms turned upwards. Looking through the bush I see we're above the cemetery; the women are praying for the souls of the dead.

On the way I see the children drinking from a stream next to the track. I'm thirsty too, but daren't drink the cool water as I'm unsure whether it's safe. A little later, at the next stream, my dry throat makes me change my mind, and I take a scoop of water with my hands and raise it to my mouth. 'No, no, not that water!' the children scream. Why one stream is alright and not the other is a mystery to me, and no one explains why, but I've already swallowed the water. Could one sip of the wrong water make you sick? Surely not? I decide that from now on, I'll only drink water where the others do, and not choose my own stream.

The path is getting steeper; it's hot, the sky is blue and speckled with the odd cloud, and the verdant mountain landscape around us gets more impressive with every step. The track narrows as we go around a corner and reach a wide, fast-flowing stream. We walk alongside it for a bit, which isn't easy as it's narrow and slippery, and if you were to fall you would hit large boulders on your way down to the shallow water. The children laugh at me as I awkwardly clutch bushes and stones, anxious about tumbling down. I watch in admiration how the women forge ahead regardless of the narrow path.

When we cross the stream – I manage this more elegantly, hopping over three boulders to reach the other bank unscathed – I can hear the goats: the air is filled with bleating.

It's only now I stop concentrating and look up that I see where the climb has brought me: a large sandy pasture, strewn with boulders and a few small trees and scrubs, bounded by the stream on the right. About a dozen men are driving a few hundred goats towards the highest part of the plot, where around thirty women stand facing each other in two rows, forming a narrow corridor between them. They open their cotton saddle bags and pull out funnels, empty yoghurt pots, soft drink bottles, and white plastic jerry cans. They place the bottles and jerry cans behind them, supported between stones. Some women put large plastic aprons on.

One of the goatherds sits on top of a couple of large stones in between the women, and then it starts: the goats are driven down this 'milking corridor,' and when a woman sees one of her goats, she grabs it by the hind legs and milks the animal with her skilled hands. Using a funnel, the milk is poured from the pot into an empty soft drink bottle, which is emptied into a jerry can when it's full. Goats are distinguished by a plastic ear clip, a dash of blue, green, yellow or red paint on the horns or a triangular marking in one of the ears.

The goatherd in the middle knows exactly who owns each goat, and pulls them in the right direction or gives them a smack on the rump if they don't leave the milking corridor fast enough after being milked. Milked goats run out of the corridor, where goatherds make sure they don't mix with the unmilked livestock higher up. I watch this fascinating spectacle from a distance, sitting on a stone. The bleating of the goats is drowned out several times by army helicopters zooming across the valley in front of us, occasionally even skimming over the *yayla*. Nobody pays any attention.

Every day, one or two of the women from the group prepare food for everyone. After milking, blankets are spread out next to the stream and stream water boiled in blackened kettles over a fire for tea. Dolmas (stuffed vine leaves) and filled pastries are served with fresh bread from plastic tubs, and people drink water from the stream. The women rinse their buckets and plastic bottles downstream, pack the saddlebags, and load the donkeys and mules. We're back in the village around noon.

Banners at the Cemetery

The rituals of daily life have remained unchanged for generations. In December 2011, the female relatives of the air strike victims added one to their routine: in the afternoon before the Islamic day of rest, they visit the graveyard together. Pakize, dressed in her habitual dark skirt, black shirt and blue headscarf, invites me along.

I'm staying at her place for a few days and am making great friends with her children, especially the two youngest, Mahmut and Hülya, who even insist on placing their mattresses next to mine at night. Not a recipe for a great night's sleep, but all the more fun getting up in the morning. On our way to the graveyard, Hülya walks next to me. She takes my hand and gives me such an affectionate smile that my heart melts at once.

The first part of the way is the same as going to the *yayla*: we walk up the sandy path that leads out of the village from Pakize's house. Two more women join us along the way, also dressed in dark clothing. Shortly afterwards I hear rapid little footsteps: Mahmut is running after us. He takes my other hand.

The cemetery has changed since the first time I was here four months ago. The graves have not yet been marked by headstones, it's too early for that, and the colourful sea of plastic flowers is still just as overwhelming. What's new are the banners strung between the trees. One calls for the 'killer state' to provide answers, another reads, 'We curse the Roboskî massacre, we want those responsible brought to justice.' There are Kurdish flags.

Pakize and her children go to Osman's grave. She rearranges the flowers a little, sweeps the stones around the grave and prays in silence. The children, all of whom have come except Özkan, the eldest, also say their prayers, hands held out in front of them with the palms facing up. Afterwards, they fill some empty soft drink bottles lying around at the cemetery tap and go round all the graves with living plants. Everyone lends a hand except Mahmut, who's busy climbing a tree.

The graveyard soon fills up with family members. I look around and sure enough, there is Semire, the quiet girl I spoke to during my first visit to the village. She's with a woman who's clearly her mother – they are like two peas in a pod – and some aunts. I go to her as she prays at the grave of her little brother Bedran. We embrace. She looks better than she did the first time, when Bedran had barely been dead a week – mentally stronger, her eyes not as wide with bewilderment, not as hollow and empty anymore.

Semire and her family want to know what I have written about the air strike, and why I am back in the village. I tell them I want to find out more about what exactly happened, and get to know the village better. I tentatively broach the subject of Servet Encü, the survivor of the bombing I was originally meant to stay with, but who has emigrated to

Iraqi Kurdistan. He is an uncle of Semire's, so these women are likely to know all the ins and outs.

'He went to Zakho because he found a job there,' one of Semire's aunts tells me. She says it a bit too forcefully, and I find it hard to believe he moved his wife and children, some of whom are still in school, to the small town across the Iraqi border just for a job. Surely the employment situation must be about the same as here?

'Is it really easier to find work there?' I ask. 'I've heard he didn't feel safe anymore. Isn't that true?' Semire's mother says something about Servet getting phone calls, but doesn't get the chance to finish her story before her family members intervene, hissing something to her in Kurdish. There follows a rapid exchange I don't understand, and from then on Semire and her mother keep silent. Servet went there to work, and that's all the family will say.

Pakize's Tears

That evening, I talk with Pakize. Her neighbour's boy Burhan is visiting. Burhan, in his twenties, is the son of Osman's foster mother Belkiz. I don't find all the Turkish-speaking villagers easy to understand because some of them have a thick Kurdish accent, but Burhan's Turkish is perfect, and he speaks clearly and calmly. He's prepared to interpret between me and his half-brother's widow.

It was around five o'clock in the morning after the air strike that Leyla, the wife of Osman's brother Mehmet, called at Pakize's house. Pakize had hardly slept a wink. 'Osman often went on smuggling trips and had never been back later than 11 o'clock at night. That evening, he just didn't show up. I stood at the window for ages waiting for him to come home.'

She would lie down and take a short nap now and again, then continue to pace restlessly up and down the house and look out of the window. What did she think had happened? Pakize: 'Perhaps the group had been arrested, fined and taken to the army post, or maybe he'd been shot at and was wounded,' she said. It had never happened to him before, but she knew these things went on, and it could easily be her husband's turn this time.

Leyla broke the news without mincing her words: 'The smugglers have been bombed and everyone is dead.'

In the weeks that followed, Pakize was never left alone. Leyla stayed with her at first, holding her when she cried. The children woke up, and together they went to Belkiz's house. RojTV was airing the first footage of the tragedy. Pakize: 'There was no need to tell the children what had happened. The TV did that.'

She never saw Osman again. 'I was told his body had been blown to pieces, and it was better for me not to see him again.' She remembers the days after the bombing like a haze of grief in which she could only cry; she was looked after, the children were looked after, and she was haunted by images. Asleep or awake, she kept seeing the faces of all the men and boys who had died. The faces didn't give her a moment's peace. She couldn't go back to living in the house she'd shared with Osman. 'I needed my family around me, I couldn't bear being in my own house. I didn't dare go back.'

In the early years of their marriage, Osman and she lived with Belkiz's family. The house they were to move into had been built by Osman's father but had become run down. Osman spent eight years painstakingly renovating it. When it was finished, they moved in with Özkan and Esra, and Sinem, Hülya and Mahmut were born in the years that followed.

The whole family lived in the living room, day and night. The other room was hardly ever used – too cold in winter, too warm in summer. It contains a wardrobe with a pile of mattresses and blankets next to it. Leaning against the other wall is a huge bag of sugar cubes and another bag, also almost a metre tall, full of cucumbers. That's it. A small window looks out over the verdant valley and the army post on the hill opposite. On the windowsill is a broken hand mirror, a comb and an elastic band.

Pakize shows me photographs of their wedding; she was only fourteen, Osman twenty. Pakize wearing a glittering white dress, the female guests shimmering gowns and the men traditional Kurdish outfits. 'I didn't know what was going on, I was just a child,' Pakize says.

Despite marrying young, they were happy together; they never argued, and Osman was a good father who looked after his family as best he could. After Mahmut was born, Osman had himself sterilised. Pakize: 'He decided five children were plenty for us. I refused to take contraceptives, so he went in for the procedure. He went to a doctor visiting the village.'

After the bombing, Pakize didn't set foot in her house for two months. Then she felt it was time to go back. Pakize: 'For the children's sake. It was better for them to return to our own place.' All the women of the family accompanied her, including her mother and sisters. Weeks earlier, they had come over from Silopi, a small town close to the Iraqi border like Gülyazı, but further to the west.

The women cleaned Pakize's house from top to bottom. There was tea, there was food, there were tears. Then everyone went back home except Pakize's mother, who stayed with her daughter for another month.

Pakize has now been alone with the children for about five weeks. 'They can be difficult to control,' she sighs. I see what she means. Around suppertime, the children wreak havoc in the house. '*Reeena*,' Pakize sometimes shouts at them, 'sit down!' But it's no use. The pillow-fighting, hair-pulling, horsing around, jumping, squealing and screaming continues, sometimes until it ends in tears. Pakize usually lets them blow off steam while she's preparing supper or making tea. Esra proves herself a worthy eldest daughter by helping her mother the moment she is asked. Sitting on the floor in the hall, she's chopping cucumbers into tiny pieces and stirring them into a large bowl of yoghurt.

It only takes a word from their mother for the others, too, to swing into action getting supper ready – Hülya obediently sets out the cutlery on the plastic rug the family eats on, Sinem puts the bowl of rice on it – but things only really start calming down when the meal begins. More often than not, hell breaks loose again afterwards. If I didn't know better, I'd think they were just a lively bunch. Pakize: 'They used to settle down the moment their father came home.' She can't always summon the energy to be both father and mother.

The Air Strike as a Pawn in a Political Game

Pakize is not a woman of many words, great displays of emotion or lengthy speeches on what was done to her and her children, and why. She doesn't even respond 'because we're Kurds' to my question why she thinks the bombing took place, but says, 'I don't know, and perhaps we never will. But God knows everything and that comforts me.'

I've wondered whether I wouldn't be better off finding a different family to stay with, one whose relatives also died in the massacre, to talk in more depth about life before and after the bombs. Many families in the village – and many of the women – are far more articulate than Pakize, and better at expressing their emotions. And they speak Turkish, which would make communicating easier.

But I dismiss the idea, and visiting the village time and again in the months that follow, I feel no inclination to change my mind. This is partly because the bombing is increasingly becoming a pawn in a political game. This polarisation started to become apparent in the first days after the incident, but the government's handling of the situation has only increased it; the secrecy, the investigation commission that doesn't get to speak to important decision-makers, and the venomous – not to say downright boorish and callous – comments by government officials.

The Interior Minister İdris Naim Şahin takes the cake in late 2012. It's one of those moments that make me doubt my command of Turkish, because I simply can't believe what I'm hearing on the news. Şahin says in a live interview with the NTV news station – who allow him to talk without posing a single critical question – that the victims of the bombing were like 'extras in a film,' that they were engaged in illegal activities for the PKK when they died, and that legal action would have been taken against them had they been caught alive during their mission. In this context, he announces, 'we see nothing to apologise for.'

A few days after Şahin's comments, Prime Minister Erdoğan adds insult to injury by using the Uludere incident to take a cheap shot at abortion: 'Every abortion is an Uludere,' he says. The public debate about Şahin's words has not yet died down, and Erdoğan cleverly makes use of it to give his party a more humane image. This is the game he and Şahin are playing. Şahin's role is to make callous remarks that will keep the ultranationalist AKP voters happy, then Erdoğan reprimands his minister and comments on the same subject to satisfy the more moderately nationalist AKP voters.

Such political games are salt in the wounds of the victims' relatives, and all inhabitants of Gülyazı and Ortasu. Their grief is ignored by the large, established Turkish parties, all of which are more or less nationalist. Only the pro-Kurdish Peace and Democracy Party (BDP) speaks up, in this case by vehemently condemning the government insinuations. 'The AKP uses abortion to divert public attention from the Uludere bombing,' BDP leader Selahattin Demirtaş lashes out.

This is exactly the kind of political polarisation I'm trying to avoid by getting an impression of everyday life in the villages. The BDP is widely supported in Gülyazı and Ortasu; in the summer 2011 elections, the party achieved its greatest victory to date. Staying with the most eloquent villagers would not necessarily mean I'd get to record more emotions and individual opinions, but probably only that I'd hear more of the party's views.

Pakize and Osman always voted for the Kurdish party, too, but Pakize is anything but an activist. She always joins the gatherings of relatives commemorating the dead, and the protests against the poorly conducted investigation by the parliamentary commission, but she never stands at the front, never shouts slogans, never cries with theatrical, long-drawn sobs. Not on the Thursday I accompany her to the cemetery nor on any other occasion I witness in months to come.

Every time I come across an image on the internet of any kind of gathering in the village to do with the bombing, I search them for Pakize. I know she's there, but she's never on the photograph, or only as a barely recognisable background figure. A young, humble, deeply religious widow, Pakize is intelligent but unschooled, a mother of five and a villager, and does not have a ready story. Perhaps not the first choice of a Western journalist, but I'm glad she crossed my path. She represents an important group: Kurdish women who have lost someone in the conflict, and who generally bear their grief in silence with the help of Allah and their families.

The Rash

To my regret, I'm unable to stay in Gülyazı for the month or more I had planned. After a fortnight, I can no longer ignore the drama that is taking place on my arms and legs: they are covered in red pimples, and they itch. I thought I felt something crawling around in my bed the first night but tried to pretend I hadn't, especially after inspecting the mattress in daylight without finding anything. And even if there were invisible creepy crawlies living in my mattress, what did I care, I told myself. In my opinion, no journalist worth her salt should be daunted by some bug or its bite.

But on a Saturday morning roughly two weeks later, the handful of spots have become a rash covering my arms, legs and shoulders. Pakize pulls a worried frown when she sees them, Çiğdem claps a hand before her mouth and blames the 'changing weather' – an event that must have slipped my notice – and Belkiz says I should go to the hospital immediately. I am not the type to run to the doctor's, but I find the bumps are worrying me; not to say sending me into a bit of a panic.

The only minibus running from this part of Gülyazı to Şırnak, the province's capital, left hours ago at seven o'clock this morning. It's around ten now, and after some deliberation, Belkiz's son Burhan says he'll help me get a lift. Fed up and angry, I pack my bags, hug the children – except

Mahmut, because the little monkey is nowhere to be found as usual – and kiss Pakize and her neighbours goodbye.

Waiting on the square with the shop and internet café, we're soon picked up by a car heading towards the main road down below. During the short ride, Burhan reassures me that he knows just about everyone in the area and will find a suitable driver to take me to Şırnak. His reassurance is unnecessary, as I'm not the least bit worried. Partly because I trust Burhan, but also because of the last time I left the village and my assistant Beyda, Aziz the fixer and I were given a safe and comfortable lift by the very first lorry to drive past. Burhan explains his strategy: he will only hail vehicles registered in Şırnak (whose number plates begin with 73) or one of the neighbouring provinces that have a road going to Şırnak: Hakkâri (30), Siirt (56) or Mardin (47).

A lorry comes thundering up: a Siirt number plate. Burhan and I raise our hands and it stops. There are two men in the cabin. Burhan addresses them in Kurdish, which the men, who turn out to be two of the many Arabs living in Siirt, don't understand. The conversation switches to Turkish. Yes, they're on their way to Şırnak, and yes there is a free seat, as long as I don't mind squeezing in between them in the front. Burhan nods at me and I tell the drivers, 'No problem.'

They jerk their heads at my suitcase. 'What's in there?' 'Clothes, notepads and a laptop,' I answer. 'Nothing illegal?' Nothing illegal, I promise. The back is opened, I put in my suitcase, say goodbye to Burhan and climb into the cabin. Arabic music is playing.

I am of course taking a risk as a woman by getting into a lorry with men I don't know, but as I learn on the way, giving me a lift is risky for them, too. They trade in toys and household articles, driving around the area every day to sell their wares to the shops in the villages along the road. The lorry is full of balls, dolls, toy cars, china, pans, cutlery, towels, hat stands – you name it. 'Our van gets inspected at almost every army post,' the men, who turn out to be brothers, tell me. 'If you're smuggling cigarettes in your suitcase, we're in for it. You do know that a lot of smuggling goes on around here, don't you?'

Sure enough, the lorry is inspected at two of the four army posts, and so is my suitcase. I notice the two men are nervous about it, but I was telling the truth about its contents. We stop a couple of times on the way to deliver goods or collect cash owed to the salesmen by shop owners. The brothers treat me to a small tub of ice cream at one shop and a fruit flavoured drink with a straw at the next. Roughly two hours later, they drop me off in Şırnak, on the road that leads to the hospital. I thank the drivers and they wish me a speedy recovery. Wheeling my suitcase after me, I walk the short way to the entrance of the colossal state hospital.

Chapter Four

The Mountains

Something doesn't make sense. Şırnak province doesn't have many roads but plenty of army checkpoints, some of which are very thorough when it comes to inspecting vehicles, and yet smuggling is the main economic activity in the region. You might go unnoticed by the authorities on the small trails in the mountains, but after that, the goods are transported in lorries. The lorries sometimes make the headlines when they are intercepted, but that happens very rarely compared to the annual amount of trade in the area.

Let's just say that it doesn't take a rocket scientist to work out that the authorities must not only allow small-scale smuggling operations such as the ones conducted in Gülyazı and Ortasu, but turn a blind eye on a much larger scale, too. Proving it is another thing, however.

Scouts and Smugglers

The next time I visit the villages, I decide to go on the smugglers' trail myself. The rash that forced me to leave Gülyazı early last time has cleared up of its own accord. At Şırnak state hospital, they gave me a jab in the buttock without a clear diagnosis, and without result; a newly fledged dermatologist at the Diyarbakır academic hospital prescribed pills and a lotion for scabies, which proved to be the wrong diagnosis; and at a private clinic in Istanbul, an infectious disease specialist and a dermatologist unanimously agreed that it was some kind of allergic reaction, and left it at that.

Unfortunately, I still haven't found out what it is I am allergic to. Using a sheet sleeping bag hasn't helped at all, allergy pills have helped a little, and taking along bottled water instead of drinking from the stream makes no difference. With each visit, the rash on my limbs makes its appearance sooner and takes longer to disappear. This doesn't prevent me from visiting the village, but I do regret that it forces me to leave after a short while.

Anyway, off to the mountains. To get there, you don't set out from Gülyazı but from its neighbouring village Ortasu, on the road to the border. The bombing is officially called the Uludere air strike after the

Turkish name of the district in which Gülyazı and Ortasu are situated, but the Kurdish community prefers calling it Roboskî, the Kurdish name for Ortasu – it was closest to the bombing.

I've made quite a few acquaintances in Ortasu too, one of whom turns out to be closely involved in the smuggling. He's one of the three people who keep records of each smuggling trip, are in touch with the people placing the 'orders,' and make arrangements with the suppliers in Iraq.

A man in his early forties, he's also a 'scout,' one of the ten to fifteen men who keep watch during each trip as the smugglers lead their packed mules back across the Turkish border. Three footpaths run from the border to the slightly larger dirt track leading to the village, and the scouts scan the area with binoculars from the hilltops. Operating alone or in pairs, they use walkie-talkies to communicate with each other and the smugglers. This way, the scouts guide the smugglers back to the village, choosing the safest possible route: *there are soldiers hidden along that path, that one seems safer, and don't go there because I think we saw something move there too.* As the army can listen in on the open system, smugglers and scouts always speak in Kurdish.

He didn't want to take me at first. Too dangerous, he said. But after making my own risk assessment, I decide to insist. The scouts themselves don't smuggle anything; so as long as I'm with them, *I* can never be caught with smuggled goods. I'll take along my official Turkish press pass, a pen and a small notebook to prove that I'm on a journalistic mission. The scouts always stay well on the Turkish side of the border, so there's no chance of me inadvertently breaking the law by crossing the Turkish-Iraqi border, which would give the authorities the right to throw me out of the country. I have the phone number of the Dutch embassy in Ankara, which is open twenty-four hours a day, and thanks to the many army posts in the area, my phone always has a signal. What could possibly go wrong?

Angel, my interpreter, reminds me of the well-known Turkish journalist who accompanied the smugglers and wrote a story about it for the national newspaper *Milliyet*. She says the article got the local soldiers into trouble because their superior officers believed they should have prevented the journalist from doing his work. The journalist was fined 2,000 lira (around 800 euros) for illegally crossing the border, and so were the smugglers he was with.

'Perhaps *you* won't get into trouble,' Angel adds a little testily, 'but others will.' I'm not too bothered by the idea of some soldiers getting a ticking-off from their officers for neglecting their duties and letting me get on with my work in the area. I don't want the smugglers or the scouts to be fined because of me, but they can always choose not to take me along if they think there's a real risk of that happening; I'll let them be the judge of that.

Around seven o'clock in the evening, my contact and some other scouts hop into the trailer of a tractor and disappear around the corner of the dirt track on their way to the border. No, he's really not taking me along. Waving to Angel and me, he promises to call me when they're on their way back with the smugglers, so I can watch. Yeah great, I mutter, resisting the impulse to run after them and leap onto the trailer.

Angel and I drink buckets of tea and polish off a large bag of sunflower seeds. About two and a half hours later, my phone rings, 'We're coming, meet us at the path!' We run through the village to the road the scouts took when they left. It's pitch dark. We stop at the corner and listen – is there something coming?

My God, something's coming. We hear the hooves before we see the outlines of the pack animals. Four slim, strong legs apiece, balancing a massive shape: one bundle on the left, one on the right, and one on top. The mules are going at a brisk pace and the smugglers leading them by their reins are running alongside them. They tear into the village in groups of between three and ten animals, then stop at one of the first houses. The smugglers immediately start unburdening the mules. I'm in the middle of it. The bundles, wrapped in indestructible orange plastic tarpaulin, fall to the ground with a muffled thud. Each mule carries three of them, a weight of over 100 kilos. Women are coming out of the house bringing tea for the smugglers, whose work is done and who are resting on the broad front steps of the house. A moment later, the dusty ground is strewn with packets of cigarettes. I count around thirty mules, which adds up to ninety bundles and well over 3,000 kilos in total. At a closer look, I can read the brands on the packets: Gauloises, MM and Prestige. There is also Mahmood tea.

A large delivery van turns onto the yard. While most of the smugglers are leading their mules home, the ones that have stayed behind start loading the goods into the van in the sparse light coming from inside the vehicle. I notice the number plate starts with 44: Malatya province, which borders on Diyarbakır in the west and is considered mixed territory rather than purely Kurdish. While the bus is expertly crammed full of tea and tobacco, another group of mules clip-clops past the yard. I notice their load looks different, barrel-shaped, and edging closer I can make out a sloshing sound. Petrol. Instead of loading it into vans, the smugglers take it home and sell it from there.

'Any problems?' I ask my contact as we walk back to his house after he's wrapped up the business part of the trip. 'None.' All three paths were open, the soldiers left the smugglers alone and there wasn't even a surveillance drone patrolling the area that night. He said the next trip was planned on the following night and that his twenty-year-old son was joining it. 'So you're going to be a scout again tomorrow?' I ask as insinuatingly as I can.

On the Smuggling Trail

Around six o'clock the next evening, he hands me a traditional Kurdish men's outfit: baggy trousers and a jacket with lots of pockets. Wearing my black shirt, his son's beige socks, and sturdy shoes with a heavy tread belonging to another son, I'm ready to go on a scouting mission with him.

'Did you know these were guerrilla clothes?' he asks. 'I thought that was a Turkish preconception,' I answer in surprise. Grinning, he points out the differences between his clothes and mine. His have buttons at the bottom of his trouser legs, mine Velcro. His trousers have two normal pockets, mine two additional ones, again with Velcro. His jacket has two pockets and mine four, plus an inside pocket on each side. 'What you're wearing is the guerrilla version,' he says. 'Mine is just traditional Kurdish clothing.'

The inside pockets have convenient zips, perfect for keeping my passport, residence permit and press pass. You never know what papers the soldiers we might meet would want to see, or what it would take to prove my identity. I slip a notepad into the outside pocket and a pen into my trouser pocket. My own clothes would have been completely unsuitable, as the only things I usually take along to the village are long skirts, sneakers with hardly any grip, and flip-flops.

The two of us set off, climbing the broad dirt track leading out of the village, but soon take a right turn down a path I wouldn't even have recognised as such. Rushing through woody shrubs, we hear a zooming noise above our heads: drones. After a while, we reach the top of a hill with a stunning view of the border region. He points out three paths to me. There, at the lowest point between two hills, is the spot the bombs were dropped. On the hilltop to the left of the site where thirty-four men and boys were killed, is a clearly visible army post.

The smugglers have already crossed the border into Turkey, I gather from walkie-talkie conversations. We peer into the darkness but can't make them out. They keep hidden behind the shrubs as much as possible, and are very good at it. The drones, too, are invisible. The evening sky is clear, but the unmanned aircraft are small and high up. Only their humming reaches us. Strange to think that whoever is watching the footage from that buzzing bluebottle can see *us*.

We carry on, until the scout suddenly orders me to leap behind a shrub. We kneel, peering out cautiously from behind the bush. 'Look,' he says, pointing to the hill across the valley, 'soldiers.' I can see them too, on the next hill, less than 500 metres away. They're moving around too much to be inconspicuous. 'Have they seen us?' I ask. 'Undoubtedly. They have special equipment, so if we can see them with the naked eye, they're bound to see us too.' We stay in hiding for a bit, and after conferring with the other scouts by walkie-talkie, decide that the two of us should move back a little. 'You won't be able to run very fast on this terrain,' the scout says, 'so we should get out of here now rather than wait and risk the soldiers coming after us.'

I just about manage to keep up with him on uphill paths, but don't do quite as well downhill. I keep slipping on the loose stones. We sit down again at a spot we walked past earlier. He takes two packets of fruit juice out of the plastic bag he's carrying and hands me the cherry juice. I'm given *kek* to go with it, a piece of industrially produced cake. Dusk is falling and the first stars twinkle in the sky.

The light is fading quickly, and scanning the area, I think I can see something move on a hill to our left. At that moment, one of the walkie-talkies crackles to life. 'Come on, they're here!' my companion says, and we leap to our feet. I take another look and see them threading their way along the mountainside: a long line of heavily loaded mules led by men. We dash through the undergrowth towards the line, the sound of hooves getting ever louder. We reach a slightly broader path and I stand to one side to let the animals pass.

Without a moment's hesitation they thunder past me at breakneck speed, over the rocks and shrubs towards the village, balancing their scrawny, heavily loaded bodies on four spindly legs. How strong they are.

Some of the smugglers stop for a moment when they see me. 'Hey *abla* [sister], welcome!' they say, and some shake my hand. A moment later, they're gone again. The scout tells me to come along, but following the mules and men I find I simply can't keep up with them. The two of us slow down to my pace. We soon lose sight of the procession and moments later, even the sound of hooves has faded away.

Supporting a family here means running a marathon on rocky terrain – closely watched by drones from above and soldiers on the ground and from army posts on the hilltops – picking out paths where many other smugglers have been shot at and thirty-four of them were killed in a single night.

By the time the scout and I arrive at the house in the village where the transfer takes place, most of the mules have already been unloaded. A large group of smugglers is sitting on the front steps of the house drinking tea. Some start clapping when they see me, and I'm given some appreciative slaps on the shoulder. It makes me laugh, but I'm also a bit dazed, as if the world order has been turned upside down: surely I'm not the one due respect here?

My last remaining doubts on whether the state tolerates smuggling have disappeared. Not just because of the soldiers I saw – and who saw us – on my trip with the scout, or because the army post on the hill is a stone's throw from the smugglers' daily route and the site of the massacre, but also because of what I've seen of day-to-day life in Ortasu.

Every afternoon, men and boys ride or lead mules along the main road towards the path to the border in plain sight. They don't look nervous, they just go about their business, even though the very same road, from the main road to the border, is also used by army trucks driving up and down to and from the army post on the hilltop.

Smuggling, the Government and the PKK

In Diyarbakır, I find out what happens to the smuggled goods next from S., a Kurdish journalist who has worked in the region for roughly thirty years. I promise to quote him anonymously – S. has been imprisoned for his work several times and is afraid of being arrested again if he gives me information under his own name. Not without reason: the majority of the dozens of journalists locked up in Turkey work for the Kurdish media.

S. doesn't beat around the bush: 'The leaders of the smuggling parties agree on certain time slots in which the army posts let smuggled goods through. When lorries drive past on the agreed night at the agreed hour, the military staff turn a blind eye. Sometimes, a commanding officer gets into the lorry with the smugglers and waves to his subordinates, who of course would never dream of inspecting a vehicle with their commander in it.'

Can I trust such a statement coming from a Kurdish journalist? The Kurdish press is known for its activism and political bias towards the PKK – isn't he just using this as an opportunity to vilify the army? But S. is more than happy to provide the whole picture, placing his accusations in a logical context.

On Turkey's borders with Iraq, Iran and Syria, smuggling has been a source of income for generations, but it really took off in the 1990s. S. says, 'It was part of a strategy to recruit village guards. In places where people who became village guards had no other job to supplement their income, smuggling was implicitly allowed. Many village guards depended on this extra income, as their pay was insufficient and even decreased as time went on. In many cases, the father became a village guard and the sons smugglers.'

Not everyone was given the choice whether they wanted to be a village guard. There are many known cases of chieftains enlisting all the men of their clan for the system, collecting the weapons and the money and then paying some of their income to the men who actually wielded the weapons. This still happens today – the old tribal system has by no means disappeared and the chieftains loyal to the state are still making a good living by cooperating with the authorities.

In places where the clans are less powerful and don't rule over 'their' village guards, 'head guards' are appointed. They must see to it that the village guards in their area do their job properly, and are usually the ones who communicate with the local army commanders. The head guard of Ortasu, for instance, is tipped off by the army post when a military strike is planned against the PKK and smuggling trips should be postponed for a few days. I never got to speak to him – except for one occasion on which he let me know in a few words, swigging a huge, frothing glass of *ayran*, that he did not want to speak to the press.

The smuggling trips are often organised by the chieftains, head guards or other middlemen, who occasionally cross the Iraqi border legally to broker deals and settle the financial side of things. Journalist S.: 'Then the local smugglers carry out the deals. They're paid by the chieftain, the head guard or some middleman.'

S. also explains the situation in Gülyazı and Ortasu, villages he consistently calls by their Kurdish names Bejuh and Roboskî: 'The inhabitants of Bejuh and Roboskî belong to the Kesuran and Goyan clans, who aren't that powerful. Some of the villagers don't belong to any clan and therefore don't have a leader. This means they don't work for a chieftain but for themselves. The village guard or other middlemen are the organisers.'

The smuggling system had been in place long before the government played any kind of part in it. The Turkish state officially controlled the southeast at the time, but didn't make its presence felt: in large parts of the district there were hardly any roads, few schools and other state institutions, and the army was not always present, either. The chieftains were generally loyal to the state, brokered economic deals with the government, squeezed their subjects dry and thought nothing of suppressing their own people so as not to disturb that lucrative balance.

The PKK taking up arms *has* disturbed this balance, but has also created a new one: the state has been slotted into the existing system, as it were. Deals are still made with the chieftains, though the emphasis no longer lies on the use of the land as in former times, but on the ultimate goal of defeating the PKK. In this, the chieftains and the state are united, as the PKK, an organisation based on communist ideals that fights the Kemalist state system as well as exploitation by the ruling class, is a common enemy.

According to the state's reasoning, allowing smuggling activities is one way of fighting the PKK, since people who earn an income – young men in a job – are less likely to join the rebels. It is also a way of wielding power: anyone who is disloyal, for instance by neglecting his village guard duties, is the first to get into trouble if smugglers are arrested.

It is therefore in the state's interest not to make the fight against smuggling a priority, but to maintain the balance: giving local people the chance to earn an income with semi-legal activities while at the same time enforcing a certain degree of loyalty. In order to keep this balance, cross-border trade must not only be allowed but facilitated, by letting the majority of smuggled goods pass. Only if there is a reason for intercepting a particular smuggling haul, for instance to demonstrate to the country that the state is cracking down on illegal activities, does the trap sometimes snap shut.

Back in Ortasu, I ask the scout who took me along to the mountains the night before what is going to happen to the packets of tea and cigarettes. How will the van make it past the checkpoints? He claims the smuggled goods never go anywhere near a checkpoint: the traders avoid them by doing other legs of the journey by mule, too. He says, 'there are more mules waiting further on.'

I look at him with raised eyebrows. 'Really? I was told the army posts sometimes turn a blind eye.' 'Absolutely not,' he insists, pouring me yet another cup of tea. 'Completely unthinkable. The authorities take a strong stance against smuggling, they really have nothing to do with it.'

'But,' I argue, 'they tolerate it here in the village, don't they? Wouldn't it only be logical if they didn't always intervene further down the road either?' Without supplying any arguments, he resolutely dismisses the idea again. I should forget what I've heard.

In the following months, I talk to several people in Gülyazı and Ortasu – and in Diyarbakır – about the transport. It appears that both stories are true: some of the smuggled goods are taken past the checkpoints, some on mules.

The Marijuana Fields of Lice

Journalist S.'s account is also supported by a journey I took to Lice, the 'cannabis district' of Diyarbakır province. In July 2012, the army conducted 'the largest operation ever' against 'the drug fields of the terrorist PKK': 500 million liras' worth of cannabis plants were destroyed and a few dozen people arrested. The operation involved 1,500 soldiers, 500 policemen and 500 village guards, and sixteen tanks and four helicopters were deployed.

On such occasions, the army usually invites Turkish journalists, and a select few are taken up in army helicopters in the early hours to witness the operation from the outset and to get the best photographs. The images show burning piles of marijuana, tanks, helicopters with swishing blades, cameramen running towards them, and the 'nerve centre': a table under some trees, covered with communication equipment and maps of the area and surrounded by the commanding officers coordinating the operation. On television, reporters with flying hair and tanks in the background, shouting to make themselves heard above the helicopter noise, are accompanied by action film music. The message is that the terrorist organisation has been dealt a heavy blow.

Not one TV station or newspaper bothers to go to the villages in Lice and ask the inhabitants for their views on the matter. Except the Kurdish press, which reports on the devastated villagers: 'Those were our fields, the PKK has nothing to do with them. How can we make a living now?'

About a week later, I set off for Diyarbakır. I'd wanted to go to Lice from the moment I heard of the marijuana operation on the news, but since I was in Istanbul at the time and unable to drop everything and leave, I only arrived in the area around ten days later. It wasn't too late to find out about the marijuana fields – there were plenty of those left – but it was yet another piece of news to do with the Kurdish question that made me wish I had been closer by.

It is around that time I take the decision to move to Diyarbakır. How can I seriously think of specialising in the Kurdish question if I stay in my office in Istanbul? It's true that there are more Kurds in Istanbul than in any other city, but Diyarbakır is the beating heart of Kurdistan. From there, I can reach every part of southeast Turkey in a day, I can soak up the atmosphere of the town and surrounding countryside, talk with the inhabitants out in the streets, visit the park, the different neighbourhoods and the market every day. I need to let the idea sink in and think of a way of realising it, but taking the decision feels good. Just as in 2004, when it first occurred to me that, as a freelancer, I could work in Turkey.

On the morning I set out on my marijuana mission in the minibus from Diyarbakır to the small town of Lice, there is upsetting news: the PKK has blown up an army convoy with a remote-controlled roadside bomb, killing two soldiers.

Lice is not only well-known for its marijuana fields but also for the PKK's strong presence in the mountains of the northern part of the district. Because the PKK camps in the Qandil Mountains on the Iraqi border are always in the news, it's easy to forget that many PKK militants are on Turkish soil, especially in the mountainous regions such as the northern districts of Lice and Kulp in Diyarbakır province, but also Bingöl, Dersim/Tunceli, Van, Şırnak, Batman and Hakkâri provinces.

In the following days, I speak with dozens of inhabitants of Lice and surrounding villages, and with local politicians. The problem is that the politicians all belong to the pro-Kurdish BDP party, which controls all the local municipalities, and will never admit that the PKK has anything to do with the marijuana fields. One BDP member in a village in Lice even says, 'The PKK condemns drugs because they are bad for our young people. It would never get involved with drugs.'

The inhabitants, too – a majority of whom vote BDP – won't hear a word against the PKK. 'The fields belonged to the villagers,' they say unanimously, just like the Kurdish press. They explain that the cultivation of marijuana, like the smuggling, preceded the war between the state and the rebels. When the war started three decades ago, the cultivation and trafficking became more lucrative, and according to the villagers, drug-related activities have increased noticeably in the past decade.

'The AKP,' a local politician says, 'launched a programme around that time to help people return to the villages they had been banished from in the 90s, but there was concern that young people in particular would join the PKK if they didn't have an income. That's why they tolerate the drug plantations. Anything rather than seeing the young go to the mountains.'

He estimates that between ten and fifteen per cent of the people in the Lice district are financially dependent on the marijuana plantations. The others make a living in other forms of agriculture, or work at the animal feed plant near the town.

There is a large army post just outside Lice, and exploring the area on foot and by car, I notice other strategically situated military posts. I can hear the buzz of drones circling invisibly high above my head – the army is on the lookout for the perpetrators of the bomb attack. This is a war zone, and I don't think the inhabitants are exaggerating when they tell me that the army knows every inch of the province. And, as every inhabitant tells me, that they know exactly where the marijuana fields are. They pose the – to them – completely rhetorical question, 'Why do they only destroy some of the fields now and then, and not all at once? They could make quick work of them if they wanted to.'

It is rhetorical because the inhabitants are convinced that the local military authorities profit from the drug trade by confiscating part of the crops or collecting their share in cash. And it's not just one villager saying this, but all of them. I call the BDP headquarters in Ankara and speak to Evren Çelik, member of the international committee of the pro-Kurdish BDP, who doesn't mind being quoted under his real name saying, 'The police and gendarmerie are part of a network that cultivates and trades in marijuana. Everyone knows that. It's been going on since the 80s, when the war made the marijuana trade more lucrative. People were forced to leave the area, and those left behind had to make money and find a way of living with the military presence. That's how the networks of villagers, village guards and army staff came about.' Just like the villagers, Çelik is adamant that the PKK has *ab*so*lu*tely nothing to do with the marijuana trade.

Back in Istanbul, I speak to Gareth Jenkins, an analyst at the American Central Asia-Caucasus Institute who specialises in the relationship between civil and military power and in issues concerning security and terrorism. He claims that where drugs are concerned, neither side of the conflict is as lily-white as they pretend to be. 'I don't think the gendarmerie taking a share of the drugs income is common policy, but it is easy to imagine individual soldiers supplementing their income by confiscating a portion of the plants or taking a share of the profits. The PKK also makes money with the drugs trade, but not as much as the government claims. Donations to the PKK are partially financed by drug money, but the rebels themselves do not haul or sell drugs.'

He says that the PKK is also known to levy 'taxes' in regions where its presence is strong. 'But that is not the same as marijuana fields being in the hands of the organisation.' He then adds, 'I have often heard that locals are forced to donate money to the police and the army as well as the PKK.'

Remarkably, the 2011 annual report of the Federal Office for the Protection of the Constitution (Germany's domestic security agency), also published in July, contains twenty-three pages (from a total of 500) dedicated to the PKK. Under the heading 'Financial and Economic Activities' it states that the United States consider the PKK a drug organisation, but that there 'are no indications that the PKK is directly involved in drug trafficking in Germany.'

This sentence sparks many, often outraged, reactions in the Turkish press. Is the 'largest ever drug operation against the PKK' a response to this? Is Turkey trying to prove that the PKK really is involved in the drug trade? That may be stretching it a bit – an operation like this is not planned in a week. According to the Turkish press, preparations took nine months. The air strike took place exactly nine months after a PKK attack killed more than twenty soldiers in Hakkâri province.

The operation coinciding with the publication of the German annual report is quite a coincidence, all the same. The Turkish government, and especially Prime Minister Erdoğan and the Minister for European Affairs and main EU negotiator Egemen Bağış, say the EU is not doing enough to support Turkey's war against terrorism. A war that is in Europe's interest too. For, as Bağış puts it at a press conference for foreign journalists I attend in 2011, PKK drugs are 'poisoning Europe's youth.'

The smuggling in Şırnak and the marijuana growing in Lice have both been going on for generations, and have, since the outbreak of hostilities between the PKK and the state, become part of this struggle. Everyone with any power in the region profits from and allows it. The PKK because it brings in money, the state in order to keep young people from joining the guerrillas, the traffickers to get rich.

Only the villagers have no power. They do all the dangerous, dirty work. They are the ones who really suffer when the state decides it is time to display some decisive action against the PKK, and, watched closely by the Turkish press, plucks a lorry full of smugglers from the road or burns down a marijuana field.

That they point an accusing finger at the state and absolve the PKK of any guilt shouldn't come as a surprise, since their sympathy lies with the guerrillas.

The PKK, a Child of the Turkish Left Movement

It has taken me some effort to get a clear picture of the PKK's history. It's easy to be prejudiced by the way the organisation is portrayed in the news today, what it represents to various groups of people and the labels it's been given, ranging from 'terrorists' to 'freedom fighters.' This is the way it's seen in today's context. But in the 1970s, when a group of Turkish and Kurdish leftist revolutionaries organised living room meetings that laid the foundations of what became the PKK in 1978, Turkey was a very different country.

The future PKK originated around 1972 or 73. In 1971, the Turkish army staged a second coup d'état, in which the active left movement of the 70s was hit hard, with many of its members killed or locked up. The constitution implemented by the army after its previous coup in 1960, which guaranteed various social rights and made it easier to form political parties, was reversed after the 1971 coup.

Important left wing and Kurdish factions from the 60s, such as the Revolutionary Eastern Culture Centres (Devrimci Doğu Kültür Ocakları, DDKO; 'Eastern' was a way of avoiding the word Kurdish, which would automatically have made the party illegal) and the Workers' Party of Turkey (TİP) were prohibited. The old administration, which included such icons as the intellectual Musa Anter and the Turkish sociologist İsmail Beşikci – both active members of the DDKO – was silenced, its members arrested and sentenced to long-term imprisonment or death by hanging. Devastating as this was, it also created conditions that made it possible for new groups and leaders to emerge.

It was against this background that the ADYÖD, the left wing revolutionary Ankara Democratic Higher Education Association, was founded in 1973. In an internal election, Abdullah Öcalan (a dropout political sciences student and former land registry employee) was voted into a top position. The ADYÖD was an attempt to re-organise the revolutionary left, and even though the party was prohibited only a year after its foundation, the debate it sparked was intense.

Joost Jongerden, a sociologist, anthropologist and university lecturer at the University of Wageningen in the Netherlands, is one of the few people in the world to have researched the origins of the PKK. He takes me back in time. 'The right of self-determination of peoples and the struggle against colonialism were important topics that were discussed intensively in left wing parties. One of the questions was what exactly constituted a colony and colonialism, and subsequently whether Kurdistan was a colony of Turkey. Öcalan's group considered Kurdistan a Turkish colony – or rather an international one, because it was being colonised by several countries. Most left wing parties disagreed, arguing that colonialism is a phase of imperialism. Turkey, itself a semi-colony of the US, could not be an Imperial power and therefore couldn't colonise others. In their view, Kurdistan was therefore not a colony of Turkey.'

After ADYÖD was prohibited and the association tried to regroup, Öcalan decided not to join again but to found his own group instead. This group, which called itself the Kurdistan Revolutionaries, took a radically different approach from other organisations at the time. Joost Jongerden: 'Others, such as the Kurdish groups TKSP, KAWA and Rizgarî, attracted attention by founding real political parties with, for example, their own publication, while the Kurdish Revolutionaries developed quietly on the political sidelines, building a foundation. They debated, recruited members and created a loyal, devoted group in living room meetings, endlessly talking about theory and tactics, self-criticism and reflection.'

Öcalan wanted to learn from the mistakes of the revolutionary left, especially the two radical student movements THKO and THKP-C. The leaders of both movements were killed in the early 1970s: the now legendary Deniz Gezmiş was given the death sentence and hanged, and the other, Mahir Çayan, was killed in a gunfight with the army together with eight others. Joost Jongerden: 'Öcalan criticised such groups for revolting against the state before having the weight to do so. The Kurdish Revolutionaries took a different approach.'

The last words of Gezmiş, whose picture still crops up regularly in Turkish student circles and at all kinds of demonstrations, illustrate the struggle of the left in those days: 'Long live a wholly independent Turkey. Long live the noble ideology of Marxism-Leninism. Long live the struggle for independence by the Turkish and Kurdish people. Down with imperialism. Long live workers and villagers.'

Those could have been Abdullah Öcalan's words, though saying so would be considered blasphemous in Turkey's current 'left' movement. The succession of coups, including that of 1980, have inflicted almost irreparable damage to the Turkish left. Incidentally, the PKK probably survived the 1980 coup thanks to the groundwork they did in the 70s, which made the group strong and resilient. The parties that call themselves left today are in fact often Turkish nationalist, sometimes even ultranationalist. Seeing them waving their Deniz Gezmiş flags makes you wonder whether they have any idea what their idol's last words actually meant, and whether they realise that the man they hate so profoundly, Abdullah Öcalan, draws on the same ideologies.

Joost Jongerden: 'The struggle of the Kurdish Revolutionaries, based on a common ideal in those years, was actually a struggle for freedom, as defined in terms of class and nations. The idea was that the liberation of Turkey could only be achieved once its colonial ties with Kurdistan were severed. This was in keeping with the theory that a coloniser could not be free as long as a power relationship existed between it and its colony. In short, Kurdistan was the key to the liberation of Turkey.'

According to the Kurdistan Revolutionaries, the right of autonomy of the colonised, the Kurds, and the liberation of the coloniser, Turkey, translated into the foundation of a new state: Kurdistan. The group was led by three Turks and three Kurds. None of this was put in writing – not even when the group finally presented itself to the left movement in 1977 – until two years later, when the PKK had been founded and Öcalan presented a manifesto.

On 15 August 1984, the PKK launched its first attack against the state, targeting army posts at Eruh in Siirt province and Şemdinli in Hakkâri province. Immediately after the attacks, the group distributed pamphlets reading, 'Democrats and revolutionaries in Turkey, workers of Turkey, the

HRK is fighting the barbarity looming over your lives and futures like a dark cloud,' appealing to them to join them. Somewhat confusing, this sudden name change to HRK; the Hêzen Rizgarîye Kurdîstan, or Kurdistan Liberation Units, was the PKK's armed faction at the time. The cooperation between the PKK and other revolutionaries in Turkey in fact never got off the ground; the Turkish left wing was hopelessly divided, the PKK were quickly and effectively labelled terrorists and separatists by the state and the media, and that was that.

As the story of its formation makes abundantly clear, Joost Jongerden writes in one of his articles, the PKK should not primarily be defined in military terms: 'the PKK is first and foremost a political organisation,' he writes, 'spurred on to the use of violence by conditions that did not allow any (legal) alternative means of genuine political expression.'

Students in the Kurdish Movement

He grabs his orange shirt and tugs at it. 'This,' he says without a hint of irony, 'is not my shirt. The fact that I happened to put it on this morning does not make it my property.' It's the summer of 2012 and I'm sitting on the roof terrace of a tea shop in the eastern town of Van with student R. (twenty-four). He's an active member of a Kurdish students' association I got in touch with through my network. I wanted to speak to him about his volunteer work helping victims of the earthquakes that devastated Van in October and November 2011, about which I was hoping to write a story. The conversation soon turned from the earthquakes and R.'s volunteer work to the PKK.

'Make that 12 years,' he says when I ask him how many years of detention the prosecution has demanded against him. Two court cases are pending against him for 'being a member of a terrorist organisation,' and in both cases the prosecution is demanding six years and three months. A couple of weeks ago, he and eight other suspects were imprisoned for four days, but the judge ruled that they be allowed to await trial in liberty.

'But don't think for a minute they managed to break our spirits in prison,' R. grins, eyes sparkling with delight. 'The nine of us shared one cell. We walked up and down, talking politics. Three steps, turn, three steps back. One of us would make a statement and we'd discuss it.' Sometimes the discussions were interrupted by the guards, for instance when they fetched someone for questioning. 'I knew I'd been shadowed for years. You just notice. The little clicks on the line during telephone conversations, men that keep following you.'

It's the reason we're in this café. The conversation we started on the university campus the day before was cut short after five minutes, when a couple sat down at a table behind us and R. immediately recognised the man as a snoop. I hadn't realised, only noticing R. had suddenly gone very quiet. 'Have you changed your mind about talking?' I asked. 'No, but I'd rather do it without that man in the white shirt at the next table. Come on, let's get out of here.' In the spacious top floor of the café we select a corner table below the speakers, so the music drowns our conversation and we're far away from the staff at the bar. Here, it's just the two of us.

It became clear during the interrogations that he *had* been shadowed for a long time: they knew a lot about him, including his volunteer work after the earthquakes. R.: 'They asked, "Why did you distribute blankets?" Well, what could I say? Because it was winter, the people lived in tents and were cold. That's why.'

The question is illustrative of the row that flared up around humanitarian aid after the earthquakes: Van is controlled by the pro-Kurdish BDP party, but the provision of emergency relief after a disaster like this is coordinated in the capital Ankara, where the AKP are in power. Kurdish political leaders complained that the cooperation didn't go anywhere near as smoothly as in the neighbouring Erciş at the epicentre of the earthquake, where the municipal council is controlled by the AKP.

It's an age-old problem in Turkey: local authorities and mayors belonging to the governing party in Ankara – no matter which one that is – can count on far more support from central government than those from opposition parties. This is no different under AKP rule. R. had been shadowed for some time, and once he was arrested, even his volunteer work for earthquake victims was politicised.

The 'terrorist organisation' of which the prosecution claims R. is a member, is the KCK, Koma Civakên Kurdistan, or Kurdish Communities Union. It is an umbrella body for Kurdish organisations in Turkey, Iran, Iraq and Syria, founded by the PKK. Abdullah Öcalan is the leader and other high-level PKK members sit on the board, such as Murat Karayılan, the highest-ranking commander in the mountains until July 2013, and Cemil Bayık, who in the same month succeeded Karayılan as commander on the ground. Like the PKK, the KCK is considered a terrorist organisation by Turkey.

Around 4,000 politically active Kurds are standing trial in the KCK case, many of whom have already spent months, even years, in custody. The figures don't get any more specific, as no one knows exactly how many people are being persecuted for their ties with the KCK, and how many of them are waiting for their verdicts behind bars. With trials being conducted all across the country, the case is simply too large and obscure for an observer to know all the details. Not even the lawyer handling the case for the BDP party office in Ankara can provide the exact number of those persecuted.

R. doesn't seem too concerned about his trial. He talks about his few days' imprisonment in glowing terms, because of the great solidarity he felt and the intensive discussions that helped sharpen his mind again. 'Doesn't it make you angry to be asked about distributing blankets?' I ask. He answers, 'No. You have to be ready for anything, you know. This is what we're up against. And I was ready for it.'

As a teenager, he leaps back in time, he was not 'ready' yet. He grew up in a village near Van, and his parents weren't politically active. A bright student, R. won a government grant for free education when he was sixteen. There was an opening at a secondary school in a town in the Black Sea Region, and he became a boarder there.

'I knew nothing about politics, I thought the PKK were terrorists,' he says. 'But I was given a hard time anyway, and was beaten up more than once – simply because I was a Kurd from Van province, though I didn't realise that at the time.' The Black Sea Region, where the ultranationalist MHP party always does well in elections, is well-known for its Turkish nationalism. R. endured the two years of his schooling there without telling his parents about the violence. 'Just imagine, they might have come round with a large group of clan members to teach the bullies a lesson, and then left me alone with them again. Far too dangerous.'

He won a place at the University of Antalya via an entrance exam and studied civil administration. He grins as he reveals the career he might have had if he'd completed his degree: 'I could have been a governor.' Governors are government officials, like the governor of Uludere who was assaulted in Gülyazı. The governors in the southeast have a reputation for making life difficult for the Kurds; they have the right to prohibit demonstrations, for instance, and they have some say in how police and riot police are deployed.

R. joined a left wing student club, in which Turks and Kurds studied various revolutions in the history of the Republic together. 'Eventually of course, the PKK came up, and we discussed it. Living in the Black Sea

Region changed my opinion of the PKK. If I was beaten up by nationalists, the police would arrest me instead of them, and then give me another beating. When I was living with my parents I'd be appalled by news about soldiers being killed fighting the rebels, but in that period I started to understand more about the PKK.'

But the association was being watched, and there was nationalist violence on the campus too. It peaked between 4 and 6 April 2008, when a group from outside the university spread panic on the campus. One of the main suspects Ömer Ulusoy turned out to be a member of Idealist Youth, a network of local youth factions of the ultra-nationalist Grey Wolves, which are closely linked to the MHP. A tattoo of a sword on his forehead, he opened fire on the students around him. 'I watched it happen,' R. says. 'I didn't feel safe at the university after that, so I transferred to Van. I'm studying economics here.' Nowadays, he says, nothing surprises him anymore. He's ready for anything.

The PKK – to Join the Struggle or Not?

In the past years, R. has read everything he could get hold of about the PKK, or, as he prefers to call it, 'the movement': 'I try my best to live according to the movement's ideology.' He believes this essentially means doing his best to love his country and facing up to his own flaws. He seeks to become the best human being he can. 'And this is not just about Kurdistan,' he points out repeatedly. 'In fact, it doesn't have anything to do with being a Kurd. In a narrow sense, it revolves around the Kurdish question, but actually it's just as much about being human.'

This is the moment he tugs at his shirt, solemnly declaring it isn't his. 'Having too many possessions isn't good either, or throwing away food, because that contributes to the capitalist system and the starvation of others. And if a workman dies at a shipyard in İzmir tomorrow, I will have to do something about that. If I don't, I fall short. What can I do? Organise a demonstration with the students' association and put out a press release demanding more rights for labourers, for instance.'

'You're very hard on yourself,' I say. 'No, no, on the contrary,' he objects. 'Living the best life you can lightens the load. It sets you free; and only once you're free can you help to free the people of the world. It's all about a higher goal.'

To him, an independent Kurdistan is not one of the aims of the struggle. 'The PKK, too, has given up on that,' he adds, scrupulously following the party's lead: when Öcalan declared that an independent Kurdistan was no longer the goal, every true member of the movement immediately relinquished that demand. R.: 'I think it's no more than logical. Kurdistan would be a nation state like Turkey, and look at the misery that has caused. Not something to strive for.'

But, he adds, the struggle is still important. 'It is our fundamental right to live in our own culture, speak our own language and be in control of our own lives. And since the system wants everyone to conform, fighting for your culture means fighting the system.'

I ask him if he ever considered going to the mountains. He answers that joining the PKK is 'his fervent hope.' So is he considering it or not? 'Circumstances,' he says, 'determine whether or not you go, and my circumstances aren't favourable.' What circumstances does he mean? 'I have shortcomings,' he says.

Kurdish television channels such as RojTV and NûceTV, and the music channel MMC that is broadcast from Europe via satellite, portray PKK militants as men and women walking through beautiful landscapes in full kit including Kalashnikovs, playing volleyball on alpine meadows, dancing traditional dances in large circles or singing songs. They have even been observed playing on improvised swings; gliding through the air in slow motion on a plank fastened to a tree with two lengths of rope. The violence, deaths, loss of comrades and maimed bodies are never shown, nor the hardships endured in the harsh weather conditions high up in the Turkish or Iraqi mountains. They are heroes – saints, almost – who have found a freedom in the mountains of Kurdistan they never knew in Turkey, and are putting up a manful – or womanful – fight for their people.

'But doesn't killing people go against the principles of humanitarianism?' I ask. 'Their main aim is not to kill people,' R. answers, 'but they are, of course, an armed group. They have to carry weapons in order to defend themselves, not to spread death and destruction.' 'But don't they sometimes launch an attack?' 'Yes, they do attack. There's a war going on. After the Uludere air strike, they started hitting back. Revenge. It's war.'

He tells me about friends of his who disappeared. One day only five or six months ago, an old friend from his village was suddenly gone. He's a PKK member now. R.: 'When we were doing the earthquake relief work, we showered at someone's home. RojTV was on, showing footage of a PKK funeral. The man they buried used to be one of my best friends as a boy. I couldn't concentrate on my work after that, memories of him kept flooding in.'

'How are you different from your old friends?' I want to know. 'Why did they go, and not you?' Now that we're talking less about party ideals and more about his personal choices, R.'s voice keeps getting softer. 'My friends,' he says, 'had stopped doubting. They were ready to sacrifice themselves.' I have to ask every question explicitly before he goes on. 'What doubts do you have?' 'I've never been asked that question; I don't know.' I don't believe him, at the very least he's put the question to himself. I say as much, and his eyes fill with tears as he continues. 'You know,' he says, 'it's not as if everyone born and raised there just goes off into the mountains one day. You have to give yourself, but only once you have done a lot of thinking and know exactly who you are. You have to confront yourself. And that's my greatest fear. I can't do it. I might find out that I'm a guerrilla, and go. But it's just as possible I'll turn out to be someone who, despite everything, feels comfortable living in the system.'

A Suspect in the KCK Case

Shortly afterwards, I meet a student in Gülyazı who reminds me of R. Slightly younger and less ideologically sound, but just as heavy-going, just a serious. I'll call him H. H. is also a suspect in the KCK case, but because of (legal) activities in a different town and at a different university. He became a suspect for organising a commemoration meeting for the victims of Saddam Hussein's poison gas attacks on the Kurdish village Halabja in 1988.

I met H. in Pakize's house, where he called one evening because he'd heard a foreign journalist was staying. We talked about the bombing, but the conversation soon turned to him, the student who spends his time as a village goatherd instead of attending lectures in the city. He'd be arrested the moment he showed up on the campus, suspected of 'being a member of a terrorist organisation' or 'spreading propaganda for a terrorist organisation' – that is, the KCK/PKK.

We're sitting on the floor in Pakize's house, drinking water. Pakize and the children are away visiting family, and H. and I can talk undisturbed. He tells me he's a member of a Kurdish students' association: 'Many universities in Turkey have associations like that. The authorities keep a close eye on them. At the beginning of this year, when I happened to be away, they arrested the whole group on suspicion of being members of and spreading propaganda for the PKK. I was told about it on the phone and decided to avoid the university by staying in the village for the time being.'

But, I ask, surely the police could collar him here just as well? 'The arrests happened about a month after the bombing,' he explains. 'I'm hoping that the police won't have the nerve to turn up here of all places to arrest a student. I feel reasonably safe. But I can't leave the village, I can't go anywhere. They'd recognise me at the nearest checkpoint and turn me over to the authorities. The only place I ever go is the village pastures, where I tend the goats the women come to milk every day. The path there leads through open country with no checkpoints.'

To H., Gülyazı is an open-air prison, where he grieves for the two cousins he lost in the bombing. He doesn't believe for a minute that the parliamentary investigation will uncover the truth about the thirty-four killed smugglers. 'Why should they reveal the details about a deliberate mass murder?' he asks. He, too, is convinced the bombing wasn't an accident; he, too, says it happened 'because we are Kurds.'

The first evening we meet, H. speaks at length about the Kurdish question. Starting with the rebel leader Sheikh Said in the 1920s up until today's PKK leader Abdullah Öcalan, he unfolds the history of the Kurds in Turkey, frequently linking it to his present situation and that of the village. A recurring theme is the lack of freedom to be yourself. His students' association, too, has seen many attacks by nationalist fellow students. They are protected by the police, who, if called in, arrest the Kurdish students. It's a lack of freedom to express your views without automatically being labelled a PKK propagandist. His murdered cousins were forced into smuggling by poverty, and paid for it with their lives.

Courtroom Farce

In early April 2012, I go to the Diyarbakır court to attend one of the hearings in the KCK case. The hearings are taking place throughout the country, from Erzurum in the east to İzmir in the west, but the one in Diyarbakır is the largest. There, 151 people are standing trial at once, around eighty of whom are present on the day I visit. The others have been allowed to follow their case in liberty (though some of them have come to the courtroom to support their fellow suspects) or could not be moved from the prison to the court due to ill health.

I spend the whole day watching the farce performed before my eyes with slack-jawed amazement. The players: the judge, the public prosecutor, the suspects and a legion of gendarmerie officers and members of the public (consisting of the suspects' family and friends). The suspects are seated facing the judge, women on the left, men on the right, and are surrounded by gendarmerie officers – judging by their tender age, all soldiers doing their military service. The male and female suspects are divided by more gendarmerie officers. The prosecutor is seated to the left of the suspects, the dozens of lawyers on either side. The public gallery, which is six rows deep and seats a few dozen people, is enclosed by a low balustrade.

A deafening noise erupts when the suspects are escorted in. The visitors are jostling at the balustrade and the suspects at the cordon of gendarmerie officers, and all are shouting to one another. *How are you? How is the family doing? Father, mother and the children? Nice to see you! So good of you to come!* They wave, blow kisses, greet each other touching their hands to their hearts with a brief nod.

I see several familiar faces, such as BDP parliamentarian Selma Irmak from Şırnak, and Muharrem Erbey,* a human rights activist and head of the local office of the independent human rights organisation İHD in Diyarbakır. When the judge switches on the microphone and opens the session, everyone sits down.

The courtroom is by no means silent, though. The suspects might as well be sitting in a teashop. They chat, turned around in their chairs to face each other, and the men and women communicate through the cordon of gendarmerie officers. Some of the suspects are napping, turned around with their heads on the backs of their chairs and their arms on the armrests, or leaning on the shoulders of the people next to them. None of them shows even the slightest interest in anything the judge says.

There is one brief period of relative silence at the very beginning of the session when the judge calls out the names of the suspects, who are required to confirm their presence. They do so in Kurdish: '*Ez livirim!*,' 'I'm here!' They aren't supposed to answer in their own language, but the sentence is too short for the judge to switch off the suspect's microphone from his control panel before it has been uttered, something he does regularly later in the day: when a suspect is asked a question, they answer in Kurdish, too. After about eight words, the judge turns off the microphone. The suspect carries on talking without a microphone for a bit, until his or her lawyer goes on in Turkish. The minutes secretary notes that the suspect answered in an 'unknown language.'

* Muharrem Erbey was released from jail on 12 April 2014. The court case against him continues.

In the 'lawyers' room' during one of the breaks, I speak with Mehmet Emin Aktar, head of the lawyers' association in Diyarbakır. The small room is crowded with lawyers, all dressed in shiny black robes with burgundy collars and dark green lapels. Endless cups of tea are served in a tiny kitchen in a corner, and there's a fridge full of juice and fizzy drinks.

Playing the devil's advocate, I ask Aktar whether the judge isn't right not to allow the suspects to speak Kurdish. Shouldn't the right to defend yourself in your mother tongue, which does actually exist in Turkey, primarily apply to people with no command of the official language? Such as foreigners, elderly Kurds, Arabs and others who speak little or no Turkish? All of the suspects in the courtroom are highly educated Kurds, often more fluent in Turkish than Kurdish or Zazaki. So why do they insist on speaking their mother tongue?

Aktar answers that that would probably be appropriate in a democracy but not in Turkey, and certainly not in the KCK case: 'This is a purely political trial, with the aim of silencing the Kurdish political movement. There is no evidence to speak of, all the suspects are being persecuted for legal activities. And you expect them to do something as apolitical as speaking Turkish? Of course they insist on their right to use their own language. And according to international conventions, they do have that right.'

The fact that there isn't a shred of evidence against the suspects becomes very clear that day. All of the sessions this week are devoted to reading out the charge, which is several thousand pages long. The judge doesn't make the slightest effort to deliver a captivating recital but reads in a tired, monotonous voice. The 'evidence' consists mainly of (often illegally) tapped telephone conversations about trivialities. At least, most of it is trivial; a conversation about a meeting might sound like this:

'Hello how are you, fine and you, are you coming tonight, yes I'll probably be late, are the others coming, yes, and do we need anything except the forms, no I don't think so, well, see you tonight then, take care, you too.'

And so on, for hours on end. The suspects and audience sometimes laugh out loud at certain passages because the evidence in the conversation being read is so ridiculously scant ('Are you bringing tomatoes?') and the judge intervenes: 'Silence please, this is no laughing matter.' After such reprimands the suspects keep quiet for a short while, but the buzz of voices soon rises again.

In the breaks, the rituals of communication are repeated: suspects push against the row of gendarmerie officers and the audience gathers behind the balustrade, calling, waving, greeting. I'm in the middle of the throng, observing and listening, until someone draws the attention of BDP MP Selma Irmak to me, telling her I'm a Dutch journalist. Irmak places her hand on her heart and nods at me. Foreign reporters seldom attend the trial, as there is hardly any interest in it in Western media, and the presence of any foreign journalists is welcomed. I make the same gesture, and hope that Irmak can lip-read my silent 'Take care of yourself.'

What surprises me most are not the conversations between suspects and the public gallery or the sleeping and chatting going on in the dock, but the incredibly relaxed atmosphere in the courtroom. I had expected something far grimmer. The suspects are polite to the judge (even if they address him in an 'unknown language'), the people in the public gallery are never unfriendly to the gendarmerie officers (in fact they completely ignore them), the lawyers never raise their voices when speaking, the male and female guards at the entrance to the courtroom search the visitors and turn bags inside out without anyone getting angry.

At first, I put this down to resignation. The suspects don't have any influence on their trial at all, the lawyers don't harbour the illusion that they can actually do anything to help their clients, the people in the public gallery have only come to see their loved ones and speak to them if possible, not to engage in politics.

'They're Ruining Our Lives'

I realise later that resignation doesn't come into it – these persecuted politicians, human rights activists and leaders simply do not recognise the court. The system that is condemning them does not offer what a legal system should: justice. To Kurds, it epitomises the state, which has never in the history of the Republic protected them, but on the contrary has denied their existence, suppressed, assimilated and murdered them. The defendants, their families and the entire community view the KCK case as just another chapter in a long history of suppression.

This also becomes clear to me during a conversation I have with H.'s parents in Gülyazı some months later. I have often urged H. to explain to me what exactly has kept him from going into the mountains until now. The question still intrigues me: why do some young Kurds go and not others? What makes one group different from the other? The first time I asked H., he said, 'Who said I *won't* go?' – after which I'm always relieved to see him when I visit the village.

One day, he adds that he doesn't go because his parents won't allow it. 'So you've asked them?' I want to know. 'No, of course not,' he answers. 'That's taboo. But I know they wouldn't allow it.' I ask him for an interview with him and his parents on the subject. Out of the question, he says. 'You can go ahead and talk with them about it, but not while I'm there. It just won't do.'

One afternoon, I enter his parents' house. H. is grazing the goats on the *yayla* with some other men from the village. I already know his mother, her house is on the way to Pakize's. I always enjoy playing and talking with her grandchildren, and every time I walk past her house, she invites me to come in. We can't really talk if I'm without my interpreter, as she only speaks Kurdish. But we have a way of understanding each other all the same. She pours tea with the word *dixwe*, which means 'drink' (or rather, 'eat'; the official word for 'drink' is *vedixwe*, but the villagers don't bother with such details), and then just keeps topping up my glass. We sign and exchange looks, sometimes I hold her hand or she holds mine.

That day, I tell my interpreter to explain to her that I want to talk about H., that I've had several long talks with him (which she knows) and that his story has moved me. That I sometimes worry about him, because he's exactly the kind of young Kurdish man who would go to the mountains: highly educated, knowledgeable about Kurdish history, traumatised by and angry about what the state has done to him and his family, and committed to the struggle. Is she worried he will leave?

'I've told him several times not to go to the mountains,' she says. 'That it is better to end up in prison than murdered by the army.' But can she be sure he won't go anyway? 'He's a human being,' she says. 'He's young, he thinks about life. I'd understand it, and maybe someone will persuade him. We're trying to solve his problems so he can get his degree. He has a good future ahead of him.'

A son or daughter taking to arms is usually a nightmare for Kurdish parents, and few of them actually allow their children to go. At the same time, parents can't help being proud of a child who chooses to join the PKK. I ask H.'s mother how she would feel about it if he disappeared one day. 'We wouldn't be angry,' she says.

Her husband has come in, a short, quiet and friendly man whose tanned and wrinkled face usually has a melancholy expression but can unexpectedly break out in an almost childishly happy smile. He always wears dark-green, traditional Kurdish clothes: baggy trousers, a shirt, a green jacket or smock and a broad length of cloth wrapped tightly around his waist. His head is invariably covered by a black and white checked scarf. Tired, he lies down on one of the elongated cushions against the wall, using his folded green jacket as a pillow.

When he hears what we're talking about, he sits up. 'You know,' he says in Kurdish, 'we try to give our children a good, traditional upbringing. We teach them our values, make sure they find a good partner and get married, and we help them look after their family. And then the state comes along, bombs and persecutes them. This legal system is not ours, this government is not ours, it doesn't represent us in any way. They are ruining our lives.'

My Position as a Journalist

H., journalist S., R., a scout and a head of a village guard, local politicians, villagers, smugglers: they won't be the last to appear anonymously in my book. As a journalist, I'm not happy about that, as one of the golden rules of journalism dictates that I avoid anonymous sources as much as possible; mentioning peoples' names increases credibility.

It isn't the first time I'm at odds with the golden rules of journalism when writing about the Kurdish question. Or, in other words: having won my spurs as a journalist in a democratic country, I'm finding the Dutch approach to journalism often falls short in Turkey. The Turkish government is not transparent, no one takes responsibility for their actions, civil servants are fired if they ever (and I mean, *ever*) talk with the press, and the people who only agree to talk to me anonymously are justified in fearing they will face arrest otherwise.

It means having to make your story all the more convincing and tying up any loose ends. And sometimes holding your own against clients who don't know much about Turkey, or who refuse to take into account the different way things are done here.

An example: I tried to sell the story about the marijuana fields to a website written in English. It was a hot topic: the 'greatest strike ever against the PKK's marijuana fields' had just taken place and was covered mainly from the government's point of view.

The site didn't want it though, because none of the villagers or local politicians was named in the piece. Serious allegations, if made anonymously, simply don't pack much of a punch, so I added Evren Çelik's voice, the BDP member in Ankara, who confirmed the allegations directed at the local army posts without insisting on anonymity. The site still didn't want to publish, unless the Turkish government or the army were given the chance to put their side of the story. I had incorporated quotes made earlier by Minister for EU affairs Egemen Bağış, as well as the government's view as published in the Turkish press, but that wasn't enough for the editor, who wanted a direct response to the allegations by a ministry or the army.

And so the story has remained unpublished. I tried my best, of course; I emailed the AKP, the Ministry of the Interior and the prime minister's office. But whatever you do, their lips are sealed on a topic like that. This gives them exactly what they want: the other side of the story is not told.

Everything I have found on the subject in foreign media reflects the government's views, frequently quoting AKP members (who are keen to support the claim that the fields belong to the PKK), journalists from Anadolu Agency (AA, the large, semi-official Turkish news agency whose reports always obediently follow government lines), police academy instructors (civil servants who wouldn't dream of deviating from the officially approved story), or army commanders involved in the operation, put forward by the AA. And perhaps the occasional very short quote by a BDP politician arguing in favour of economic investment in the southeast, but that's about it.

Or it's a 'single-column item,' a short news item whose source is revealed by the phrase 'the Turkish press organisation Anadolu Agency reports.'

This is a bad situation, giving every story a criminal – in the Turkish press even terrorist – slant. And that is only one aspect of it. I consider it my duty as a journalist to do my utmost to tell the *whole* story. Luckily, we journalists aren't easily discouraged. I didn't accompany the scout in Ortasu for the thrill of it, but to witness a smuggling trip with my own eyes and find out whether there really are so many soldiers and drones – and what I saw has proved that the army keeps a close eye on the route and that, just as everyone keeps telling me, they usually leave the smugglers alone.

I sometimes pretend to be more naive than I really am so I can gauge people's reactions. For instance when talking to inhabitants of the Lice district, I'll say, 'I'm Fréderike, a journalist from the Netherlands. I've heard that some PKK marijuana fields were destroyed here a couple of days ago?' Invariably, the astonishment at such ignorance is written all over their faces – and that astonishment speaks volumes. Then the stories come out. *So you don't know what's really going on? Take a seat, have you eaten? Have some tea, and listen – but you didn't hear this from me!*

And when they tell me that the marijuana fields are often situated right next to the road, I don't just take their word for it, I check. That wasn't possible during that first research trip, because drones were circling above the area looking for the perpetrators of the recent PKK attack. My contact in the village called me to say it was too dangerous to wander around the countryside. But I returned a few months later and I've seen them, the fields along the road.

It was another reason for me to return to Gülyazı and Ortasu so often. If I hadn't kept going back to Pakize and her children, all I'd have had to go by would have been her understated remark on her financial situation after losing Osman in the bombing, 'It was difficult then, it's even more difficult now.' I wouldn't have witnessed the poverty.

Coming out of her house one morning, I saw a deep hole of at least four square metres in the small yard between her house and that of her brother-in-law (Osman's younger brother) and sister-in-law Çiğdem: the improvised septic tank had imploded because of recent heavy rains and a merciless downpour the night before. The village is not connected to a sewer system, and the only affordable solution was filling the hole with concrete. This is what Abdulkarim, Hüseyin (Belkiz's husband) and Burhan (Hüseyin's son) were busy doing. Little Mahmut made attempts to climb up the large shovel whenever it was put down.

And I will never forget the time Pakize's eldest daughter Esra asked me to go to the shop with her. I didn't understand why, but let her persuade me out of curiosity. She browsed through the imitation gold jewellery and selected a necklace. Would I pay for it? I refused, explaining that I couldn't just buy her such a necklace, since I didn't know if her mother would allow her to wear it. I was also a little surprised at her, as she was usually such a humble girl; what did she want jewellery like that for? I showed her things I'd be prepared to buy for her instead: notebooks, coloured pens, stickers. She didn't want them.

Ambling back home without having bought anything, she suddenly whispered, 'It was meant for Mother's Day.' Not a holiday that usually features very prominently in my calendar, I had completely forgotten it was the next day. Back in the shop, Esra paid for the necklace with a beaming smile. Only to whisper something to me again on the way home, 'I'd rather exchange it.' I waited as she ran back and then returned with a package containing three vegetable peelers. At home, she ripped two pages out of an exercise book, wrote 'Dear mama I love you very much' on one of them in Turkish, rolled it up in the other with the peelers and sealed the parcel with sticky tape. The next morning she interpreted the letter for her mother, who put away the peelers in the kitchen drawer with a smile.

Am I Becoming Too Pro-Kurdish?

It's probably what you get for systematically making Kurdish voices heard and presenting the conflict and everything to do with it from their perspective: some nationalist Turks will think you're a 'terrorist whore' and won't hesitate to tell you. Qualifications like that are like water off a duck's back to me, but I sometimes get asked critical questions I can't dismiss as easily. 'Are you sure you're not getting too pro-Kurdish?' a Turkish colleague asked me in a personal Twitter message.

Am I becoming too pro-Kurdish? Am I, as someone else put it, 'anti-Turkish'? Such accusations are always made by Turks, who take a black and white Turkish nationalist view of me and my work. They imply that I've become part of the conflict, that I am 'on' one side and 'against' the other. Which I'm not. And having neither Kurdish nor Turkish blood, I can't be defined in terms of nationality either. I'm an outsider. A journalist with an interest in the human rights angle, specialised in the Kurdish question.

Even in the Netherlands people sometimes think I'm taking sides. I once had an argument with an editor of a magazine, who wrote in an email, 'It seems to me you are not being completely objective.' She was right, in a sense – the topic I was broaching showed my priorities – but that was not what she meant. She meant I wasn't on the ball as a journalist. That I was becoming a kind of activist instead of seeking to write a balanced story.

The article in question was about the Kurdish language in education. Since 2012, children from the fifth year onwards – when they are eleven years of age – have been able to choose Kurdish as an optional subject in state schools. I wanted my story to reflect the view of children, too. Kurdish schoolchildren. But the editor insisted on including Turkish ones, and I didn't agree to that. What would Turkish children have to say about this, indoctrinated as they are at school with Turkish nationalism? It might have provided interesting quotes and reflections for an in-depth article, but this was a news item of roughly 700 words. But my main objection was that this would present the issue as a conflict between Turks and Kurds, which it isn't. The Kurds are not fighting the Turks, but a system that denies their existence, assimilates, suppresses and murders them.

The real issue underlying these examples and accusations is balanced journalism. I can agonise about such things: for weeks after this incident, all I could think of was how to practise my profession as conscientiously as possible, and where to draw the line between journalism and activism.

I've chosen to let one of the duties of a journalist play a crucial part in my work, namely giving a voice to people who are usually not heard. Recording the story of ordinary Kurds, their daily lives, their past, their choices, their losses, their pain. And doing that in the most balanced way possible. No one would take me seriously if I wrote down everything I was told indiscriminately, without researching any claims. This includes claims made by the state as well as the Kurds: 'The Uludere smugglers are the terrorist's helpers,' as well as 'The PKK has nothing to do with the marijuana fields.'

And then there's a great deal that remains unpublished because it just won't wash. If I were an 'activist' journalist for the Kurdish cause, I probably wouldn't think twice about declaring that Turkey has used poison gas against Kurds; you only have to follow enough Kurdish activists on social media to see such accusations pop up regularly. As a professional, I don't go along with such serious allegations, as it has never been proved beyond doubt that Turkey used poison gas – not recently, that is; it was almost certainly used in Dersim.

I became aware of how fiercely certain activists believe in such allegations when I tweeted about being on my way to hospital in Uludere because I was covered in a rash. 'Could it be caused by residues of poison gas that may have been used in the bombing?' someone asked in all seriousness. 'Don't be daft,' I answered, 'this place is crawling with bugs.'

My work on the Kurdish question has been my greatest journalistic challenge yet, and it has helped me become more aware of the essence of my profession: the search for truth. We like to say it 'lies somewhere in the middle' but that isn't true at all. The truth, nuanced and complex though it can be, hardly ever lies in the middle, but is hidden somewhere in a jumble of information, opinions, observations and research, and it is up to journalists to unravel that jumble. In the most famous revelation in the history of journalism, the Watergate scandal (the bugging scandal that forced American President Nixon to resign from office), the truth didn't lie in the middle, either: the offices were bugged, end of story.

The Kurdish Press Fills a Vacuum

In Turkey, journalists can go in search of the truth too, but getting it published is a little trickier.

The Turkish media almost all belong to large corporations. Media conglomerates are also construction giants, telecom titans and banking and insurance colossi. Newspapers serve an economic rather than a journalistic purpose. This intrinsic link between commercial and political interests in Turkey forces the media to stay within the accepted limits of the current political discourse. Straying too far from the government's course means missing out on government tenders. In an effort to maximise newspaper circulation and television ratings, editors pander to the tastes of the average Turkish newspaper readers and television viewers by serving up a tried and trusted mix of news and opinions covered with a veneer of polarisation, sensationalism, sex, sexism and nationalism. By reporting just one side of the Kurdish question, the Turkish media kill two birds with one stone: sucking up to the government while serving bite-size chunks of nationalism to the readers.

I once asked a reporter for a major Turkish newspaper ('Please don't mention my name in print or I'll get fired') why they never just ask ordinary Kurdish people for their opinions. 'Because we're afraid of what they would say,' she answered. 'And we can't print it anyway, so why bother?' She was ashamed of it, realising full-well how un-journalistic it was, but, as a novice reporter at the bottom of the ladder who was glad to have found a job after completing her degree in journalism, what could she do?

The Kurdish media are part of the Kurdish political movement. The PKK is at the heart of this movement, and has permeated it with its ideas. This means Kurdish journalists aren't always able to tell the whole story either. Returning to the issue of the marijuana fields: Kurdish television stations and newspapers showed angry and distressed villagers saying that those were *their* crops the army burned down, that their source of income has been lost and that the PKK has nothing to do with it. But neither RojTV nor the *Özgür Gündem* newspaper made any mention of the fact that the PKK *does* take a slice of the profits.

Yet labelling the Kurdish press as pure PKK propaganda wouldn't be fair, just as you can't do justice to the Turkish press (who can match RojTV's over-the-top glorification of fallen fighters, but then with Turkish soldiers) by portraying it as just a state propaganda machine. I think they both have a role to play on the Turkish media scene. Turkey is not a fully fledged democracy, and its press doesn't function as would befit a democratic system. When the Kurdish media were founded in the 1990s, Kurdish affairs did not even feature in the Turkish press. Most Turks knew nothing about the thousands of villages that were being torched in the southeast; they thought the Kurds who moved to Istanbul, İzmir, Mersin and Adana at the time were economic migrants rather than refugees fleeing atrocities inflicted on them by the state.

The Kurdish media filled a vacuum. Hardly any Turks read or watch them, but for Kurds, they are the only source of news concerning them, and their only chance to say their piece and be heard. True, Öcalan features somewhere on the front page of *Özgür Gündem* every day, and true, Kurdish TV stations paint a romantically free picture of life in 'the mountains,' portraying the PKK rebels as demigods, but there is also real and trustworthy news coverage. News that doesn't make the Turkish press.

Such as that Friday evening in November 2011, when a young Kurd hijacked a ferry with about twenty passengers on board near İzmit (a short distance to the southeast of Istanbul) and forced the skipper to sail towards Imralı, the island on which Öcalan is held prisoner. I was visiting friends in Diyarbakır at the time. We were watching an entertainment programme on a Turkish station when I read the news on Twitter. 'A ferry hijacking, the hijacker wants to go to Imralı!' I said, and we zapped over to RojTV, where the news of the hijacking was already being broadcast. We checked all the Turkish news stations, but weren't in the least surprised to find nothing. There was a very brief report some time later, eventually followed by a slightly more detailed account once the hijacker had been shot dead by security forces.

I tweeted the RojTV news in English, which brought in quite a few new followers that night, especially Turkish ones. The Kurdish stations (broadcast in various languages including Turkish) can only be received with a separate satellite dish most Turks don't have. Many wouldn't dream of switching over to RojTV anyway – a Turkish friend of mine with an interest in the Kurdish question would get into terrible trouble with her family if she switched the television to the 'terrorist station' RojTV at her parents' house.

Suggesting that I am biased is ignoring this journalistic reality, as well as what I'm trying to do: making the best use I can of my privileged position as a foreign journalist, unhindered by the authorities and the limitations of the Turkish media, in order to shed light on the largest killing of civilians perpetrated by the Turkish state in recent decades.

The key figures – the AKP government and the Turkish army – won't speak to me, and certain important documents are not even available to the parliamentary investigative commission. I have to find other ways, all the time questioning my journalistic integrity, and have come to the conclusion that only if I failed to share with my readers all the pieces of the jigsaw I have been trying to put together would I be failing as a journalist. Then those in power, responsible for the murder of thirty-four civilians, would get away with it all too easily.

The Air Strike: a Deliberate and Targeted Operation

Meanwhile, the parliamentary commission investigating the Uludere bombing is not making any headway. Even the commission's chairman İhsan Şener complains about being hindered from doing his job. In July, he tells the Turkish press, 'I don't believe the government is sharing all its information and documentation with us.' For instance, there is a report on the incident drawn up by the Ministry of the Interior that was immediately classified 'SECRET.' The highest military authority won't reveal everything about what happened that night, either.

Şener has had to postpone the publication of the commission's report twice already – the April 2012 deadline wasn't met, and the subsequently promised presentation in June also fell through. Then September came and went without the promised presentation, which Şener finally decided to postpone until January 2013, after the first anniversary of the bombing, so the report wouldn't be 'used for political purposes.' Two days before the commemoration, on 26 December, he reveals the possibility that the army's chief of staff Necdet Özel may have given the order for the air strike, adding that there had been no evil intent, but that the bombing had been the result of 'a succession of errors.'

In the course of 2012, various members of government give their opinion on who ordered the bombing. On 20 May, Prime Minister Erdoğan claims it was the General Staff: 'On the question of giving instructions in this matter, the system has operated the way the system always does. The security forces acted on the authority they had been given to look after their own needs and interests.'

In other words, he's referring to something the Armed Forces said immediately after the bombing, that permission for cross-border military operations has been issued annually by the Turkish parliament since 2007. The question is, what are the so-called 'rules of combat,' i.e. the rules that determine whether and to what degree soldiers are permitted to use violence in a given situation? The answer seems impossible to find.

But then a different question intrigues me more anyway: why? Why were civilians bombed to death? Until there is an answer to this, I refuse to believe the bombing was an accident, the result of a succession of errors, or whatever else it has been called. I arrange a meeting with the BDP MP Ertuğrul Kürkçü, a member of the parliamentary investigative commission. Of those who are prepared to speak with journalists, he has the most inside information, knowing all the unclassified documents the commission has studied.

We talk in late February 2013 (the presentation of the commission's report has been postponed from January to March) at his office in the parliament building in Ankara. Kürkçü has also concluded that the bombing was no accident, *and* he knows why it happened. I'm on the edge of my seat.

Fehman Hüseyin, alias Bahoz Erdal, a high-ranking PKK commander – this is all about him. He read this in the report the Ministry of the Interior drew up shortly after the bombing. It was declared confidential, but the members of the commission were allowed to look at it; and no more than that, Kürkçü says: 'We were allowed to read the report and make notes in closed meetings. Photocopies or photographs were prohibited.'

Kürkçü noted the most important information, including that about Fehman Hüseyin. Kürkçü: 'The members of the ministerial investigation commission spoke with the local commander of the 23rd division of the military police İlhan Bölük. He stated that the only political and military target in the region was Fehman Hüseyin. According to intelligence, he was staying just over the border in Iraq, and the PKK was planning attacks on police posts along the border.'

This rhymes with the explanation the army gave shortly after the bombing, that they had been informed the rebels were planning retaliation attacks for the considerable losses they'd suffered. PKK units were thought to have been sent into the Sinat-Haftanin area, the region in Iraq where the Uludere bombing took place, to prepare the attacks.

But the same report by the Ministry of the Interior seems to contradict that claim. In it, several army officials declare that the region is, on the contrary, 'relatively calm,' and that there is 'no terrorist activity.' The chief of intelligence of the Şırnak province police force, Baris Çolak, says, 'According to our information, this particular area is not known as a region in which terrorists are active. It is used by smugglers.'

As it turns out, the intelligence on PKK units congregating in the area is based on rumours, and an observed increase in the use of radio communication equipment in the region compared to the same period in previous years. The ministerial report states that such information does not justify a military operation without being supported by other intelligence.

Ertuğrul Kürkçü: 'Based on intercepted conversations, the decision was taken to carry out a ground operation at the border. A PKK unit was thought to be crossing over to Turkey, possibly including Fehman Hüseyin. The operation was going ahead as planned until it was suddenly aborted at around 9 pm, when all soldiers were ordered to return to the barracks. That's why the villagers who heard the bombing and went to the site around 9:30, encountered soldiers on the way.'

I check the newspaper archives. In the days after the bombing there are speculations that it was not just smugglers who were hit, but also members of the PKK, and the name Fehman Hüseyin is mentioned several times. Later, once it has been established that all victims are ordinary civilians, the name disappears from the columns. Yet it is the key. Ertuğrul Kürkçü: 'The Uludere massacre was a deliberate and targeted operation with a calculated risk of civilian casualties, for the sake of possibly killing a single PKK leader. Had they been successful, no one would be talking about the dead civilians anymore. They would have been dismissed as PKK helpers. The strike would have been celebrated as a victory.'

A victory that was sorely needed: politicians had sworn revenge after twenty-four soldiers died and twenty-one were injured in a PKK attack in Hakkâri province on the night of 18 to 19 October. The attack made the headlines in Turkey because it was the largest, claiming the most victims, in months. Two days later, the publishers and editors-in-chief of the news media were summoned to Erdoğan, where they agreed to comply with the government's publication restrictions and set up guidelines on how 'terrorism' should be covered.

When there are so many casualties in one day, the Turks get out their flags and hang them outside their houses to express their grief over the dead soldiers and to show their support of their country. The photos of the fallen soldiers (usually young men doing military service) dominate the papers and news broadcasts for days, as do the pictures and TV images of their weeping relatives at the funerals, at which a flag is invariably draped over the coffin. The country lives and breathes revenge. The Uludere bombing was that revenge. At least, it was meant to be.

Kürkçü doesn't have any solid proof, simply because all the crucial documents are secret and the top decision makers refuse to speak to the commission. Kürkçü: 'But based on the information we do have, as well as witness testimonies and common sense, we arrive at this result.'

The Man Politically Accountable: Prime Minister Erdoğan

There are of course other theories. One of the people I've discussed them with is Gareth Jenkins, analyst and expert on civilian-military relationships. The theory that civilians were deliberately killed to intimidate all Kurdish citizens strikes us both as too simplistic. Jenkins: 'There are more effective ways of intimidating a civilian population, and they have been used in the past.' He is referring to the many 'disappearances' of Kurdish activists and civilians in the 1990s, the burning down of villages, the torture practised in prisons.

And the intimidation has not ended: at the KCK trials, civilians are tried for exercising their democratic rights, and that is extremely intimidating. Turabi Kişin, a Kurdish colleague of mine who was imprisoned for several years because of his work in the 90s, is currently behind bars again in an Istanbul prison.* At our last conversation one evening in Diyarbakır, he only dared to whisper, glancing nervously over his shoulder all the time. About a month later in January 2012, the police clapped him in irons at Ankara airport on his way home from a reporting trip to Hewlêr, in the Kurdistan region of Iraq. At the time of writing in late 2013, he is still imprisoned without charges. *That* is intimidation: frightening people with things that can actually happen to them – and an air strike on the Turkish-Iraqi border doesn't fall into that category.

Gareth Jenkins: 'There have been suggestions that the PKK intentionally leaked false information to the Turkish internal and military security

* Turabi Kişin was released from prison on 12 May 2014. The court case against him continues.

forces about a PKK unit crossing the border, deliberately putting the lives of Kurdish civilians on the line. That would be good propaganda for the Kurdish movement.' He himself is not convinced by the theory: 'If you're planning something like that, you pick a more stable target than a moving group of people on a dark winter night. And taking a broader view, the PKK depends on the local population for supplies – especially in wintertime – both on the Iraqi border and in Turkey. They wouldn't risk that.'

I find it unlikely, too. Would the army really launch such an operation, based purely on intelligence picked up from the PKK? Besides, in its almost thirty-year history, the PKK has never been the cause of so many civilian casualties in one go, even indirectly. It's true the organisation has killed civilians, including Kurds, but never like this, and most of these murders took place in the early years of the PKK (and the Kurdistan Revolutionaries), between the 1970s and 90s. The victims were usually village guards, feudal leaders, members of families or clans opposed to the PKK, or else PKK members who had turned against the movement, criticised the organisation or its leaders or were suspected of doing so. Never just a random group of Kurdish civilians.

I think of what my colleague S. in Diyarbakır said about the relationship between the PKK and the village guards of Ortasu and Gülyazı: 'The village guards of Roboskî and Bejuh were never a PKK target. They were made village guards against their will and have never been called into action.' Incidentally, most of the victims of the bombing weren't village guards, as you are only eligible to become one when you come of age.

Jenkins says the most logical explanation is that the bombing resulted from an intelligence report or an analysis made on the basis of images supplied by American drones. 'If the analysis was made on the grounds of information from a human source or intercepted radio conversations, it must have been known for some time before the attack.'

And, on the prime minister: 'Erdoğan may have been aware of such a report or analysis, but he wouldn't usually be consulted on what action to take on the basis of it. He may have had a part in formulating the rules of combat in operations on and across the Iraqi border, but any later decisions are taken on the strength of these instructions; his permission is not needed for every attack.'

According to Jenkins, how high up the chain of command the decision for the bombing was taken depends largely on the nature of the 'evidence' with which the bombing was justified. Jenkins: 'The earlier the decision to attack was made, the likelier it is that someone in the higher ranks was involved in taking it.'

If the 'Fehman Hüseyin theory' is correct, it would mean Prime Minister Erdoğan probably knew of the rumours that a PKK commander wanted to cross the border in the area but not about the decision to mount an air strike that night, since that now appears to have been taken at the very last moment.

This does not absolve Erdoğan of his political responsibility, however, as the army is controlled by the government. Which I believe puts paid to the theory that the army carried out the bombing to get Erdoğan in trouble. The last-minute decision was simply taken too quickly for that – the bombing was not that meticulously planned.

But I believe an incident that happened in the summer before the bombing shouldn't be ignored, either. The top army commander Işık Koşaner and the commanders of the land forces, air force and the navy all took early retirement at their own request. This happened shortly before the annual meeting at which military promotions are decided, and for the first time, the tables were turned: President Gül and Prime Minister Erdoğan imposed their will on the army officials instead of following their suggestions, as had been the custom. What was the argument about? The army officials put forward colleagues for promotion who were suspected of involvement in planning a coup, and Gül and Erdoğan refused categorically. For the first time in Turkish history, the army officials did what democratic values dictate in such a case: they threw in the towel. The 'early retirement' is seen as the turning point at which the great political power of the army finally came to an end. Kosaner's successor Necdet Özel may not be a dyed-in-the-wool democrat – every high-ranking serviceman started his career in the days that coups were staged and it was generally felt that the government was at the army's beck and call – but he does seem to bow to the political powers. As do the new commanders of the army, air force and navy.

Moving to Diyarbakır

Early September 2012, I decide to put my money where my mouth is and move to Diyarbakır. I keep my Istanbul apartment, however: I love the spot, my landlord has only increased the rent once in seven years (which means I'd have to pay a few hundred lira a month extra for a similar apartment if I returned to the city later) and I can find subtenants to keep costs down. Besides, the rent in Diyarbakır is ridiculously low: sharing with a friend, we pay 325 lira a month, which translates to a monthly rent of around 65 euros for me alone.

I take the bus. It takes twenty-four hours where a flight would have been an hour and a half, but I can take more things with me without having to pay for extra luggage. Not that I'm taking that much along, but my two carpets alone exceed the twenty-kilogram baggage allowance on a flight. I pay for two seats so I can sprawl out and be carried to the southeast at a nice, leisurely pace.

Late that evening, it must be around midnight, I'm standing with a pile of my things in front of the concrete block I'm going to live in on an empty, dark and quiet street, when a young man appears as if out of nowhere. 'Good evening,' he says. 'Need some help?' 'Yes, please,' I answer. I pick up my bag and rucksack and wheel my suitcase after me as he takes the other suitcase and swings a carpet wrapped in a bin liner over his shoulder. We go inside, he puts my things in a neat pile at my front door, wishes me *good evening Madam*, and is gone.

If only my neighbours in Üsküdar could have seen this. My nice neighbours, who looked at me in disgust a couple of months ago, when I told them I'd spent a few weeks in Diyarbakır and Şırnak. I wish they could come with me to this part of the country and see for themselves how beautiful it is, how verdant in some places and rough and barren in others, and how friendly, helpful and hospitable the people are.

Hospitality is such a hackneyed word, but I feel more of it when I'm among Kurds than anywhere else in Turkey. It is deeply rooted in their culture, but I think the 'polarised identity' has helped to bring it out even more; and to divide the 'outside world' into people who support the goal of the group and people who don't. A visitor to their country who listens to their stories is automatically counted among the 'supporters,' and welcomed with open arms.

This doesn't mean, however, that anyone who doesn't support them is hated or even disliked. There is no anti-Turkish sentiment here, and I have never heard Kurds cheer when soldiers are killed fighting the PKK. On the contrary, Kurds frequently say the soldiers are as much 'their children' as the rebels. That is often literally the case: Kurds are also obliged to do military service, and don't always survive it either. The Kurdish media don't gloat when soldiers are killed, in contrast to Turkish TV stations, who endlessly repeat army-issued images of attacks on PKK camps.

In late August 2012, an army minibus was driving along the road from Şırnak to Hakkâri when, in a twist of fate, it had an accident near Ortasu and Gülyazı. The villagers rushed out to help. The utter astonishment of the Turkish media reporting on the villagers' helpfulness towards soldiers, of all people, speaks volumes about the Turkish attitude towards Kurds. What had they expected? That the villagers would rush up only to stand by and laugh?

Turkish public opinion is dominated by the 'terrorism problem.' While the existence of Kurdistan is stubbornly denied in Turkey, many Turks don't realise that they themselves never cross the border of that non-existent country. Not in their thoughts, not physically, and not even by switching to a Kurdish television station or reading a Kurdish newspaper from time to time. The southeast is a no-go area where terrorists live, where there is only violence and where Turks are hated.

Though standards of education are rising dramatically in Turkey, the highly educated do not always take a critical stance towards their country: in Turkish universities – which are still under the supervision of the Council of Higher Education (YÖK) and where there is no academic freedom – critical and independent thought is not a priority. Equally, having a degree does not always mean knowing English: most graduates still only speak one language, and are unable to read or watch foreign media.

When I meet Turks who *have* started to doubt the things that were hammered into them all their lives, I always ask them how they have freed themselves from the state truths. Invariably, they have spent time abroad, for instance in a university exchange programme, or are also part of a minority. A Turkish colleague in Istanbul once confided her bisexuality to me. 'Believe me,' she said, 'it is enough to change your view of Turkey.'

Bedel Encü: to the Mountains

I've never seen Bedel Encü (sixteen) before. That is to say, I don't recognise him on the photograph his mother Beydin (fifty-two) shows me on her battered little mobile. 'Look,' she says, 'he's blond, and tall. More handsome than the others.'

It's summer 2013. Bedel left two and a half months ago. He suddenly ran away while he and some others were fetching sand close to the border – the whole family was helping to build a house. 'A few days later,' Beydin says in Kurdish, 'the organisation let us know on the grapevine that he really had joined them.'

Bedel is the first child from Ortasu and Gülyazı to join 'the organisation,' i.e. the PKK, since 28 December 2011. His friends Savaş, Bilal, Muhammed and Orhan, all fifteen years old at the time, were killed in the bombing. Bedel was also a smuggler, had been since he was twelve, but happened to stay at home that night. His eldest brother Kadri (twenty-three): 'The five of them did everything together. Going on picnics, or to the internet café. They had plans for the next day, too.'

The family lives just outside Ortasu, on the dirt road leading to the border. They heard drones and army helicopters that evening, but that wasn't unusual. Even the three army trucks driving past the house and blocking the road further down didn't alarm them: the roads used for smuggling were regularly cordoned off.

Kadri: 'We were eating nuts and dates. Shots rang out, but that didn't worry us too much, they're a familiar sound in these parts. But then we suddenly heard an incredibly loud blast. We almost jumped out of our skins. Bedel was scared to death. His best friends were there. He was shaking all over.'

Bedel spent more time at home after that, and became withdrawn. Had he ever talked about wanting to go to the mountains? 'No,' Kadri answers, 'that's not something you talk about. You just do it.' His mother: 'But he *was* very quiet that morning.' Do they worry about the baby of the family? Kadri: 'No, we know who he's with. He's given emotional support, the same as all the members, because everyone has to leave their family behind and that's always hard. Did you know they teach you reading and writing if you've never learnt how? And they play volleyball. Yes, it's possible he'll have to kill someone.' Then comes a simile I've heard before: the PKK kills in self defence, as a response to the state aggression that has been directed at the Kurds for decades; like a woman violently fending off a rapist.

Beydin says she does worry sometimes. 'When I'm at home, I often cry. I think of him and imagine I can hear his voice.' Kadri spoke with his youngest brother in a dream: 'I asked him, "Bedel, are you coming back home?" He answered, "No. I will not leave this path."'

Chapter Five

The Earth

They are standing in a line from the graveyard entrance to the gravestones: the female relatives of the air strike victims. Each of them is holding a portrait of a loved one she has lost. Coming from the official entrance of the graveyard lower down, a group of women climb the hill. They are surrounded by a small army of journalists aiming their camera lenses at their leader in particular, a simply-dressed woman in black trousers and shirt, a denim jacket and a white shawl. I'm already at the cemetery, watching the scene from a distance.

The woman visiting is Selvi Kılıçdaroğlu, wife of the leader of the main opposition Republican People's Party (CHP), Kemal Kılıçdaroğlu. She and a number of female CHP parliamentarians have come to show their support for the relatives of the Uludere bombing. And not just on any day: it's 13 May, Mother's Day.

This morning, Pakize unwrapped Esra's gift to her and put the peelers in a drawer. After breakfast, we left for the cemetery. Pakize is standing in the line; she has Mahmut with her, who is remarkably quiet today. I'm standing a little distance away with Hülya, Sinem, Esra and some other girls, Özkan has joined some friends.

Selvi makes her way down the line of relatives. She takes some of the portraits in her hands, comforts and talks to the women, occasionally wipes a tear from her eyes and completely ignores the press. The women pray at the graves. Selvi joins in, the white shawl now covering her head.

Afterwards, minibuses are waiting to take everyone the short distance down to the part of Gülyazı that lies on the main road. Lunch is served in someone's house. Shoes are piled high outside the door, and long rugs have been put out on the floor inside, set with countless plates of rice, dishes with chicken pieces and bowls of salad. Bread is handed around. Selvi Kılıçdaroğlu and the CHP parliamentarians are seated in one of the rooms, sharing a rug with women from the village. The other room is also crowded, and children are running around everywhere. The CHP women have brought gifts: toy cars for the boys, dolls for the girls and brightly coloured clothes for the women.

Selvi talks to the press. She tells them she will do everything to make sure the memory of the bombing is kept alive. That the investigation will have to be thorough, and that the government will have to issue an apology. I ask the relatives what they think of the visit. Each and every one of them says they appreciate Kılıçdaroğlu's coming. 'She feels with us, that is nice,' one of them says, expressing the general mood. 'But we don't think there's much she can do in Ankara. The CHP is not a ruling party and has little say in parliament. But we are glad about the media attention her visit will generate.'

During our chat after lunch, one of the women crumples up the skirt with the gaudy flower print she's just been given and pretends to throw it out of the open window with an angry face. 'A flowery, colourful skirt, the very idea,' she grumbles. 'Don't they know we're in mourning?' The Turkish press doesn't see this, and neither does Selvi Kılıçdaroğlu or her colleagues, who have just left the village. But the relatives of the Uludere victims have every right to be satisfied with the media attention given to the visit: it features on all the large TV stations that evening, and all the big papers the following day. Selvi Kılıçdaroğlu is quoted extensively and the grieving relatives hardly at all, but that's a mere detail. For the time being, the air strike has been saved from Turkish oblivion.

The Parliamentary Investigation: More Questions Than Answers

In March 2013, the parliamentary investigative commission presents its report.

It is full of things that don't seem relevant to an investigation searching for the truth behind a bombing.

It states that there are sufficient primary schools and one secondary school in Gülyazı and Ortasu, that there are paths leading up to the *yaylas*, that steps are being taken to install a sewer system and a reliable water supply and that the provision and manning of the health centre are being improved.

It says that the entire population, regardless of belief, race or politics, is deeply saddened by the incident in which thirty-four civilians died. There's a list of people and organisations that visited the villages to make sure the relatives were not left alone, and to share their grief.

It says that the governor of Uludere district, among others, was the victim of aggressive and provocative actions in the days after the incident. That village guards were present during the funeral as a measure against acts of provocation by the separatist terror organisation. It says that shrouds in 'various colours' (the Kurdish colours red, green and yellow) were draped over the coffins, a provocation by the terrorist organisation that made some people feel uncomfortable.

The bombing gets a mention, too – remarkably, however, only in the form of claims without any evidence to back them up. No documents, no sworn testimonies, no independent analyses.

The most extraordinary story by far is of an anonymous informant who supposedly approached the authorities five days after the air strike, claiming two PKK rebels he met in north Iraq confided in him that they had joined a group of smugglers on the night of the bombing, in order to cross the border into Turkey for a family visit.

'See, here,' says Levent Gök, MP for the largest opposition party CHP and a member of the investigation commission. I've arranged to meet him in his office at the government building in Ankara. Piled high in a corner of the room are copies of a report on the bombing he wrote himself, out of frustration with the official investigation. He picks up one of them, thumbs through it and points at a passage on one of the first pages: 'That's the story of the informant.' I mark it with a circle and pore over the piece at home.

First, I read the testimony of another informant, K.A., which was printed in the official commission's report at the end of the chapter 'Evaluations and Conclusions.' K.A. is allegedly a PKK rebel who turned himself in to the authorities three days after the bombing and made a deal with the prosecutor: in exchange for information, he would not be charged. K.A. describes a conversation he had in north Iraq with two other PKK militants, referred to by their aliases Cudi Gui and Kazım. He quotes Cudi Gui telling him that he and Kazım had been part of the group of smugglers killed in the incident. Apparently, they wanted to cross the border to visit family in Turkey.

When the group, approaching the Turkish border, heard aircraft noise, the two rebels detached themselves from the others. According to K.A., Cudi Gui said they were hiding behind some rocks when the bombing started. Once the planes had left after dropping the fourth bomb, the rebels checked on the group of smugglers and found them all dead. Then they turned straight back to their base in Iraq because they expected soldiers to appear at the site of the bombing shortly afterwards.

The official report states that the informant's testimony was given on 2 February 2012 (over a month after the bombing) at the public prosecutor's office in the border town Silopi and at the Serious Criminal Court in Diyarbakır. In February 2013, the story suddenly appears in the papers, based on undisclosed sources. There is no proof that the informant even exists, however, and neither is his account supported by, say, the video images taken by the drones.

Until then, the commission had based its investigation of the footage supplied by the drones in the so-called 'ASELSAN report.' ASELSAN, Turkey's largest defence company, is owned in large part by the government-run Turkish Armed Forces Foundation. There were ASELSAN experts present when the commission was shown the aircraft footage in February 2012. In March 2012, three months after the bombing, the firm sent the commission a report of its findings, affirming that the images taken after the air strike show people going to and from the site of the bombing but not who they are or what they are doing; that is difficult to determine from images taken by infrared cameras. But that villagers went to the site after the bombing to rescue the wounded and recover their dead is certain, and not denied by anyone.

The commission agrees unanimously with ASELSAN's matter-of-fact expert account, which is to become one of the sources for its own report. On 14 November 2012, the commission decides to start writing it.

Levent Gök claims that the AKP members of the commission altered the ASELSAN report findings to fit in with media coverage about the informant in February 2013. The AKP's interpretation of the images can be found in the final report, in the analysis of the minutes between 00:26 am and 00:31 am, two hours after the end of the bombing. ASELSAN's minute-by-minute account is completely free of interpretation, merely mentioning 'persons' going from north to south or south to north, and how many of them there are. In the commission's final report, the people walking around for five minutes at half past midnight have become the PKK rebels Cudi Gui and Kazım.

The report adds that Kazım's real name is Ferhat, and that Cudi Gui, whose real initials are B.E., lost two brothers in the bombing – this would make his surname Encü, in common with twenty-six of the victims.

Levent Gök calls the sudden appearance of the informant 'a lifesaver' for the commission's AKP members. Just what they needed, in other words, to support the hypothesis that rebels used the route, or even that there were PKK members among the smugglers that night.

Gök points out that this new, unauthorised interpretation of the drones' images is inconsistent with the informant's account. He writes that if the fourth and last bomb was dropped at 22:24 pm and Cudi Gui and Kazım, as they allegedly told K.A., took to their heels straight after the bombing, then how could the drones have filmed them running away two hours later?

Something else is puzzling me. Before returning to Iraq, the rebels supposedly established that all the smugglers were dead, but there were three slightly injured survivors and eight severely injured ones, of whom one survived and seven eventually died after being taken to the village by the locals. Could the men who called themselves Cudi Gui and Kazım really have failed to notice eleven survivors?

The identity of informant K.A. – if he even exists – is impossible to establish. The official report of the investigation commission states that he was released after giving his testimony. Vanished without a trace.

'And *here*,' Levent Gök says again, still thumbing through his own report, this time pointing out statements by İlhan Bölük, commander of the 23rd division of the military police in Şırnak.

Bölük made the statements in – I can't help it – yet another report, commissioned by the Ministry of the Interior. Written soon after the bombing, it was declared a state secret with even greater haste. The members of the commission were allowed to read it on several occasions, but after each session of poring over the document (making copies or taking photos was prohibited), they had to hand it in again.

In this report, İlhan Bölük states that the only political military target in the area was the PKK commander Fehman Hüseyin, alias Bahoz Erdal. This supports the theory that the government was out to kill him. He says that besides being used for smuggling, the route taken by the smugglers is 'used daily by the locals for such activities as gathering herbs and fire wood.'

Bölük also says that the group's lack of concern about the bombs and the shots preceding them was seen as proof of the assumption that they were PKK militants. They simply continued on their way after the shots, which is what rebels would do because they'd know they were only fired as a warning. But in the ministerial report, local Major Mehmet Ölçensoy says, 'I have my doubts about that. It was this feeling of ambiguity that prevented us from celebrating the destruction of the terrorist elements.'

Member of the opposition Levent Gök also quotes statements made by the chief of intelligence of the Şırnak province police, published in the ministerial report: 'As far as we are informed, the area in question is not known as a region in which terrorists are active. It is used by smugglers.'

Since the official report of the parliamentary commission makes no mention of the secret ministerial report, it doesn't include such crucial statements by local security staff, either.

Important questions are not addressed in the final report: Who analysed the images by the drones and who determined that they show a group of PKK members? What were the official rules of combat in place for cross-border operations on the Iraqi border? Why did the bombing continue after villagers had told the soldiers that the people being murdered were smugglers, and after the village chief of Gülyazı had phoned the nearest army post? Why was the bombing carried out at all? Who gave the go-ahead for the operation?

The Investigation: Dominated by Secrecy

I keep in touch with Ertuğrul Kürkçü of the pro-Kurdish BDP after our interview, and he contacts me in March to let me know the report is finished. He's already read the final version but cannot provide me with a copy, not even if I give him my word as a journalist not to publish anything about it until it has been officially released. That's because he does not have it. Kürkçü: 'We weren't allowed to take home the end product of our own commission because of fears it would be leaked to the press ahead of time. I've no idea when the official report will be presented, that can change at a moment's notice.'

According to Kürkçü, secrecy has been the dominant theme of the fourteen-month investigation: 'Many of the meetings were closed sessions, including the one in which we looked at the drone images, even though there was no legal reason for that. I wanted to get the whole picture, so I submitted a request to see the images made by the unmanned American aircraft above Iraqi soil, but it was rejected – the investigation could be manipulated by foreign powers.' He grimaces helplessly.

The secrecy also prevented commission members from speaking to people such as any army officials ranking higher than local commanders – including the commanders of the air and land forces and the Chief of

Staff of the army – as well as the top politician in charge, Prime Minister Erdoğan.

Another consequence was that certain evidence, if it even existed, was not made available to the commission. Such as confirmations of the number of walkie-talkie conversations that were tapped, which only appear in the report in the form of oral statements made by local army commanders; proof of the existence of the anonymous informant, a tape recording of his testimony or the possibility of tracking him down for questioning by the commission; photographs of the surrounding area and a detailed contour map, including army posts, of the couple of square kilometres in which the tragedy took place.

The official report doesn't actually contain any conclusions at all, just findings on the security situation in northern Iraq, Fehman Hüseyin and his alleged presence in the area, an anonymous informant and his conversation with Cudi Gui and Kazım, the footage recorded by the drones, the exact times the small aircraft took off from which airfield, and so on. It is rehashed information, mentioned earlier in the report and now presented as the conclusion. Its only sources of information are local commanding officers and other local authorities. Why exactly this is hailed as conclusive evidence while the experiences and accounts of relatives and survivors are not, remains unclear.

For a long time, I'm so engrossed in the details of the official report and its alternatives by the opposition parliamentarians Levent Gök of the CHP and Ertuğrul Kürkçü of the BDP, that the greater significance of the official report only dawns on me very gradually: this is not the report of an investigation into the bombing, but an account of the security situation in that part of north Iraq. In the eighty-three pages of the report, the word 'terrorists' appears eighty-six times and the word 'terror' ninety-two times.

It surprises me at first to find the name of PKK leader Fehman Hüseyin, as he is key to the bombing, but in fact the AKP commission members use him to underpin their 'accident theory' rather than to shed light on what actually happened. What is worse, the link with the security situation and the 'terrorist threat' is made so much of in the report that it throws suspicion on the victims and villagers, dismissing them as terrorist helpers.

In Turkish public opinion, terrorists – and to Turkish nationalists that includes terrorist helpers – deserve no mercy. You only have to make the connection between Uludere and the struggle against terrorism once, or mention that the victims and their relatives have ties with the PKK, to effectively nip any potential empathy in the bud. Which also prevents such pesky questions as what exactly happened that night, and why.

Whether Erdoğan knew about the Uludere bombing before it happened is anyone's guess. CHP commission member Levent Gök is convinced he did, pointing out that the bombing took place on the exact day of the monthly National Security Council meeting, at which the country's political and military leaders discuss current affairs. 'It's very unlikely they did not discuss the alleged presence of PKK member Fehman Hüseyin in the area, and what to do about it,' he says.

But there's no way of knowing. Whether and to what extent the details of a possibly imminent operation were discussed that afternoon depends, among other things, on the rules of combat in force for the area, and those are still unclear. Besides, the exact moment at which the decision for the bombing was taken is uncertain: given that it started out as a ground operation until the ground troops were suddenly told to retreat, the bombing may well have been a last-minute decision. There is nothing about that in the official report.

I try to find out more by speaking to Lale Kemal, military expert and journalist for the *Taraf* daily newspaper. She makes the cautious statement that the parliamentary Uludere commission 'did not succeed in finding the truth,' and adds, 'that is partly because of the power of the army, which is still not under control in Turkey. Prime Minister Erdoğan's good working relationship with the army may give the impression he's in control of it, but he's not. In a fully fledged democracy, the army would probably have proceeded with more caution. An incident like Uludere would be thoroughly investigated. But in today's political set-up, nobody is able or willing to ensure the army makes all the information available.'

Kemal does not want to comment on the question of whether the bombing was an accident. 'But even if, as the government claims, it was an accident,' she says, 'it was a foolhardy accident. And imagine it was true that there were PKK members among the smugglers, is that a reason to bomb them, if they're not about to launch an attack? Human life has absolutely no value in this country.'

The AKP members of the commission decide by a majority to publish the report on 20 March 2013. İhsan Şener tells the Turkish press that there was no evil intent, that the reason for the bombing lay in communication flaws between civilian and military authorities and that the accident happened in the context of a serious terrorist threat from north Iraq.

The Turkish press obediently reproduces this, and many journalists embellish their articles with passages mentioning the presumed but unproven presence of PKK rebels in the group of smugglers. Some say that the report was passed by a majority consisting of AKP members and rejected by all three commission members from an opposition party. Not a single one of them does their own research or asks commission chairman Şener a critical question.

Newroz 2013: the Peace Process Begins

The report publication date could not have been more strategic. The next day, 21 March, is Newroz, the most important Kurdish festival, the start of spring and the Kurdish New Year.

The run-up to Newroz 2013 in Diyarbakır is intense. From the end of 2012 Erdoğan's government has communicated openly with PKK leader Öcalan, through the intelligence service MİT, about ending the war between the PKK and the state, which has lasted almost thirty years. For a long time Öcalan has not been allowed to receive visitors on the prison island of İmralı, where he has remained since his arrest in 1999, but from the new year boats suddenly start travelling back and forth over the Sea of Marmara from Bursa. Öcalan's lawyers are still not permitted to go to İmralı, but Öcalan's brother Mehmet and pro-Kurdish BDP MPs are. They consult with the imprisoned Kurdish leader on peace process strategy, bringing messages to and from the PKK in the camps in Iraqi Kurdistan and representatives of the Kurdish political movement in Europe.

People have been buzzing for weeks about what will happen at Newroz. A declaration from Öcalan will be read out, that much is clear, but they can only guess at its content. Is this a definitive ceasefire and surrendering of weapons, after the PKK's many temporary ceasefires in previous years, to encourage political action from the government to solve the Kurdish question and end the violence? A withdrawal of the PKK from Turkey? Has the government pledged to set Öcalan free, or will he be placed under house arrest as an intermediate step towards freedom someday?

The celebration of Newroz is always either on 21 March or the Saturday afterwards if that's more convenient, and it's held on the same day in most places. The pro-Kurdish party generally organises the festivities, always including speeches by politicians. This year is different, however:

in order to attract as many people as possible to Newroz in Diyarbakır, where Öcalan's announcement will be read, the festivities in the southeast and in Istanbul, İzmir, Adana, Mersin and all other cities with Kurdish residents take place the week before. No one is forced to choose between Newroz at home and the historic event in Diyarbakır.

It's still early on Thursday 21 March 2013 when I arrive at the enormous Newroz venue in Diyarbakır, dressed in a cheerful floral skirt and T-shirt (spring has arrived). The press has been advised to arrive in good time in order to get through the crowds to the reserved area just by the podium. Music is already playing, the finishing touches are being made to the podium, there are balloons, food, flags and streamers and enormous pictures of Öcalan and early PKK veterans who have lost their lives. Somewhere in the middle of the area stands an enormous fire basket, where the traditional Newroz fire will burn later on.

As I stride towards the stage, I suddenly hear someone behind me say, 'Feride!' I often use this name in Turkey because Fréderike is awkward for many people to pronounce. I turn, and have to think for a moment because the two women are so out of context here, with the initial hubbub of the festival, in the big city: they are mothers from Gülyazı who each lost a son in the bombing. We embrace and talk briefly. They have a place on the VIP stand by the podium, they tell me, and we agree to see one another there a bit later.

The grounds are soon full, and dozens of Turkish and international journalists are gathering in the press area, separated from other guests by fences where people are already waving Öcalan flags. There are lots of people I know, the atmosphere is friendly, tea flows continually, the sun is shining – I should have worn my flip-flops – and the VIP stand fills with BDP politicians, foreign guests and important figures from the Kurdish movement. A place is symbolically reserved for Sakine Cansız. Born and brought up in Dersim, one of the founders of the PKK in 1978, she was shot dead, along with two other politically active Kurdish women, in Paris in January 2013. All my colleagues take a photo of her empty chair, as do I, at the same time realising that she would not have been here even if her heart were still beating. Turkey was forbidden territory to her.

The police are nowhere to be seen: after all, the peace process has begun. For once the Öcalan flags and pictures of champions of the cause who have died over the last thirty years are not seen as reasons to start a fight. The Kurdish movement has its own marshals, who are always present at events and demonstrations and perfectly capable of calming incipient disturbances with the help of bystanders.

At mid-afternoon it's time for Öcalan's message. I climb behind the screens to the highest platform beside the podium to look over the crowds: hundreds of thousands at least, perhaps even the million I keep hearing people claim. Beside me some men are occupied tying balloons in the Kurdish colours into bunches to release after the speech. On the other side of me I can see between the constructions, through to the podium. There Pervin Buldan, a BDP MP, is beginning to read out Öcalan's message in Kurdish – her Kurdish is not brilliant, I hear from those around me. When she's done, her colleague Sırrı Süreyya Önder reads out the Turkish version. The crowd is almost silent but the flags do not stop waving for a second.

The news is as follows: 'We have now reached the point where we say: silence the weapons and let ideas and politics speak,' and, 'It's time for our units to withdraw over the border.' Also: 'Turks who know the old Anatolia as Turkey should know that they have lived alongside the Kurds as far back as a historic agreement of brotherhood and solidarity under the flag of Islam.' In other words, Kurds and Turks, and all other groups that make up Turkey and are named in the speech, should move together towards a new future.

The hundreds of thousands respond with frenzy, balloons rise into the air and a machine throws silver glitter over the crowd. Music breaks out and there is dancing.

The two mothers from Gülyazı sit on the VIP stand, each holding a photo frame to her chest containing the photos of all thirty-four dead boys and men from their village. No one pays any attention to them. As for me, I hardly dare to ask them how they feel. They shrug and say nothing.

Ceasefires and the Oslo Process (2008-2011)

I have often reflected on Newroz 2013. In one day, in barely five minutes, the Kurdish political movement switched from supporting the armed struggle to supporting its end. I am reminded of what human rights activist and Kurdish politician Leyla Zana said in 2010: 'The weapons are the Kurds' insurance. As long as the Kurdish question exists, the weapons are their guarantee.' I also think of what Gültan Kışanak, and Selahattin Demirtaş, leader of the BDP in parliament, said during a press conference I attended in 2012: 'Have you ever seen an armed organisation with a political aim lay down its weapons before any concession is made by the other side?'

I felt the urge to raise my hand retrospectively: 'Yes, now I know an organisation like that!' Of course, the PKK did not definitively lay down arms on 21 March 2013 and weapons were not handed in, but Öcalan's words did not allow much space for a return to violence. Not that I would want that, not that I don't welcome every ceasefire, because every life spared counts, but I can't quite get my head around the story. Why now, without any pledge from the government? Did the Kurds suddenly not need any insurance?

I believe the answer lies in the fact that Öcalan's words at Newroz were nothing new. At the start of the 1990s, a peace process was already set in motion, on the initiative of President Turgut Özal, with Jalal Talabani, Kurdish leader in Iraq, as intermediary – at the time directly negotiating with Öcalan was a bridge too far. The PKK leader announced a ceasefire and extended it, but before anything firm could be started, Özal died of a heart attack. 'Murdered!' said many Kurds, and although there is no proof, the death of the president is still a recurring theme in news in Turkey.

In the months before Öcalan was arrested, on 15 February 1999, he also advocated an end to violence, and negotiations as a means to a solution. In the autumn of 2013, I heard a direct witness talking about it during a private mini-conference in Istanbul on the situation of Kurds in Turkey, Iraq, Iran and Syria. The conference was held under the 'Chatham House Rule,' meaning that you don't reveal who attended or who said what, but there was a professor who spoke with Öcalan for hours when he was deported from Syria in 1998 and was staying in Italy. That professor said, 'Öcalan was already convinced then that the armed struggle was ineffective, and he was particularly frustrated that the Turkish state was not open to dialogue.'

It's easy to be cynical about it. Öcalan was in a tight corner in Italy: Syria had dropped him after twenty years of hospitality, his arrest was imminent, many countries would not allow him onto their territory, and he was seeking asylum but was being passed from country to country like a hot potato. No wonder, you might think, that he declared the armed struggle doomed to failure at a moment like that to save his own skin.

But that's talking in retrospect. From a detailed report of the time between his departure from Syria on 9 October 1998 and his arrest in

Nairobi, Kenya, on 15 February 1999, available in the book *Blood and Belief* by Aliza Marcus, it appears that Öcalan himself was still convinced he would find asylum somewhere.

When he was staying in Italy, from mid-November 1998 to mid-January 1999, he had not foreseen that a couple of months later he would be in solitary confinement on İmralı Island near Istanbul. Turkey requested his extradition, but Italy, like many other European countries, refused to deliver prisoners to countries with the death penalty. As a detainee, imprisoned in a strictly guarded apartment on the edge of Rome, he continued to lead the PKK, spoke to journalists, received sympathisers and exchanged thoughts with all sorts of visitors, including the professor I later met in Istanbul.

In fact, irrespective of whether Öcalan advocated peace or war at this point, he was sentenced to death – later commuted to life imprisonment.

Öcalan's arrest plunged the PKK into crisis. In August 1999, two months after he was sentenced to death, he ordered PKK troops in Turkey to withdraw and end the armed struggle. This was supposed to be followed by dialogue with the government leading to a definitive peace accord. The demand was no longer a Kurdish state, but full cultural and political rights for the Kurds.

The withdrawal had tragic consequences for the PKK: the army did not plan on letting the militants go without a struggle and repeatedly attacked the guerrillas, resulting in many deaths.

The dialogue did not get off the ground. A couple of commitments may have been made, such as concessions towards Kurdish in the media, but they were far from sufficient to satisfy the demands of the Kurdish political movement, which wanted complete freedom for the Kurdish language.

Moreover, the commitments were made without negotiation. The government – since 2001 under leadership of the AKP, which is also in power now – went to work on its own initiative, and the old Kemalist elite still firmly held the reins of state power, including the judiciary. The Kurdish political movement was silenced: in 2003 the pro-Kurdish HADEP party (People's Democracy Party) was banned by the Constitutional Court on a charge of 'separatism.' This was not the first time that the highest court had opposed Kurdish politics: in 1993 and 1994 it banned the predecessors of the HADEP, HEP and DEP on the same grounds. Neither was it for the last time, as in 2009 the DTP – HADEP's successor and the current BDP's predecessor – was to follow suit.

In 2004 Öcalan declared that he had failed in his attempts to gain rights for the Kurds through democratic means. The ceasefire was broken and from 2006 violence welled up, leading to negotiations in 2008: in September that year the Oslo Process started in complete secrecy, with representatives of the PKK and the Turkish intelligence service MİT meeting in the Norwegian capital to negotiate peace. Direct talks with Öcalan were part of the process: MİT representatives travelled to the prison island of İmralı several times.

In order to support the process, the PKK observed several ceasefires, sometimes unilaterally and for months on end. The Oslo Process never led to concrete results, and in July 2011 it ended abruptly. The government blamed the PKK: in mid-July the organisation attacked an army post in the province of Diyarbakır, killing thirteen soldiers and making further negotiations impossible. The PKK blamed the government, claiming that it had failed to bring concrete proposals to the negotiating table in Oslo. They blamed the same lack of government initiative for the intermittent violence during the negotiating process. The PKK declared an end to the ceasefire in February 2011, but respected it in practice until the elections in June.

The Oslo Process was secret for a long time, but in summer 2011 recordings of failed negotiations were leaked and Erdoğan was forced to admit to talks with the PKK. In order to avoid accusations of being soft on the PKK, he opted for a radical policy change: the faction would be dealt with harshly.

A period of unprecedented violence ensued. Based on counts from public sources the well-known International Crisis Group came to the conclusion that 928 people died in the fighting between July 2011 and Newroz 2013: 304 state actors (soldiers, police and village guards), 533 PKK members and 91 civilians, including the 34 from Uludere.

'Democratic Modernity'

Despite the violence and many deaths, over the past four years or so an important change has taken place in the population: the government admitted to talks with the PKK and the Turkish people did not protest. There were no large-scale demonstrations, and the AKP, which won the general elections in June 2011, did not lose support in opinion polls. It was mainly the opposition parties in parliament, the CHP and MHP, which tried to capitalise on the talks the government conducted with the 'terrorist leader' and 'baby murderer' – to little effect.

This made the renewed peace process possible. Prime Minister Erdoğan did not wait for a press leak, confidently announcing in mid-December 2012 that the government had been in direct talks with Öcalan for a month.

For the first time since Öcalan's imprisonment in 1999, pro-Kurdish BDP parliamentarians received permission to visit Öcalan. The boat to İmralı was reinstated (since the summer of 2011 no one had been allowed to visit him, and every visit request from his lawyers was refused under the official pretext that the boat was out of service or the weather on the Sea of Marmara was too bad). BDP members consulted with the Kurdish leader, liaising vigorously between Öcalan, PKK camps in Iraqi Kurdistan and the Kurdish movement in Europe, and setting out in person for PKK camps in the mountains for consultation, all in preparation for Newroz and subsequent steps in the peace process.

For the first time since the foundation of the Kurdistan Revolutionary Party, and later the PKK, Öcalan found and grasped the chance to address all the people of Turkey on the cause he had been fighting for since 1998: an end to violence and beginning of political dialogue. In his Newroz speech, after announcing the ceasefire and withdrawal from Turkey, he states, 'This is not the end of our fight, this is the beginning of a new sort of fight.'

That day all eyes in Turkey are fixed on Diyarbakır, everyone is listening to Öcalan, and for the first time since the foundation of the PKK, the leader addresses a Turkish audience: 'Our fight was never directed against a particular race, religion, sect or group, and it never could be. Our fight has always been against oppression, ignorance, injustice, lack of development and all forms of pressure.' And, 'On the occasion of Newroz I call on all people with Armenian, Turkish, Assyrian, Arabic and other backgrounds to see the light of freedom and equality as clearly as the Kurds do.'

As related by the two BDP MPs, Öcalan reflects at length on the shared history of Kurds and Turks, especially in the period of the foundation of the Republic of Turkey and the preceding years. He refers to the fact that Turkish and Kurdish soldiers were martyrs side by side during the First World War and in the subsequent fight for independence for the newly forming country, and that it was Kurds and Turks together who founded the Grand National Assembly. 'From our shared history there flows a mutual need to shape our future together.'

The ball was firmly in the government's court.

Öcalan's wish to silence the weapons and engage in dialogue was nothing new, but isn't his call to build a free, democratic and egalitarian country together, where there is space for all identities, rather far from the founding ideals? After dropping his demand for an independent Kurdistan, has he also given up his demand for self-determination within Turkey?

Why does he mention only that ideal which he calls 'democratic modernity,' without talking about any of the other issues: self-government, education in Kurdish to save the language from decline and to allow the connection with ancient Kurdish culture to exist, the hundreds of Kurds who are imprisoned for political reasons, citizens who instead of being protected by the state are killed with impunity? Why does he want to be a leader for all, rather than for the Kurds? How can Kurds work with Turks towards a real democratic society if they have no complete rights? Shouldn't that fight be fought first, instead of sketching future ideals now that can only be realised in several generations, if ever?

I would love to grill him on these topics in an interview, but unfortunately there is as yet no space for journalists on the boat to İmralı.

The Unsolved Murders of the 1990s

Since the autumn of 2012 there have been gravestones on the thirty-four piles of earth in the graveyard in Gülyazı, all in black granite with matching surround, still covered in plants and colourful plastic flowers, but heavy, dark, oppressive all the same.

Thousands of Kurds, killed in violence, lie like this in the ground of Kurdistan, some in graves tended carefully by their relatives, as in Gülyazı, but many others buried without a stone, without even a marking for their final resting place, often with many bodies dumped together. There are similarities between these deaths and those of Uludere: the state is responsible for them, and refuses to investigate the true circumstances. Both the relatives of the murder victims of the 1990s and those of Uludere request attention for their fate on a weekly basis. In Diyarbakır and Istanbul the 'Saturday Mothers' meet every Saturday, in Gülyazı the female relatives meet every Thursday.

They carry photos of their fathers, husbands, sons or daughters, from whom they have not heard of since, but they hardly ever make it into the newspaper or TV news. Attention for the dead from Uludere tailed off after the first year. The list of unsolved state murders is long, and continually growing.

Human rights organisation İHD has produced a map of Turkey marking all mass graves in the country with a little flag. There are flags scattered all over the southeast of the country: mostly red, meaning 'suspected mass grave,' and occasionally yellow, meaning 'opened mass grave.' Suspicions are based on testimony from witnesses, inhabitants of neighbouring villages, and repentant murderers.

The İHD study is so thorough that they have drawn up a list of locations, combined with year of burial, and the number of people thought to have been buried there.

The İHD list of mass graves in the province of Diyarbakır is long, and somewhat unfathomable when it comes to geographical names, as some villages are referred to by their Kurdish names, others by their Turkish names. In any case, since 1993 around thirty people are thought to have been buried near the village of Zera, two near Erkenci since 1995, and seventeen near Koska since 1998. Bitlis province: thirty-three people near the village of Kokarsu since 1994, four near Cakalsogut since 1995, twenty-seven in a water depot since 1997. Şırnak province: twenty-four people near Giver since 1994, and fifty-two people in anonymous graves in the municipal graveyard of the town of Silopi. The oldest suspected mass grave dates back to 1925, in Bingöl province, belonging to a family whose house was set on fire at the time of the Sheikh Said Rebellion. The list also includes mass graves from 1937-1938, which are thought to contain the remains of around 250 people: the three graves lie near the villages of Çemişgezek and Alicik in Dersim province.

The İHD list records a total of 253 mass graves with a suspected 3,248 bodies.

The Army Death Squads

The group responsible for the most murders is JİTEM, a Turkish army anti-terrorist intelligence service, founded at the end of the 1980s in the fight against the PKK, and probably disbanded at the end of the 1990s or beginning of this century. That roughly coincides with the period in which a group of ten provinces in the southeast of Turkey (called OHAL in Turkish) were in a state of emergency, and were effectively inaccessible, putting the authorities above the law.

JİTEM was an illegal organisation and the Turkish army continues to deny its existence, but there is overwhelming evidence to the contrary. One of the founders, General Veli Küçük who retired in 2000, has admitted that he stood at the cradle of JİTEM, and, more revealingly, there are accounts from former JİTEM agents who eventually fled Turkey. The best known is Abdülkadir Aygan, who started out as a PKK fighter, was later recruited by JİTEM, and now lives in Sweden as a political refugee.

In interviews with various international media organisations he revealed JİTEM's methods, as did at least two of his former colleagues. The Turkish-manufactured white Renault Toros in which they prowled the OHAL region were feared by the people. I still hear people talk about them sometimes: when a car like that showed up, you could be certain more people would disappear without a trace. Anyone stopped by JİTEM in a Toros would not come back alive. Abdülkadir Aygan said, 'We usually murdered people at night, when there were no soldiers. No one survived our interrogations.'

The illegal group's main targets were not PKK members, who were dealt with by the army and air force. JİTEM targeted Kurds who had confirmed or suspected connections with the PKK, who harboured sympathy for the movement (often ordinary citizens), Kurdish intellectuals and sometimes people at random.

The most famous JİTEM murder is that of the writer and intellectual Musa Anter, a veteran of the Kurdish political movement: he was convicted for the first time in 1959, for a poem he wrote in Kurdish, and spent a total of almost twelve years of his life in prison. On 20 September 1992 Anter was lured away from a conference by men who said they needed his help to solve a conflict about land ownership, and was shot dead.

The murder of Anter, or Apê Musa (Kurdish for 'Uncle Musa'), and the investigation into it, still often features in newspapers. His image can be seen all over Kurdistan, and an important journalism prize named after him is awarded on the anniversary of his death. As for the thousands of other victims of JİTEM, you only hear of them if a mass grave is opened somewhere or remains are identified. In Kurdish newspapers you then see a photo of the reburial, with one of the family members holding a little bag containing what is left of the body after all those years.

On my travels I sometimes hear about those who have not yet been dug up and identified. A woman once approached me with a photo in her hand, after a political meeting in Diyarbakır. She asked where I came from and whether I had a moment for her. She told me that one day the police came knocking on the door for her husband – it was the early 1990s and they had just been married. He was not home, but decided to go and inquire at the station for himself later that day. If he didn't, they would simply come back later, he reasoned. 'I told him not to,' the woman told me, 'because we knew people sometimes just disappeared, but he went anyway. He said, "I haven't done anything wrong, they can't accuse me of anything, so why *wouldn't* I go?"' It was the last she heard of her husband.

There were politicians at the meeting who were close to the ruling AKP party. That was why she had come: I had already seen her earlier that morning, showing her husband's photo to one of the politicians and asking if he could help her in her search.

A Centre of Expertise for Disappearances

JİTEM abandoned bodies, often unrecognisably maimed with acid, in fields and rivers, under bridges, and in pits on the premises of Turkey's national oil and gas company, near the military base at Silopi on the Iraqi border. These 'death pits' gave the dumping grounds their symbolic name. In an interview at his office in Diyarbakır in January 2012, human rights lawyer Tahir Elçi told me that sometimes a body was found, 'which the authorities would take away and give an anonymous grave in a random graveyard.'

In January 2012 a mass grave was found during renovations in the heart of the old town of Diyarbakır. There was a rumour that it was a grave from the 1990s, as the site was right next to the JİTEM office. Elçi was unable to talk about this during our interview: 'We know JİTEM was there,' he said, 'we know there was torture and people died, but we don't know for certain if this is a JİTEM grave. It could be from the Sheikh Said Rebellion in the 1920s, or a grave for murdered Armenians, or something else.'

The human remains were investigated by the forensic laboratory. Two months later it was announced that they were at least 100 years old, and that animal bones had also been found. Scepticism remained: many people did not trust the official conclusions.

Tahir Elçi, one of the founders of the Turkish section of Amnesty International and a member of the Turkish human rights group İHD since the start of his career in 1991, said of such investigations, 'Society needs to believe that the government has done everything in its power to expose the truth and punish the culprits,' and he knows that confidence is absent. He judges the forensic lab to be reasonably reliable at present, but more is needed for the truth.

Elçi: 'As lawyers we depend on the public prosecutors, who have to give permission to open a grave and lead the investigation. Ten years ago the willingness simply was not there, and now you have to be lucky with your prosecutor. Unfortunately there is no policy.'

Elçi and other lawyers working on missing persons and mass graves feel there should be a national centre of expertise, with a DNA database to compare genetic material from family members of missing persons with disinterred remains, where lawyers, prosecutors and forensic experts can exchange information.

With a centre like that, graves could be opened and investigated without a family making a specific inquiry. Elçi gives an example: 'Two weeks ago a soldier gave information to the prosecutor regarding a murder in Silopi in 1993. I was called in, as it was pretty certain which missing persons were involved; it was a case I was in charge of.' Generally, however, it is a question of families who have no idea where their husbands or sons were murdered and dumped. Elçi: 'Families looking for the remains of their loved ones have to make a request through a lawyer to the public prosecutor to be allowed to dig in a specific place, but the locations of possible mass graves are not always that specific, often it's an entire region.'

You can ask witnesses from that time for information, but people are still often too afraid to speak. What helps is carefully keeping up with the newspapers. I had spoken to Elçi on the phone before, for a story about the 'death pits' in 2009. At the time Abdülkadir Aygan, a repentant former JİTEM member, had given a newspaper interview revealing new information about a murdered Kurd whom Elçi had been searching for for years on behalf of the family. On this basis he was able to pursue legal proceedings.

Another big problem for disinterment is the fact that the government does not carefully observe the Minnesota Protocols. These protocols were drawn up by a group of forensic experts, lawyers and human rights specialists, and apply internationally as the standard for researching extra-judicial killings and genocide, among other issues.

They give rules on best practice for reopening mass graves, collecting evidence of the identity of the victim, culprits and circumstances of the killing, autopsies, and points of attention in these kinds of killings. The rules also recommend the establishment of a special, impartial investigation committee when it comes to killings for which the state may bear responsibility.

In practice, human rights organisations in Turkey are faced with an impossible dilemma. The killings are committed by the state, but the conflict in which they happened continues, so the government will not take the initiative in setting up an independent committee.

Many human rights activists also agonise over whether to open a grave as quickly or as carefully as possible. Speed is crucial to ensure DNA of the highest quality, whereas diligence is important in order to prevent DNA damage or contamination. Opening a mass grave with a digger, as has happened, may mean human remains cannot be photographed in their original positions, and impede collection of as much material as possible that might provide DNA, such as hair near to skulls.

For this reason, the İHD working group for mass graves does not always submit an application to open a grave. Tahir Elçi does not see this as an option: 'Available DNA has to be safeguarded, even if the international standards aren't always followed.' So much time has passed already. Elçi: 'I grew up in Şırnak province, which was in a state of emergency until 2000. The lawless situation made it dangerous for citizens to seek legal help against human rights violations. Many cases only got started after 2000.'

Elçi is personally moved by the issue, not only because he himself is a Kurd, and witnessed – and experienced – many horrors as a young lawyer in the 1990s in Şırnak province: in 1993 he was arrested with fifteen colleagues and imprisoned and tortured for a month by the gendarmerie. He has been arrested several times, there have been plots to murder him and he has been impeded in his work.

In March 2012 he was present when a mass grave of special importance to him was opened: it is highly probable that his brother Ramazan lay there. The grave was found through interrogation of the only soldier to stand trial for the death squads of the time, Cemal Temizöz. The identification took a long time, but news came in spring 2013: it was Ramazan, who disappeared in 1994.

When the 'Saturday Mothers' meet each week in Istanbul and Diyarbakır, they hold the portraits of the loved ones they have lost, as do the Uludere relatives in the graveyard every Thursday.

I have added the bombing of Uludere on 27 March 2013, just a week after Newroz, while Turkey was still bathing in the afterglow of the peace declaration, to the unsolved killings committed by the state. That was the day on which the parliamentary human rights committee, under which the Uludere group was a subcommittee, accepted the investigation report. The three opposition members, Levent Gök of the CHP, Ertuğrul Kürkçü of the BDP and Atila Kaya of the MHP, again called on parliament to reject the report, but without result.

The 500th Day After the Bombing

With a few dozen people from Ortasu and Gülyazı, I'm sitting on the rocky ground looking at the site of the bombing. We are a couple of hundred metres away; I have never been closer. Fifteen metres or so in front of us a row of soldiers are standing beside a tank. They have put up red and white tape and placed a sign in the ground: 'Military terrain, no entry.'

Directly above them, at the scene of the disaster, we can make out the small but unmistakeable figures of the victims' relatives. There are around 150 of them. They quietly asked the soldiers to clear the way for them, but when that achieved nothing, they clambered up the mountain around the blockade. The goal: to commemorate the dead at the site where they died, by leaving behind thirty-four red carnations. I also saw Pakize with her eldest son, Özkan, clambering up the mountain.

It's 11 May 2013, the 500th day after the bombing. Every day that there is no justice for the victims is counted, and on some days there is a bigger commemoration than the regular Thursday afternoon meetings. There was one on the 250th day after the bombing, when tear gas and water cannons were used to prevent the relatives from reaching the mountain pass. Apparently the soldiers have different instructions this time.

For hours I've had the feeling I'm watching a film. To the right of our group who have remained behind is the road we came by; a little further along, the minibuses and tractors are parked on flat terrain, having brought us the first short leg of the journey from Ortasu. To our right is a fenced field, straight in front of us the road to the site of the bombing with the army cordon.

While the relatives hold their commemoration above, we suddenly hear a helicopter from the right. It flies low in our direction, sinking slowly over the field just in front of us. The doors open and a group of soldiers emerge with shields and batons. Helicopters stop three times, bringing reinforcements. I recall the scene later, when I read the investigation committee's final report, in which the army explains why it did not offer helicopters to help after the bombing, to transport the wounded to hospital as fast as possible. 'There is no place to land helicopters there,' is the explanation.

The soldiers run along the edge of the field towards the closed gate. I'm astounded when one of the villagers runs up to open the gate for them. 'Why did you do that?' I ask him, surprised. 'I know how that gate opens, they might not. They're just here on military service, you know, they can't do anything about being here either.' The boys in their helmets pass close by. I see their young faces. One loses his shield in the storm whipped up by the helicopter wings.

The soldiers spread over the hills and hide between bushes. We watch them, and see one taking photos of us. I hope I'm clearly visible, so that there's proof I didn't go up with the others. That would be seen as illegal border crossing; Turkish citizens are fined, but for me as a foreigner, it would mean certain deportation and probably not being able to return for five years.

After the soldiers have spread out, one of the relatives comes down to consult with them. One of the group that has remained behind also talks to them. The villagers want to ensure they will not be arrested on their way down. The negotiator climbs up and descends, moving back and forth between the cordon and the relatives on the mountain pass a couple of times.

It goes on for hours, while we onlookers snack from time to time: some have brought bread and cheese, which they share; others forage in the surrounding area, mainly finding unripe almonds. There's not much talking, although the goats are a subject of conversation: a couple of women are annoyed at having to leave the milking to others again. If the army had allowed the commemoration to take place in the morning, there would have been no trouble and everyone could have got on with their day after an hour or two.

Eventually the result of the consultation reaches us: we onlookers will have to wait a little way further on, then those involved in the commemoration on the mountain pass can come down and the soldiers will not detain them.

We move out of the way, down the road by which we came. We sit down, nibble at a few more almonds and try to follow what is happening as best we can. We can no longer see the site of the bombing, but we can still see the mountain the commemorating relatives climbed, and suddenly we see them coming down again. We walk a little way in their direction. Many of the boys have scarves wrapped around their faces, not wanting to be recognised on the army cameras. It's an amazing spectacle: mothers in traditional clothing, with loose headscarves, arm in arm with their unrecognisable sons, both making V signs into the air. Pakize is quiet as always. This is the first time she has visited the site where Osman's life ended. 'I wanted to go for a long time,' she says. 'It made me sad to be there, but also extremely angry.'

A month after the 500th day, all of the relatives who attended the commemoration on the mountain pass receive a letter from the court: a 3,000 lira fine (more than 1,000 euros) per person for illegal border crossing. For some families that comes to a total of 15,000 lira. Pakize is only fined for herself.

No one is willing or able to pay. The appeals processes are ongoing. The outcome is uncertain, according to lawyers whose opinion I ask. In the worst case scenario, people will have to go to prison, or forfeit property to pay the fines. I would not know what you could take from the villagers' houses that is of any value, other than their TVs.

From the day after the commemoration, the smugglers resume activities on the same route to the other side of the mountain, unhindered as always. The situation is the same now: for an illegal activity such as smuggling the route is free, but woe betide anyone who takes the same route to the place a family member died to commemorate him.

Chapter Six

The Horizon

Semire sits on the floor in the kitchen cutting up a big bowl of tomatoes from the family vegetable garden in Zevîya. I sit beside her with a cup of tea. It's autumn 2012 and she has just turned eighteen. Semire stopped attending school years ago, and will probably be married before long. I'm trying for once not to talk about the bombing in which her younger brother Bedran died, just to chat, so I ask, 'Do you already have marriage plans?' She looks at me fiercely. 'I'm not getting married,' she says, 'never.' 'Why not?' I ask. She says, 'The boys are dead.'

This often happens when I try to strike up a conversation with anyone in the village: you end up talking about the bombing anyway. During the same visit that autumn, for example, I had dropped in on a family and one of the sons walked me back to Pakize's house – they wouldn't dream of letting you walk alone in the dark, despite the fact that everything is close by and there's no danger.

I had spoken with him before; he was doing well at school and studying hard in the hope of making it to university. He smuggled from time to time, the bombing had robbed him of a couple of friends. 'How's school going?' I asked, just to make conversation. 'I don't go to school anymore,' was his reply. He explained that he had been unable to concentrate during lessons over the last few months of the previous school year: 'I lost my motivation after everything that happened. My grades plummeted and I didn't pass a single subject. I wanted to repeat the year, but the headmaster would only allow it for a certain fee. We didn't have the money. So I had to stop school.'

Now he was trying to work as much as possible. He was smuggling more than before.

It was not only the lives of the families who lost sons, husbands or fathers in the bombing that changed radically, but those of the entire village community. Couples still marry, but no longer celebrate their weddings. The local BDP man Irfan shows me pictures from before the bombing: a large green pasture between the mountains, with wedding guests in an enormous circle dancing the *govend*, the Kurdish dance you see whenever there's something to celebrate or demonstrate about.

Four steps diagonally forward (to the right first), tap your left foot next to your right, then four paces back to your right, then repeat to the left. Now do it all again, linking little fingers with your neighbour and dancing up and down with them. The circle grows as people dance: you break in anywhere and join in. The man or woman at each end of the unclosed ring holds a cloth – sometimes white, but more often red, yellow and green – shaking it in the air in time to the music. It's easy to learn the *govend*, and as a foreigner you score lots of points for joining in. But in Gülyazı and Ortasu it's a thing of the past – perhaps forever.

Lamentation for Pakize's Husband

One afternoon in the autumn I'm at Mehmet and Leyla's, Pakize's brother- and sister-in-law, for lunch. Sinem and Hülya are there too. Suddenly another guest comes in; he has papers with him and is warmly welcomed. He's here for Pakize – Sinem runs home and returns a little later with Pakize. The guest turns out to be Abdurrahman Adıyan, an artist from Bursa in western Turkey. He has written a poem for the family of every victim of the bombing, including Pakize, and has come to recite it for her personally.

Lamentation for Osman Kaplan
(14 May 1980 – 28 December 2011)

the sun
had already stolen away his colour, now his cotton jacket is truly shamed
roughly the needlework of his shirt chafes at his throat
his collar worn with sweat

Osman
cherished five doves in his heart
doves in a cage in a ruin of a house

from under the door, along the windowsill came the cold
the roof leaked, the gutter dripped; he was happy nevertheless
his doves' noses might have dripped
but they weren't exposed to the raindrops
how miserable
full of sorrow was the life that flowed away

Pakize
scrubbed and wrung out his clothes year in year out
hung them in the afternoon sun, where they were smoothed by an evening
    breeze
Osman's clothes were always smoothed in the wind
until on a windy night his soul slipped out
five broken children he left behind
        and a heartbroken wife in mourning

what is it that so weighs a man down
fixes a pleading look in his eyes
the world had no space for the orphans' father
for his doves and their mother no more than a cage
broken, destitute, the cotton jacket shamed

Pakize's cries fell silent first
her eyes cold and hard
her grief a silent lament to make a stone heart bleed
not a day without a humble stream past her door
the river of time could not flow without grief

tall men, tawny, weathered
the battle with poverty had lined their foreheads
death had so often defeated poverty
it simply was so, women slim and weathered and poor
bore their sturdy children in the morning

watch out, people said to Osman
'he who does not turn up to prayer on Friday
will be alone at his funeral, no one at his table'
- don't worry aunt
'the world will know of my death, my funeral will be crowded'
the worn knees in his trousers bore witness to his prayers

dead!
your beloved memory is the last he saw
Osman, a leaf, free, torn from his branch
a prisoner now, chained to his notation.

Pakize does not understand the poem, as it's in Turkish, but later she tells me that it doesn't matter: 'I'm touched that someone has taken the trouble to write a poem about my husband. It doesn't matter so much to me that I don't understand it.'

The artist Adıyan is working on a Kurdish translation of his poems, he tells me later during a meeting in Diyarbakır. When we met in the village, during Eid 2012, he had just finished all thirty-four poems – or lamentations really. Before writing each one he talked with the family and friends of the victims. Adıyan: 'I wanted the relatives to see their murdered loved ones before them when they heard the poem. I think I succeeded in many cases.'

The poems have been collected in the book *Border Stone Number Fifteen*, named after the number of the border stone where the bombs fell.

Abdurrahman Adıyan – himself the child of a mixed Turkish-Kurdish marriage and partly raised in the Kurdish Van region – tells me that he wants his work to be a witness to his time. 'That's why I wrote a poem about the bombing just after it happened in January 2012, but I wasn't satisfied with that. So in the spring I went to Ortasu and Gülyazı, got to know the people and followed the news about it in detail.'

He tells me about the poet Ahmet Arif's 'thirty-three bullets,' which remains a testament to the memory of the incident in 1943 in which a Turkish military commander shot dead thirty-three Kurdish smugglers on the Iranian border. 'That's the power of poetry,' he says. 'It lives on years later.' In his view it was not only thirty-four people who died in the Uludere bombing, but as many families, and the entire village. He even goes as far as to say the entire region died on 28 December 2011. 'And in Turkey no one really cares. That's tragic too: the erosion of human emotions in this country.'

It makes me think of what a Kurdish writer once told me about a Turkish mother who lost her son during his military service, in combat with the PKK. That mother said her pain was greater than that of a Kurdish mother who loses her child, because Kurdish mothers have more children and can easily enough do without one. 'That's the sort of country we live in,' said the writer, who was not offended by the mother's train of thought, 'a country in which mothers talk like that.'

Poet Adıyan hopes that his thirty-four poems can help people deal with the bombing. 'At a certain point,' he says, 'it has to become history, but it's too early to talk about that now, certainly with the relatives. When I see the mothers crying… They seem so helpless and hopeless. They appeal for an apology from Erdoğan, for compassion for those who have hurt them. I find it heart-rending.'

Apologies for Dersim – and for Uludere?

For months there have been rumours that Erdoğan's apology is imminent. It would be big news, and the relatives would probably welcome it; but in my opinion, until the massacre has been thoroughly investigated, it's too soon for apologies. How can one say sorry for something while deliberately brushing the circumstances under the carpet?

At the end of November 2011 Prime Minister Erdoğan apologised for the operations in Dersim in the 1930s. Suddenly, just like that, in parliament. It's sad to say it, but despite its coming seventy-three years after the event, that apology was much too early, and for the wrong reasons.

What exactly happened? Dersim had already been a subject of debate in parliament for a couple of days, set in motion by an internal discussion in the CHP, the largest opposition party. The CHP MP for Dersim, Hüseyin Aygün, had the courage to say out loud that the massacres were planned at the time and that the order had come from Atatürk. That led to serious discussions: many CHP members of parliament attacked their colleague from Dersim, because the CHP was founded by Atatürk and CHP politicians do not acknowledge that the massacre was decreed by their great helmsman.

Erdoğan's apology was directly connected with the roots of CHP leader Kılıçdaroğlu, who also comes from Dersim and lost family members in the massacres. Erdoğan became involved in the internal CHP discussion, and he and Kılıçdaroğlu had been scoring points off each other for a couple of days already. Erdoğan's sudden apology put Kılıçdaroğlu on the spot, as he stated, 'The party who should confront this incident is not the ruling Justice and Development Party. It is the CHP who are behind this bloody disaster, and who must deal with it.'

Besides the shamelessness of political point scoring on the backs of thousands of people who have been appallingly hurt, apologies should not be issued by decree. Well-intentioned apologies first require a careful, fair and open debate of what exactly happened, why it turned out that way and why apologies would be appropriate.

Despite the apologies, official state history still maintains that there was a rebellion in the province which formed a threat to the republic and that the army quelled the uprising for legitimate reasons. If that is the case, why do they need to apologise? It must also seem strange to Turks who have been and continue to be fed the state version of history in school. Why is our prime minister apologising for a justified operation?

Apologising out of the blue is no way to confront history. Instead you should throw all historical taboos overboard and examine the issue from all sides, along with those involved. Open all archives, attribute responsibility where it belongs, pursue the culprits as far as possible, listen to people's stories and memories, and acknowledge their pain. Then apologies can follow.

That's how it should be for Dersim, and for the bombing of Uludere. The first necessary step: binning the investigation by the subcommittee of the parliamentary human rights committee. Next: set up a serious, thorough investigation. The theory I discuss in this book – that the bombing was carried out to kill PKK member Fehman Hüseyin, who was not there – is just a theory. It may be the most logical we currently have, but it remains hypothetical. The truth can only come to light once all classified documents have been released, once everyone involved talks freely, and once the state is open to any outcome – however inconvenient. Only after that can there be apologies.

I do not expect Erdoğan to be the prime minister who apologises sincerely for Uludere; it will be one of his successors, as Erdoğan is not eligible for election as prime minister in the 2015 elections. We may not have to wait so long for apologies for political gain, as in the case of Dersim. For sincere apologies, however, the entire system that made the bombing possible will have to be taken apart and reorganised, and that will take some time. In this respect past lessons from other countries are telling.

Take, for example, the lesson of Bloody Sunday, where fourteen unarmed demonstrators were killed by police bullets in the Northern Irish city of Londonderry in 1972. The bloodbath was investigated immediately – but this first investigation was only intended to cover up the massacre and protect those responsible.

The relatives and the entire Catholic community continued to demand a proper investigation for years, and that only came about after the Good Friday Agreement in 1998, which brought a definitive end to the armed conflict in Northern Ireland. Only then, after the country had changed fundamentally, could an investigation get off the ground that would really go in search of the truth.

It took until 2010 for the report to be presented. Conclusion: the shooting was not legitimate, the demonstrators who were shot in no way formed a threat. British Prime Minister David Cameron stated on behalf of the government that he was 'deeply sorry,' and only then did the relatives and the Catholic community receive justice – thirty-eight years on.

The Soweto Uprising, in which at least 200 demonstrating school students were shot dead by a police force firing at random in June 1976, teaches a similar lesson. That bloodbath was only investigated after apartheid was abolished in South Africa at the start of the 1990s: in 1996 the Truth and Reconciliation Commission commenced hearings on the events – twenty years on.

For an in-depth, independent investigation into the bombing, Turkey too will need to change fundamentally.

The State Protects Itself

My first acquaintance with the Kurdish question goes back to the beginning of the 1990s. I had graduated from the School of Journalism in Zwolle, moved to Utrecht, and become a voluntary editor of *Frontaal*, Amnesty International's now defunct monthly youth magazine in the Netherlands. Every month we had a writing campaign in which we called on readers to write letters to a country's authorities, for example to free political prisoners or track down someone who had 'disappeared.' One of the writing campaigns was about Turkey.

The case: two minors had 'disappeared' after being arrested by the gendarmerie between Gaziantep, just outside the Kurdish region, and Diyarbakır. The gendarmerie officers grabbed them out of a *dolmuş*, in possession of a stack of the illegal newspapers *Özgür Gündem* and *Azadiya Welat*. At the time they were not printed in the southeast, because that part of the country was under martial law, but they were printed in the cities just outside and smuggled into the Kurdish region. The two newspaper boys disappeared without a trace. Their family inquired at the police station but was told they were not there.

This was a perfect case for our magazine. Our readers also delivered newspapers, so we could easily relate it to their context: 'Do you have a delivery round? Well, these Kurdish boys in Turkey did too, but it got them into big trouble.' I knew nothing of Kurdish media, and we did not tell our readers that the Kurdish newspapers were not local rags but part of a political battle. That wasn't the point: it was about newspapers; those boys just transported them, that's why they 'disappeared,' and that was the injustice we wanted our readers to take up the pen for.

Such disappearances are now a thing of the past, like the random killings JİTEM committed in the 1990s, but does that really mean that anything has fundamentally changed? No. Currently Kurdish communities are not intimidated with killings and disappearances, nor are they silenced: instead they are imprisoned, hundreds at a time. The core of the problem is the same: the state is primarily out to protect itself rather than its citizens. The starting point is still the state, rather than human rights or democratisation.

There is one legal case which makes this crystal clear, and that is the case against the former general Veli Küçük. He was, as he has stated himself, one of the founders of JİTEM, the group associated with the military police which carried out killings in southeast Turkey in the 1990s. He retired in 2000 and was able to enjoy his old age, until he was arrested in January 2008 – not for his crimes in the southeast, but for alleged involvement in plans for a coup against Prime Minister Erdoğan's government.

In 2013 he was sentenced to life imprisonment.* The evidence in the case against the suspected conspirators for the coup against the AKP was weak: independent foreign experts also examined incriminating materials brought forward in the case and concluded that they were partly falsified.

So it now appears that Veli Küçük will spend the rest of his life behind bars on the basis of shaky evidence that he constituted a threat to the powers that be. He has never been brought before a judge for JİTEM's reign of terror in the southeast or the many illegitimate executions he probably has on his conscience from the 1990s, which are probably a good deal easier to prove than his involvement in a possible coup. There is not even an investigation in progress against him for his crimes in the southeast.

This is also apparent from the reforms which Turkey has so far implemented to give Kurds more freedom. There has been irrefutable progress, but this is mainly visible in a willingness to discuss the Kurdish question: Kurds are no longer called 'mountain Turks,' as they were, the status of Kurdish as a language is no longer denied, and the issue is openly discussed.

* Veli Kücük was released from prison on 11 March 2014.

However, anyone who scrutinises the concrete measures taken by the AKP government will see that these, too, are aimed at strengthening the state – those in power – and not the Kurdish community.

The Myth Regarding the Turkish Legal System

From September 2012 children in state schools from the age of eleven onwards can have Kurdish lessons (and other minority languages) as optional subjects. What does that mean in practice? Children like Özkan, Esra, Sinem, Hülya and Mahmut only speak Kurdish before they go to school, but that tends to be in a form heavily influenced by Turkish, rather than pure, correct Kurdish. When they start school, Kurdish is strictly forbidden, and they learn Turkish. Only when that is well established are they allowed to spend two hours a week learning their mother tongue from scratch – but only during those two hours, and the rest of the time Turkish is compulsory and their mother tongue remains banned.

In autumn 2013, Prime Minister Erdoğan announced that private schools could provide a full education in Kurdish. That initially seems a significant step forward, but not on closer scrutiny. In the southeast there are few private schools and most Kurds cannot afford them. More importantly, there are legal implications.

The constitution states plainly that Turkish is the only language of instruction in educational institutions. The only way to realise the plan without changing the constitution is to designate Kurdish as a foreign language, since the law makes an exception for foreign languages. This law makes it possible to run English and German schools in Turkey, for example. The definition applied is that a language is foreign if it is the official language of another country. That is indeed the case for Kurdish, which is one of the two official languages of Iraq.

For the Kurds, who have been living on land which is now in Turkey for generations, however, it is insulting to label their language as 'foreign,' and it confirms the monopoly of Turkish as the sole original mother tongue in Turkey.

There is a stubborn myth about the Turkish legal system. It states that the law is the same for every citizen, guaranteed by article 66 of the constitution: 'Everyone bound to the Turkish state through the bond of citizenship is a Turk.' The article implies that the word 'Turk' is purely a legal concept, used to describe the national identity of all citizens in

Turkey, regardless of their origin, and to declare that ethno-cultural and religious identity are private issues, irrelevant to the state.

The rest of the legal system, including the preamble to the constitution and court jurisprudence, however, undermines that idea of equality, by promoting the concepts of 'Turkishness' and 'Turkification' in many ways. To put it more simply, the entire Turkish legal system breathes ethnic Turkishness, its history, culture, religion and language.

A minor example of this Turkish hegemony can be found in the preamble to the constitution. This mentions 'Turkish national interests, the principle of the indivisibility of the existence of Turkey' and 'Turkish historical and moral values.' Recognised minorities such as Greeks and Armenians feel excluded by this, and other minorities such as Alevis and Kurds are forced to fit into the same framework.

As long as this legal system is not dismantled, it remains a case of making do with each measure the government takes to alleviate Kurdish distress. Education in Kurdish is not the only example of the way in which these measures can only be implemented using legal trickery; the same goes for all these measures.

Take the authorisation of the use of the letters *x*, *w* and *q*. These are not used in the Turkish alphabet, but they appear in Kurdish. The letters, like the Kurdish language, were never officially banned. That was unnecessary, as Turkish was always the only permitted language – banning Kurdish was also impossible because for a long time the existence of the language was officially denied.

It remains unclear how the government will free *x*, *w* and *q* from their non-existent status. It would be easiest to add the letters to the Turkish alphabet, but that would confirm the monopoly of Turkish once again, rather than giving Kurdish more freedom. In any case, for that to happen they would need the freedom to include three other letters which Turkish lacks and Kurdish requires: î, û and ê.

Kurdish State Television: Content-Free TV

It is not only in legal matters that the Kurdish language and education in Kurdish have to muddle through; in practical matters policy also lags behind. For example, there is a serious shortage of teachers for Kurdish lessons in state schools. The University of Mardin's faculty of 'living languages,' under the inspiring management of the head of faculty Kadri Yıldırım, could provide teachers at a moment's notice. Yıldırım could dust off his education plans whenever required and train teachers by the thousands at a time, but the government has so far failed to take up his offer. In fact, the Council of Higher Education is constantly scaling back the number of students.

If the faculty was initially seen as a sign that the government had serious plans to push Kurdish in the ranks of the arts, it now looks increasingly like window dressing, however impressive the work of Kadri Yıldırım and his people. They develop educational methods and reading materials, record old folk tales and poems. It's not their fault that so far it can barely be used beyond the faculty.

The Kurdish-language state channel TRT6 is often also brandished as an example of the way in which Kurds have been granted more rights. The channel went on air on 1 January 2009 and broadcasts twenty-four hours a day. Erdoğan opened the channel personally, with a sentence in Kurdish. I sometimes flick by, and it's a steady stream of contentlessness: music shows, uncritical talk shows, news as the state wants to present it.

If you want to know what's going on in the Kurdish region that the state would prefer not to show, you have to tune into the Kurdish channels broadcast by satellite from Europe. Currently Stêrk TV is the one to watch (*stêrk* means 'star'). From 2004 up to January 2012 it was RojTV, which broadcast under a Danish licence from Denderleeuw near Brussels. RojTV itself was the successor of previous channels which broadcast from Europe from 1995 and were all closed as a result of Turkish pressure.

Turkey repeatedly accuses the Kurdish satellite channels of having connections with the PKK and producing propaganda for the movement, as well as inciting hatred. Since the PKK was placed on the EU list of terrorist organisations in 2002, the Turkish pressure to silence Kurdish channels has had more support in Europe, at the expense of press freedom and freedom of expression. Kurdish satellite channels may provide propaganda and platforms for the PKK, but how is that different from Turkish channels providing platforms for the Turkish state and producing propaganda for the Turkish army?

In fact, Turkey is wrong about the channels stirring up hate. I often watch RojTV and its successors, and when I moved to Diyarbakır I immediately had an extra satellite dish mounted on the balcony railing to receive them. I have never managed to catch them broadcasting hate. On the contrary, they broadcast in different languages (including Turkish, Kurmanji, Zazaki, Sorani, Persian and Arabic) and pay a great deal of attention to cultures other than the Kurdish culture of Kurdistan. There is no cheering when soldiers die in a PKK attack, and they don't get involved in anti-Turkish rhetoric – Turkish TV could do with taking a leaf out of their book. You just won't catch them expressing opinions disagreeable to the PKK. The channels have the PKK to thank for their existence: the organisation dominates the Turkish-Kurdish movement in Europe, which gave rise to the Kurdish channels.

In other words, instead of adding to the diversity of the media landscape in Turkey, the Kurdish-language state channel TRT6 has made it more uniform. The channel is part of a tactic to silence Kurdish satellite channels, with European help.

The Kurdish satellite channels are on the ball with the news: Stêrk TV, like its forebears, works with Kurdish news agencies Dicle and Firat, which have an enormous network of local correspondents, like Aziz who accompanied me when I went to Gülyazı for the first time. One of the local correspondents, Emin Bal, from the mountain town of Beytüşşebap, around two hours' drive from Ortasu and Gülyazı, was the first on the scene after the bombing. He works among others for Doğan news agency, which belongs to the same media company that publishes big newspapers in Turkey, such as *Hürriyet* and *Radikal* – and he has a small but much visited electronics shop on the high street in Beytüşşebap. I looked him up and we talked about that night.

He says a couple of times that he really wants to leave journalism. He has two very young daughters and says, 'I could just enjoy them, spend my free time with them. I can't always take it anymore, the corpses, the misery. But at the same time I feel responsible.'

That sense of responsibility led him to take many photos from first light the morning after the bombing, around half past six. 'I was in shock,' says Bal, 'like everyone else. People cried, including me. As a journalist I should be used to it, I've seen so many corpses. But this…'

His greatest fear, says Emin Bal, was that he would be unable to send his photos. 'I didn't have internet access on my computer at the site of the bombing, so I had to go back in the direction of the village to pick up a signal. Fortunately I managed it before I reached a main road. What if I had been detained by soldiers? What if they had confiscated the material? Fortunately that didn't happen. I sent the photos to Doğan, Reuters and Associated Press, as well as various friends. It spread quickly, appearing immediately on Facebook and Twitter too.' It was Emin's photos that I saw on Twitter when I woke up the morning after the bombing.

RojTV reported on the events from around one in the morning. At the time, like most Turks, I had no satellite dish to pick up the channel. When RojTV was silenced, in January 2012, the people of Ortasu and Gülyazı were up in arms: without RojTV, how would their story have emerged? Who would have listened to them, who could have reported without censorship?

Peoples Have the Right to Self-Determination

In other words, a Kurdish state channel does not equal Kurdish freedom. Two hours of mother tongue lessons to assimilated children does not equal Kurdish freedom. It only confirms what we already knew, that the state reserves exclusive authority to give people 'rights' within the oppressive framework of the system.

Instead of the Kurds being granted such 'rights,' this ancient people which has rediscovered itself and taken shape again should be given the space to be itself. Over the past thirty years, the Kurds have succeeded in forming a nation, with all that goes with it: a growing awareness of their own identity and history, national historic heroes such as Sheikh Said and Seyid Riza, their own newspapers and TV channels, national festivals and memorial days, a reviving culture and language, and sound political organisation.

All peoples have the right to self-determination. It is clearly stated in article 1 of the International Covenant on Civil and Political Rights and the International Covenant on Economic, Social and Cultural Rights, two UN treaties dating back to 1966, and signed by Turkey. The treaties say nothing about how self-determination should be interpreted, neither does the UN define what constitutes a people, but almost no one doubts that the Kurds do. They are the largest ethnic group in the world without their own state.

Moreover, the Kurdish people demand their rights. That, of course, is the crux of the story: peoples determine for themselves the extent to which they demand particular rights. Most Frisians do not demand their own autonomous region with their own parliament, nor do they take to the streets for education completely in Frisian. The Scots have succeeded in gaining their own parliament, and the Basques in Spain demanded and received an autonomous region with Basque as the language of instruction in education. Basque children, so I am told, have spoken fluent Basque and Spanish since then.

The demands of the Kurds are not set in stone.

One demand is some form of self-government, but the precise form is open to debate and negotiation. For Turkey, however, any form of Kurdish autonomy is out of the question. The centralised state is one of the fundamental principles of the republic; although it would be logical for a country of Turkey's dimensions to have a federal system, as in Germany, for example. In fact the Kurdish movement is not arguing for a degree of self-administration exclusively for Kurdistan, but rather for the entire country. The principle of 'unity in diversity,' however, has little support in Turkey.

Another demand is education in their mother tongue, but the precise interpretation of this is not fixed, as far as the Kurdish movement is concerned. The latest proposal submitted to parliament by the BDP is for a system in which Kurdish is the language of instruction in regions with a Kurdish majority, with Turkish as a compulsory subject, so that children grow up bilingual. No other party in parliament is prepared even to discuss the matter.

But the most important demand is a new constitution to pave the way for further changes to the law. The current constitution was introduced by the military leaders as far back as 1982. It may have been amended many times, but the fundamental principle remains: the state protects itself, not its citizens.

Every party agrees that the constitution needs to change, because a military constitution is undemocratic by definition. They are also all represented on the committee working on a new constitution, which was supposed to produce a proposal before the end of 2012, but has so far only reached agreement on non-controversial points. As soon as it comes to points affecting the principle that 'Everyone is a Turk and everyone is Muslim,' the differences appear irreconcilable, and Turkish nationalism – the ideology on which the ruling AKP and opposing CHP and MHP parties are founded – proves unbending. Discussion of proposals affecting the state principles is never about rights, but about separatism. An article can only be added to the committee's proposal if there is unanimous agreement.

I often think it is as if the racist white farmers in South Africa were holding the keys to the abolition of apartheid. What Turkey needs is a statesman with the courage to say, 'If we want to call Turkey a democracy, this issue must be arranged and we are going to do that with everyone who really wants it, the rest can leave.' But Turkey does not have a statesman who is prepared to risk his own political future for peace or human rights. Turkey's prime minister loves power.

International treaties might help Kurds in the battle for their rights, but if Turkey does not sign the relevant treaties, it cannot be held to account. Examples include the 1992 European Charter for Regional or Minority Languages, and the 1995 Framework Convention for the Protection of National Minorities. These are not EU treaties, but treaties of the Council of Europe, of which Turkey was one of the founders in 1949. Only eight of the forty-seven members, Turkey included, refused to sign the minorities treaty, and more than half of the member states are signatories of the regional language treaty.

When it comes to national legislation, again, Turkey has not made a single step towards granting rights to minorities. In fact, legislation is riddled with articles gagging the Kurdish movement and suppressing Kurdish language and culture.

One of the most striking laws to the detriment of Kurds is terrorism legislation. This makes all kinds of non-violent acts and statements liable to punishment, under such vague descriptions that any random acts or utterances could be included. For years, for example, people were pursued for calling Öcalan 'esteemed Öcalan': that violated the law that made 'praising a leader of a terrorist organisation' punishable.

Journalists are 'producing propaganda for a terrorist organisation' if they write about the views of the PKK; lawyers have 'links with a terrorist organisation' because of the clients they defend and are prosecuted under the same legislation.

Both domestic and international human rights organisations – including Amnesty International and Human Rights Watch – have been calling on Turkey for years to change this terrorism legislation, as have international professional organisations for lawyers, journalists and other groups. Turkey promises reforms but does nothing.

In addition to terrorism legislation, the law regulating political life is also a source of problems. Articles in the Constitution and the Political Parties Act have been used to ban five pro-Kurdish parties since the start of the 1990s, all on charges of 'separatism.'

The case against the first party, the People's Labour Party (HEP in Turkish), began after one of their MPs, the activist Leyla Zana, added a sentence in Kurdish to her oath in parliament: 'I take this oath for the brotherhood between the Turkish people and the Kurdish people.' It was 1991 and speaking Kurdish was strictly forbidden, particularly in parliament. The clamour during her oath began as she bowed her head to read it from the paper, revealing her hair band, subtly displaying the Kurdish colours, red, yellow and green. Fellow parliamentarians beat on their desks en masse and screamed protests so loudly that her oath was almost inaudible. Her final sentence, spoken in Kurdish, caused complete and utter pandemonium in the house. Zana was imprisoned for ten years for this, convicted of high treason.

Leyla Zana is once again an MP, now for the BDP. Two other BDP MPs are now in prison: Selma Irmak and Hatip Dicle, Irmak since 2009 on charges of 'membership of a terrorist organisation,' Dicle since 2010 for 'producing propaganda for a terrorist organisation,' both so far without being convicted.* This is not the first time either of them have been imprisoned for their political activities.

The EU and the Kurdish Struggle

Why does the EU not speak out more clearly for Kurdish rights? Kurds often ask me this, sometimes at the strangest moments, as in Diyarbakır when the police attacked a mass commemoration of the arrest of Öcalan with tear gas. I took my notebook and pen out of my bag, and as we stood blinking the tear gas out of our eyes, a couple of men approached me. 'Are you a journalist? Where do you come from? The Netherlands? Why isn't the EU doing anything? Why don't they say anything? Explain it to us!'

I explained that in the 1980s and 90s the Netherlands still attached value to human rights in general and to those of the Kurds specifically, but that since then things had changed, especially in the first years following the turn of the millennium: the attacks on the World Trade Center in New York, the start of the 'war on terror'; the United States and Europe needed to be friends with Turkey, as a bridge between the West and the Arab world; and the speed with which Europe yielded to American and Turkish pressure to place the PKK on the list of terrorist organisations;

* Selma Irmak was released from prison on 4 January 2014, Hatip Dicle is free since 28 June 2014. The court cases against them continue.

the reforms which Prime Minister Erdoğan implemented at the start of his period in government – now lasting more than ten years – reforms which made Turkey an official candidate member of the EU in 2005; the growing Turkish economy, with a young population of seventy-two million people, is a wonderful market for an economically ailing Europe. 'They're playing a bigger game,' I said, 'and Europe just doesn't consider you that important in it.'

I remember the row between Turkey and the Netherlands in the spring of 1995. The Kurds set up a 'Kurdish parliament in exile' in The Hague. Turkey was enraged and recalled its ambassador, as it was of the view that the parliament in exile had connections with the PKK and should therefore be banned. The United States, which had long had the PKK on its list of terrorist organisations, also put pressure on the Netherlands, but the Dutch prime minister at the time, Wim Kok, did not flinch. He appealed to the right to freedom of assembly stated in the Dutch constitution, and said, 'Jettisoning an important part of our constitution to maintain good relations is a slippery slope.' He was right. The PKK may be a violent organisation, and yes, the Kurdish parliament in exile was a PKK-related jamboree, but the exiles were those who had declined to take up arms and were instead trying to change things by democratic means.

In the same year, the European Union awarded the prestigious Sakharov Prize to Leyla Zana, who was then in prison for the Kurdish sentence she spoke in the Turkish parliament. With this prize Europe put overt pressure on Turkey to set her free and respect human rights. It took another nine years before she was a free woman and could travel to Brussels to receive the prize.

Could Leyla Zana receive the Sakharov Prize now? I don't think so. Not because her work has changed – she returned to parliament in 2011, and has continued to work tirelessly as a human rights activist. She is still being prosecuted: in 2012 she was sentenced to ten years' imprisonment for statements in nine speeches, and the case is currently under consideration by the Supreme Court. Since the PKK is now on the EU list of terrorist organisations, she suddenly has a good deal less sympathy in Europe. The Kurdish question has degenerated from a human rights issue to a terrorism issue.

A Kurdish parliament in exile that meets in different European cities – after its foundation in The Hague, meetings followed in Vienna, Moscow, Copenhagen, Oslo, Rome and Brussels – is now completely inconceivable. The pressure on Kurdish organisations in Europe, including the Netherlands, is increasing. In 2012 alone there were two raids on Kurdish youth meetings, and those present were arrested on suspicion of PKK membership.

The arrests led nowhere in legal terms: no weapons were found, no 'terrorist training' was in progress, the second raid did not even find 'propaganda material,' and no one was prosecuted. However, freedom of assembly is under pressure, and the Turkish newspapers lap it up: PKK members arrested in Europe! The fact that the arrests never lead to prosecution doesn't make it into the papers.

These meetings are not organised by shady groups: they are members of FedKom, an umbrella organisation for eight Kurdish groups in the Netherlands, and of KON-KURD, the Confederation of Kurdish Associations in Europe.

The associations are the result of increased Kurdish awareness raised by the PKK struggle. They are active on all kinds of fronts: fundraising for the movement (to which the PKK belongs, but this flow of money has not been proven by a single European court), language education, promotion of Kurdish culture, political demonstrations, and for years a campaign to free Öcalan. When it comes to the Kurdish question in Turkey, they advocate the same thing as the PKK: full political and cultural rights for the Kurds, including some form of autonomy. Shouldn't Europe plainly support that, instead of criminalising Kurdish demands and associations, under pressure from Turkey?

An Anti-Kurdish International System

The solutions proposed by the imprisoned leader Abdullah Öcalan and the Kurdish political movement all assume a system in which the Kurds continue to be a part of Turkey, and have full rights there. This solution is based on their analysis of the problem: they were sidelined in the foundation of the republic, despite having fought alongside the Turks in the First World War and then in the Turkish War of Independence. The solutions do not seek to tamper with the existence of Turkey within its current borders, because the Kurds also fought for those borders, or, as the Kurdish intellectual Musa Anter, murdered by the state in 1992, apparently once put it, 'Why would we leave Istanbul and İzmir to the Turks?'

If you take a different analysis of the problem, however, you will come up with a different solution. One person in Turkey has been doing so, loud and clear, for decades: Turkish sociologist İsmail Beşikçi. The Kurdish question gripped him in 1961, when he did an internship in Elâzığ province, north of Diyarbakır, as part of his degree in political science. That was in 1961 – he was twenty-two at the time. After graduating, he did military service in Bitlis and Şemdinli, also in the Kurdish region, after which he specialised in sociology at the universities of Erzurum and then Ankara, and decided to study Kurdish society.

His academic career did not last long: after the 1971 coup, a criminal investigation was opened against him for the first time and he was arrested. From then on no university would offer him employment and he spent a total of seventeen years and two months in prison.

Scientific research has become almost impossible for him, but Beşikçi has never allowed himself to be gagged: he made it his life's work to articulate the Kurds' case, and is currently more outspoken than politically active Kurds, even Öcalan. 'In the eyes of the Kurds,' writes Dutch academic and Kurdish expert Martin van Bruinessen, 'Beşikçi has almost superhuman qualities: he is the only Turk never to abandon them, who has always stood up for them, at great risk to himself, personally challenging a repressive and merciless state.'

I meet the pioneer and independent thinker in September 2013 at the İsmail Beşikçi Foundation in Istanbul, which also houses a substantial library on the Kurdish question. He consented to an interview, and where I had hoped to be able to exchange thoughts for just an hour, in the end we talked for two and a half hours about the Kurdish question in general and the bombing of Uludere in particular.

According to Beşikçi, the Kurdish question originated in the 'historical mistake' whereby no independent Kurdistan was established in the years after the First World War. This is a completely different approach to the Kurdish political movement, which views assimilation and the denial of Kurds within the Republic of Turkey as the core of the problem. Logically, Beşikçi's analysis also leads to a different solution: an independent Kurdistan.

Beşikçi: 'After the end of the First World War, everyone defended the right of peoples to their own country, but Kurdistan was divided up and spread over four countries. The Kurds did not realise what rights they had, and unless they come to realise this, the problem will not be solved.'

Kurdish nationalism was discernible in 1920 in the south of Kurdistan, the area which is now in Iraq. Beşikçi: 'Sheikh Berzenci expressed his wish to become king of the Kurds, but the UK, France and the League of Nations did not listen. They worked with the Iranians, Turks and Arabs, and preferred to turn a blind eye to the wishes of the Kurds.'

That attitude has persisted in the international community, Beşikçi explains. He points to 1941, when Allied troops invaded Iran and the Soviet Union occupied northern Iran. The Soviets wanted to add northern Iran to their own territory, and in order to gain control over the predominantly Kurdish inhabitants they stirred up Kurdish nationalism. That resulted in a region governed by Kurds in the early 1940s, and the Kurdish Republic of Mahabad between 1946 and 1947. This was a satellite state of the Soviet Union and was never recognised by the international community. Beşikçi: 'So the Kurds had aspirations for their own state but the status quo was maintained and the right of the Kurds to their own country was not met.'

That was institutionalised with the foundation of the successor of the League of Nations, the United Nations, in 1945. 'The aim of the organisation,' says Beşikçi, 'was to find peaceful solutions to political problems, but for the Kurds they never fulfilled that.'

He refers to two important UN General Assembly Resolutions, 637 from 1952 and 1514 from 1960: 'The first states that the right to self-determination of peoples and nations is a prerequisite for fully enjoying all human rights. The second invokes a number of articles to put the right to self-determination into practice, while the last two articles confirm the integrity of existing states. This brought independence for fifty-seven states in Africa that had been colonised by distant powers, but not for internally colonised peoples such as the Kurds.'

He adds that internally colonised peoples are under much more direct military pressure: 'In Kurdistan the army and military equipment are always close by and immediately deployable against an armed uprising. That was completely different in Angola, for example: the Portuguese occupying force was far away, which gave the Portuguese less flexibility.'

The direct pressure in combination with an international community that does not stand up for internally colonised peoples, resulted in continuous genocide, states Beşikçi. He is referring to Dersim in 1937 and 1938, and other violent subjugations of the Kurds in the first decade of the republic, but also Halabja in Iraq in 1988. In the chemical attack by Saddam Hussein – part of the chemical campaign against Kurds and other non-Arab peoples in Iraq between 1983 and 1988 – 5,000 people were killed directly and in subsequent years many more died of complications and illness. Beşikçi: 'Colonisers such as the UK, Portugal and the Netherlands committed crimes, but never as great as the crimes against the Kurds by the countries occupying Kurdistan.'

With forty million people (estimations vary, but Beşikçi maintains that this is the figure) the Kurds are the largest stateless people. Those without a state remain invisible on the international stage. Beşikçi illustrates this by returning to the chemical attack on Halabja in Iraqi Kurdistan: 'There was no reaction worldwide and the Kurds have no platform to demand attention for it. In the same year that Halabja happened, there was an international conference on genocide in Vienna. The Kurds wanted to participate because they had suffered on many occasions, but the organisers said that only states could take part. The Iraqi government would have to represent the Kurds.'

Beşikçi calls that an 'anti-Kurdish international structure,' and illustrates his point with other armed conflicts about autonomy: 'The Algerian war lasted six years, the Vietnam war seven, and most countries founded after the Second World War came into being at the negotiating table. The Kurdish armed uprising in Turkey began in 1984 and continues today, with immense support from the Kurdish people, and at an enormous cost. This uprising could only be suppressed with the help of the international community.'

Beşikçi considers it nonsense that nation states are a thing of the past, as claimed by Abdullah Öcalan among others. 'States are still coming into existence, they're still being formed.' Moreover, 'The framework of the PKK states that they do not want their own state, but at the same time the Kurds are ruled by nation states in which their opinion is never asked.' Beşikçi thinks it is wrong that Öcalan no longer demands a state, especially since he has been in prison: 'Öcalan is not free.' Imprisonment is also the reason why Beşikçi and Öcalan have never been able to exchange thoughts directly regarding their vision for Kurdistan and the Kurds: when Öcalan was free, Beşikçi had been in prison for years, and now Beşikçi can talk freely, Öcalan is incarcerated.

An Independent Kurdistan: a Dream for the Distant Future

I put it to Beşikçi that in my conversations with Kurds I have rarely, if ever, sensed a wish for an independent Kurdistan. 'Most Kurds,' I say, 'consider an independent Kurdistan a future dream, and a distant one at that. Why do you argue for independence?' He replies that he is not telling the Kurds that they must have a country per se, but that he would like them to be more aware of the way in which the international community divides them. 'Achieving independence now is completely different from after the First World War,' he adds. 'There are more international players and far more interests than back then. But the Kurds should at least demand a federal Turkish state.'

Beşikçi explains that Kurdistan was divided up for the third time in the 1920s: 'The first time was in the beginning of the sixteenth century, when part of Kurdistan ended up in the Ottoman Empire and part in the Persian Empire, and in the early nineteenth century in the Russo-Persian War. Tell that to the Kurds you're talking to. Constantly being divided has had a great effect on the consciousness of Kurds. It has robbed them of their ability to form an identity and a vision.'

The term 'colonised mind' occurs to me. I previously saw it as appropriate to the way in which many Kurds regard education in Kurdish: many parents don't want that for their children because they fear they will not learn good Turkish, which will negatively affect their future prospects in Turkey. This is the reason why many young Kurds have little or no knowledge of their mother tongue: parents decide not to teach their children any Kurdish out of fear of repression or economic hardship, while in fact education in their mother tongue alongside intensive Turkish lessons gives children more qualifications to survive in Turkey.

That proves to be the reality in areas where similar education already exists, as in the Spanish Basque Country: Basque children grow up bilingual as a result, strengthening their own cultural identity and gaining opportunities in the future labour market. Only Kurds who are active in the political movement and have immersed themselves in this kind of background support education in Kurdish, not 'ordinary Kurds,' who have come to see the state's way of thinking as their own.

The same applies to the way in which Kurds talk about the different parts of Kurdistan. The part in Turkey is northern Kurdistan, the Iraqi part is the south, the Syrian part the west and Iranian Kurdistan is the east. This division is illogical if you look at the map of Kurdistan. The entire part in Turkey is seen as the north, when a large part of it, such as the provinces of Hakkâri, Şırnak and Siirt, along with the northern parts of Iraq, should really be seen as central Kurdistan. And southern Kurdistan, shouldn't that be the southern part of the regions now in Iran and Iraq? Why do these designations adhere to the borders of countries occupying Kurdistan?

According to İsmail Beşikçi, the bombing of Uludere is part of the continuing genocide of the Kurds by the countries occupying Kurdistan. To explain he goes back to 1960, when the Kurdish leader Mustafa Barzani (who also played a role in the defence of the Republic of Mahabad in Iran in the 1940s) wanted to start an uprising against the central authority in Baghdad for an autonomous Kurdistan. He organised a march from Barzan, in the eastern part of northern Iraq, to Zakho, on the Turkish border and closer to the Syrian border in the west, to find support for his plans.

Beşikçi: 'He did not receive much support until he reached Zakho. Villagers on the Turkish side of the border wrote Barzani a letter supporting him and joined the march. They walked back to Barzan, and on their way back the number of followers grew. The support was so great that Barzani started his uprising in 1961.'

Those villagers on the Turkish side of the border, near Iraqi Zakho, were people from the district of Uludere, from the villages that had existed before the Turkish army burnt them to the ground. Beşikçi: 'The Kurds there have always been more oriented towards the south of Kurdistan than Turkey. They became village guards in the 1980s, receiving a salary and a weapon from the state, but they never really submitted to official authority. They continued to talk their own language, and did not do enough to fight the guerrillas. Of course there was no question of the smugglers at Roboskî being guerrillas, but it makes no difference to the Turkish state.'

This, too, he places in its historical context. 'There's a story,' he says, about the end of the Sheikh Said Rebellion in 1925. The outcome of the legal case on the rebellion was that forty-seven people were to be executed, but on the morning of the execution only forty-six prisoners were brought. Someone was given the task of going to the market to fetch someone, and it was no sooner said than done. The man who was plucked from the market kept on saying he had nothing to do with the rebellion, and he did not seem to be lying. The commander needed forty-seven people, so he asked, "Does he speak Turkish?" No, he didn't. "In that case he's no use to us," he said, and the man was shot dead.'

'The Kurds of Roboskî,' Beşikçi says, 'are of no use whatsoever in the eyes of the state.'

Political Struggle and Personal Grief

In 2023 Turkey will celebrate the 100th anniversary of the republic. In the intervening years Özkan, Pakize and Osman's eldest son, will start smuggling to contribute to the family income. Pakize will not be able to stop him, she told me when Özkan had just turned twelve: 'I won't let him go yet, but I can't keep on stopping him. All the boys here do it, and he can't wait to get going. Of course I'm afraid, but what can I do?'

I can see Esra going to university. Her teacher has pushed the family to invest in her education, as she is doing very well. The family has taken the advice to heart, and they all contribute financially to make it possible – even Pakize, who lives off a sort of child benefit which she receives for each of her five children, now that Mahmut is also in school, and irregular donations from charities and private individuals. She also receives help from other people who feel involved: on one of my most recent visits, the old blue living room door had been replaced with a strong, gleaming new one. 'A present from a carpenter from a neighbouring village,' said Pakize.

Esra could just as easily be long married by her early twenties. It depends whether she is successful in the university entrance exam when she's seventeen or eighteen. If not, according to village custom, you marry soon after. It would be fantastic if Esra or one of the other kids managed to build a somewhat easier life.

But what I'm really most curious about is whether Pakize, and all the other adults who lost loved ones in the bombing, will ever deal with the tragedy that happened to them. In other words, whether Turkey, as a centenarian, will still be the rigid republic that saw the light of day in 1923, or whether something will really have changed. Will it have transformed into a state which protects its citizens first and foremost, or will it continue only to be concerned with itself.

Until that transition is made and the truth of the bombing is brought into the open, the relatives will remain playthings in a political struggle. The government will not stop rubbing salt in the wounds with nationalist rhetoric.

The Kurdish political movement is also guilty of manipulation. I was sick to the stomach when I heard the leader of the BDP, Selahattin Demirtaş, urge the relatives to accept an invitation to talk from Prime Minister Erdoğan in summer 2013. He was visiting Şırnak province to open the new airport. There were fierce reactions from a couple of villagers I follow on Twitter. Hikmet Alma, whose brother Nadir was killed, tweeted, 'We, the Roboskî families, will not demean ourselves by dining with the prime minister, who is responsible for the bloodbath and who continues to commit murder with every word he says about it.'

That same evening six relatives had a conversation with Erdoğan. Had Hikmet Alma responded too quickly and too fiercely, or was there more to it? I contacted the daughter of one of the six relatives who spoke with Erdoğan and asked her about it. She wrote to me: 'Initially we didn't want to meet Erdoğan, because since the day that the bombing happened we had called for such a meeting and never received an answer. So we refused his invitation and said, "We will not sit at the same table." Later we decided to meet him after all, as we were convinced by a person or people we couldn't say no to.'

Half a year before, at the first commemoration of the bombing, Selahattin Demirtaş – the one who convinced the relatives – still maintained that the bloodbath carried Erdoğan's signature. He would not have considered persuading the families to meet the man who he believed had signed the death warrants of their loved ones.

However, in the same month as that commemoration, December 2012, it became known that the government was directly negotiating with PKK leader Öcalan to solve the Kurdish question. A mutual ceasefire was in preparation. During the celebration of Newroz, the biggest Kurdish festival, on 21 March 2013, Öcalan read out his statement in Diyarbakır, declaring an end to the armed struggle and calling on everyone in Turkey to strive for democracy and brotherhood in the spirit of the war of independence, now almost a century ago. At the start of May the PKK began to withdraw from Turkey to its camps in Iraqi Kurdistan.

In that political reality it was expedient that the relatives meet Erdoğan – and try saying no to Demirtaş. So they went. A day later, in an interview with the independent channel İMC TV, Demirtaş said, 'The Roboskî families are glad to have met the prime minister personally. They had the opportunity to express their feelings to the person who is the most important political authority.'

'The families' comprise hundreds of relatives in total, but Demirtaş decides that they were 'glad' as a single entity. I have inquired here and there, and most relatives were not at all glad. They were deeply disappointed that Erdoğan had nothing to offer them, and one of those invited considered walking out on the conversation out of pure frustration and rage. Pro-government newspapers reported on the visit the next day as if the conversation signified an important step in the way in which the government relates to the massacre. They printed photos of Erdoğan releasing white doves at the airport opening.

What they did not report on, was the fact that the criminal investigation into the bombing of Uludere had been transferred from a civil to a military court. The relatives have lodged a complaint and begun a petition demanding a proper investigation – they have no confidence that a military court will meticulously and honestly scrutinise military actions. With all his parliamentary power, Erdoğan can change the law that makes the transfer possible, but he does not.

The translation of personal grief to political demands is an essential characteristic of a 'politicised' identity. That fits precisely with the way the Kurdish movement deals with the Uludere massacre. I understand it, but I also find it difficult to watch the way people's personal boundaries are not always respected, the lack of freedom for personal interpretation of the grief over great personal loss. Try *not* going along one Thursday afternoon to the weekly commemoration at the graveyard, or *not* queuing up when a visitor comes, carrying the photo of your lost husband or son in your hands. Try *not* listening to Demirtaş and *not* meeting Erdoğan. Impossible. The political struggle comes first.

Only once it is all over, when the truth about the bombing is plainly on the table and the Kurdish question is a thing of the past, will there be time for personal grief.

December 2012: the First Commemoration

Thirty-four black flags hang over the main road at Gülyazı. It's early in the morning. I'm staying with Pakize and her children again but I have gone on ahead to the village below. They will come later.

It's 28 December 2012, precisely a year after the bombing.

There is great solidarity all day long. The female relatives sit together, as always with the framed portraits of their dead loved ones in their laps. Little Mahmut, who just yesterday evening was playing with an enormous pair of pyjama bottoms he had dug out from somewhere, now dawdles around Pakize, hanging onto her legs, still providing a cheerful backdrop.

BDP leader Selahattin Demirtaş makes a blazing speech, spitting accusations that the bombing bears Erdoğan's signature. There is a lament by the singer Ferhat Tunç, and speeches and prayers at the graveyard. During a minute's silence at the end of the morning, the road, the verges and the neighbouring square are filled with thousands of people making a V sign in the air. More were expected but the gendarmerie has closed off the road from Hakkâri province, so that many people who would have liked to attend the commemoration cannot reach Gülyazı and Ortasu.

Part way through the afternoon someone taps me on the shoulder. I turn around: it's Servet Encü, the survivor of the bombing who fled to Zakho in Iraqi Kurdistan. 'I'm back,' he says dryly. 'Just for the commemoration?' I ask. 'No, for good. No work there.'

He confirms that he left for Iraq because the authorities put pressure on him. A while later we talk about it and he tells me about the pressure he felt he was subjected to. 'I received a call from a local army commander,' he says. 'He thought I should go to hospital for a check-up. I had been through a great deal, he said, and perhaps I needed help.'

I fail to understand him and don't see why he felt pressured by this. He explains that he suspected that the state still wanted to get hold of him, that he might be given medicines in the hospital to damage his mental health, and then the state could dismiss him as being mentally unstable and no one would take his testimony regarding the bombing seriously anymore. 'And if I didn't go to the hospital myself, they might make sure that I ended up there anyway,' he added.

The mistrust was so deep that a family meeting was arranged, where it was unanimously decided that it was better to flee to Zakho.

He has just returned on the evening of the commemoration. It has been long enough for the threat to disappear, he hopes. He missed his family, his village, his fellow villagers. One of his daughters, a teenager, stands next to him and she's pleased to be back too. She says, 'I can go back to school!' That wasn't possible in Zakho. The Kurdish spoken there was slightly different and in many subjects she couldn't follow the very different lesson content.

It's cold, especially when the sun goes down after a day of clear skies. Fires are built, with plastic chairs around them. I go and sit by one too, talking with people and drinking the tea that is passed to me. I have no idea what is on the programme for this evening.

Then someone says that 'the students' have started their procession. It turns out that a whole group of boys from the region are walking with torches from the graveyard to the village below. I walk some way in that direction, and see the torches in the distance. They gradually approach; I can already hear the slogans. 'Murderer state, answer us,' 'Kurdistan will be the grave of fascism.' When they come close enough, I suddenly see Özkan, Pakize and Osman's eldest son, at the front, with a large flag belonging to a Kurdish youth organisation in his hands. Our eyes meet. He glows with pride. I give him a thumbs up.

The youths form a circle below, leaving a large area of space open in the middle. The mothers of the victims of the bombing sit on the ground directly behind, with many villagers and visitors around them.

One of the students calls the name of one of the victims into the microphone: Salih Ürek! A boy from the circle steps forward. 'I'm here,' he calls, and falls back onto the cold ground to lie dead still. Bedran Encü! Another steps forward. 'I'm here,' and he falls and remains lying. Adem Ant! Another. Erkan Encü! And another. Şivan Encü! Muhammed Encü! Bilal Encü! Aslan Encü! Mehmet Ali Tosun! Savaş Encü! Orhan Encü! Nadir Alma! Celal Encü! Fadil Encü! Mahsun Encü! Şervan Encü! Yüksel Ürek! Cemal Encü! Cihan Encü! Vedat Encü! Serhat Encü! Salih Encü! Özcan Uysal! Hüseyin Encü! Nevzat Encü! Hamza Encü! Selim Encü! Zeydan Encü! Seyithan Enç! Hüsnü Encü! Selahattin Encü! Abdulselam Encü! Şerafettin Encü! Osman Kaplan!

Pakize has already gone home.

Post-Script

When I travelled to Bejuh (Gülyazı) for the first time on 4 January 2012, seven days after the bombing, I had no idea of exactly what had happened there, of the background of the tragedy or the people's circumstances. I also had no idea that I would return so many times to Bejuh and Roboskî (Ortasu) and eventually devote a book to it.

I am so grateful to the inhabitants of Bejuh and Roboskî for opening their houses to me, and for helping me get to know their lives, their past and their grief through their unprecedented hospitality. I would particularly like to thank Pakize, Özkan, Esra, Sinem, Hülya, Mahmut, Çiğdem, Mehmet, Belkiz, Semire, Narin, Lezgin, Faruk, Servet, Jahira and Irfan.

After more than twenty years of writing articles of a maximum of 3,000 words, the transition to a book of 75,000 words was difficult and initially extremely frustrating. It only definitively took shape after I had immersed myself in the bombing for a year. Would the penny have dropped without the help of Tanny Dobbelaar and that one effective Skype session with Femke van Zeijl? I doubt it.

Tanny and Femke were also my readers, and they did a fantastic job of that. The third reader wishes to remain anonymous. His knowledge of Turkey and the history of that part of the world where this book takes place saved me from making mistakes. And Susanne de Joode, thank you for the inspiration for the horizon!

I would not have been able to carry out the interviews for this book without the help of my interpreters, friends and travelling companions Beyda Kocagözoğlu, Delal Seven, Angel Istek, Aziz Özatça and Batu Boran. Efe Moral was always available for questions when I was wading through inextricable reports and articles in Turkish. Thanks to all of you!

Govert Schilling and Margreet Peek: big kisses to both of you for your uncomplicated friendship and that lovely house of yours. Where else could I have worked so undisturbed in the sweltering summer in Amed (Diyarbakır), and when I needed some distance from Kurdistan?

In Amed I would like to thank Ahmet Doğru and his family, and Rükiye Hemedoğlu and her husband and children: it was lovely to make friends so quickly, to have people I could come and talk to after a long day's writing, to eat with and just to be. I feel so at home with you. Gelek spas!

Various people have helped me sharpen my thoughts on the Kurdish question and shared their knowledge with me. In addition to the people whose names appear in the course of the book, these are: Feride Laçin (lawyer, Diyarbakır), Sami Tan (former director of the Kurdish Institute of Istanbul), İrfan Aktan (journalist, Ankara), Hüseyin Aykol (journalist, Ankara), Wladimir van Wilgenburg (political analyst, Hewlêr), Necmiye Alpay (Peace Assembly, Istanbul), Gültan Kışanak (politician, Ankara), Martin van Bruinessen (emeritus professor, Utrecht/Singapore), Aliza Marcus (journalist, New York), Ümit Firat (writer and politician, Istanbul), Amberin Zaman (journalist, Istanbul) and Bejan Matur (poet and writer, Istanbul).

At the end of 2012 I held a big crowd funding campaign to enable me to make this book a reality. Writer Marcel van Driel gave me a decisive kick up the ass, which is duly noted. That crowd of mine turned out to be fantastic: in a couple of weeks I had a good part of the costs of writing this book and constructing the website *www.kurdishmatters.com* (thanks Karina Meerman and Erik de Vries!), including a fee for the Kurdish and Turkish translators (thanks Abdurrahman Önen and Efe!) and my English proofreader, Barry Crooks.

That's not all I'm thankful to my crowd for. My crowd is indispensible: the support for my work and the encouragement while writing, the friendships that have arisen, the valuable stream of information, advice, contacts and opinions from all corners of the world, the coffee machine interaction so necessary for a freelancer. Deining: I'll never leave again. Facebook friends and especially Twitter followers: I feel so lucky to have you.

But the biggest thanks go to my family. Marike, Hanneke, Martin, Koen, Janet and Eefke, you're my foundation. Dad and Mum, it's thanks to you that I can do this and that I'm happy.

Fréderike

Amed, 22 December 2013

About Place Names

'Roboskî, it's the Roboskî bombing, not the Uludere bombing!' Every time I typed 'Uludere' while writing this book, I could hear some readers' criticism in my mind. Many Kurds and Turks prefer Roboskî, because it is the Kurdish name of the village closest to where the bombing occurred. The controversy surrounding the bombing soon led to a split between those who say Roboskî – sympathisers of the victims and survivors – and those who use Uludere, who are often accused of consorting with the state.

As a journalist, however, it is my task to write this book as clearly as possible, not only for people familiar with the bombing and the background and connotation of the names Uludere and Roboskî, but also for readers less at home with the subject. I would confuse them if I wrote about Roboskî.

Moreover, using the name Roboskî would, for consistency's sake, require using the Kurdish names of other towns. Diyarbakır would be Amed (or Diyarbekir, depending on how far you go back in history); Hakkâri would be Colemêrg; Nusaybin would be Nisêbîn and Şırnak would be Şirnex. Everyone would lose the plot, and no one would be able to find those places on Google Maps or in an old-fashioned atlas.

To further complicate matters, Roboskî is not the Kurdish name for Uludere. Roboskî is the original Kurdish name for the village closest to the place of the bombing – Ortasu. The Kurdish name for Uludere, the district Roboskî is in, is Qilaban. The village where most of the victims come from, and where the cemetery is – a stone's throw from Roboskî – was originally known as Bejuh, and is officially called Gülyazı in Turkish.

The only exception I have made is Dersim, the province that was given the Turkish name Tunceli in the 1930s. The massacre that took place there in the 1930s is still known as the Dersim Massacre. The name Tunceli is not used very much, and its use in this book could lead to confusion.

For the rest, I have decided to use the correct spelling for all names in this book, including letters from the Turkish and Kurdish alphabet – I also prefer my name to be written correctly, after all.

Finally, I've included the following details about letters that can cause confusion. The Turkish ı is equivalent to a schwa (⊠) – that is the indistinct vowel sound, for example, in the last syllable of London. The Turkish ğ is silent, extending the sound of the vowel that comes before it. The Kurdish î is English *ee*; the Kurdish *i* is the Turkish ı. The Kurdish *x* is the same as the *ch* in the Scottish word lo*ch*.

Crowd Funding

At the end of 2012 I launched a crowd funding campaign on *www.voordekunst.nl* and *www.indiegogo.com* in order to make this book a reality. It was incredibly heart-warming to receive contributions from (pretty much in alphabetical order):

Eefke de Jong - Alette Vonk - Annemarie Bergfeld - Anouk van Dijk - Ans Geerdink-Effting - Ariëtte Ettema - Arjen Zwart - Asha ten Broeke - Astrid van de Graaf - Audrie van Veen - Ayfer Orhan - Balen Rasool - Bas Holzhaus - Bas de Meijer - Betsie Sanders - Betsy Kits - Bruno van Wayenburg - Bülent Yokus - C. Ariaans - Canan Marasligil - Carla van Dokkum - Carole Burdon - Catherine Bayar - Christian Sinclair - Claire Berlinski - Coby den Heijer - Constance van Dorp - Cor Sanders - Corry Daalhof - Crista Vonkeman-Karaca - Deining - Derk Ederveen - Edith van Gameren - Egid Korkmaz - Ellen Segeren - Emrullah Atasoy - Erdal Kaplanseren - Eric Hennekam - Erik de Vries - Esther van Berk - Eveline Andreas - Evert van de Broek - Evin Fisli - Femke Sonnenschein - Franka Hummels - G. Rikkers - George Burggraaff - George Geerdink - Gerard Effting - Gerard Geerdink - Gerard van der Weyde - Govert Schilling - Görkem Özkaya - H.T. Wiggers - Halise Arslan - Hanneke Geerdink - Hans Goslinga - Hans Hordijk - Hans van Maanen - Hans Noortman - Harun Kaban - Hasan Baykir - Hassnae Bouazza - Heleen de Jongh - Heleen de Vries - Henk Geerdink - Henk-Jan Panneman - Hilda Algra - Hugh Pope - Ilja Geukers - Ingrid Westerduin - Irene Campari - Iris Rethy - Ita van Dijk - Jaap Ellerbroek - Jacquelin Taylor - Jacoba Visser - Jamil Fathi - Jan Dijkgraaf - Jan Nijkamp - Janet de Jong - Jeroen Wapenaar - Jessie van Loon - Jim Heirbaut - Jolet Plomp - Jolette van Eijden - Jop de Vrieze - Joris Bartstra - Judith Velthof/NAHV - Judy Landman - Karel van Koppen - Karin van Dorsselaer - Karin Kleijnen - Karine Hoenderdos - Kees Metselaar - Khenda Mustafa - Kitty Schaap - Koen van der Kolk - Koerdische Gemeenschap - Koos Dijksterhuis - Lenneke Moerdijk - Lenny Langerveld - Lex Thoonen - Lieke Lamb - Liesbet Zikkenheimer - Lilian van der Burgt - M. Hendriks - Mahir Ayhan - Marcel van Driel - Marcel van der Steen - Marein Kolkmeijer - Margreet Peek - Margreeth Geerdink-Luiken - Marianne Houben - Marie-José Effting - Marieke Baan - Marije van den Berg - Marijke Veening - Marjo Stam - Marjolein van Rotterdam - Marleen Janssen - Marlies Hanse - Marlies Mielekamp - Martie Ressing - Merel ten Elzen - Mieke Roth - Mihvan Bagok - Miloe van Beek - Miranda Apeldoorn - Miriam Vijge - Mona van den Berg - Monique de Boer - Monique van Ravenstein - Monique

Smits - Nadine Böke - Nienke Gorter - Otto Cox - Özgür Akgün - Özlem Bozbey - Pat Yale - Paul Ruiterman - Paul van der Spek - Paula Brummelkamp - Perrie Hoekstra - Peter Breedveld - Peter van der Velden - Pierre Spaninks - Rebwar Waladbaigi - Remzi Seker - Riki Effting - Roeland Schweitzer - Roos Schlikker - Sander Agterhuis - Sander Drogt - Sara van Gorp - Sedettin Senturk - Sevinc Keskin - Sevinc Rende - Susanne de Joode - Taco Ruighaver - Tanja van Bergen - Tanny Dobbelaar - Tracie Burch - Tres Melis - Trudy Nijkamp - Ufuk Can Cecen - Wendy Bosch - Wies Ubags - Willem Azad - Willemijn Bouman - Yusuf Kursat Tuncel - Yvonne Philippa - and several generous anonymous donors! Thank you very much!

Bibliography

Adıyan, Abdurrahman, *On Beş Nolu Sınır Taşı*, Miran Yayıncılık, Istanbul, 2012

Alpkaya, Gökçen Prof., İlkem Altıntaş, Asst. Prof. Öznur Sevdiren and Emel Ataktürk Sevimli, *Enforced Disappearances and the Conduct of the Judiciary*, Truth Justice Memory Center, Istanbul, 2013

Aykol, Hüseyin, *Susturulamayanlar*, Aram Yayınları, Istanbul, 2012

Ayata, Bilgin, 'Kurdish Transnational Politics and Turkey's Changing Kurdish Policy: The Journey of Kurdish Broadcasting from Europe to Turkey,' *Journal of Contemporary*

European Studies, 2011

Aytar, Osman, Şemsa Özar and Nesrin Uçarlar, *From Past to Present, a Paramilitary Organization in Turkey: Village Guard System*, DISA Publications, 2013

Bar'el, Zvi, 'Neighbors / 33 Bullets and One Censor,' in: *Haaretz*, 1 December 2010

Baumann, Timothy, 'Defining Ethnicity,' in: *The SAA Archaeological Record*, September 2004

Bayır, Derya, *Minorities and Nationalism in Turkish Law*, Ashgate Publishing, Surrey, 2013

Bozarslan, Hamit, 'Between Integration, Autonomization and Radicalisation – on the Kurdish Movement and the Turkish Left' (interview by Marlies Casier and Olivier Grojean), in: *European Journal of Turkish Studies*, No. 14, 2012

Bruinessen, Martin van, 'Ismail Beşikci: Turkish sociologist, critic of Kemalism, and kurdologist,' *The Journal of Kurdish Studies*, 2005

Bruinessen, Martin van, 'Genocide of Kurds,' in Israel W. Charney (ed.), *The Widening*

Circle of Genocide, New Brunswick, New York, 1994

Bruinessen, Martin van, 'Genocide in Kurdistan? The Suppression of the Dersim |Rebellion in Turkey (1937-38) and the Chemical War against the Iraqi Kurds (1988),' in: George J. Andreopoulos (ed.), *Conceptual and Historical Dimensions of Genocide*, University of Pennsylvania Press, 1994

Bruinessen, Martin van, 'Popular Islam, Kurdish Nationalism and Rural Revolt: the Rebellion of Shaikh Said in Turkey (1925),' in: *Religion and rural revolt*, Manchester University Press, 1984

Çandar, Cengiz, 'The Transformation of Öcalan,' http://www.al-Monitor.com, 6 January 2013

Çetin, Fethiye, *My Grandmother: An Armenian-Turkish Memoir*, Verso, London, 2008 (first published as *Anneannem: Anlatı*, Metis Yayınları, Istanbul, 2004)

Eissenstat, Howard, 'Metaphors of Race and Discourse of Nation, Racial Theory and State Nationalism in the First Decades of the Turkish Republic,' in: *Race and Nation: Ethnic Systems in the Modern World*, Routledge, 2005

Güneş, Cengiz, *The Kurdish National Movement in Turkey – From Protest to Resistance*, Routledge New York, 2012

İnsan Hakları Derneği and Mazlumder, *Roboski Katliamı Raporu*, 3 Jan. 2012

International Crisis Group, *Ending the PKK Insurgency*, Brussels, 2011

International Crisis Group, *The PKK and a Kurdish Settlement*, Brussels, 2012

International Crisis Group, *Turkey's Kurdish Impasse: the View from Diyarbakir*, Brussels, 2012

International Crisis Group, *Crying 'Wolf,' Why Turkish Fears Need Not Block Kurdish Reform*, Brussels, 2013

Jarvis, Jeff, 'All Journalism is Advocacy (Or It Isn't),' *http://buzzmachine.com*, 2013

Jenkins, Gareth, 'Continuity and Change: prospects for Civil-Military Relations in Turkey,' in: *International Affairs 83*, 2007

Jenkins, Gareth, 'Calculating Ambivalence: the Imrali process and the Balance Between Kurdish and Turkish Nationalist Violence,' *Turkey Analyst*, 2013

Jongerden, Joost and Ahmet Hamdi Akkaya, 'Born From the Left: the Making of the PKK,' in: Marlies Casier and Joost Jongerden (eds.), *Nationalism and Politics in Turkey: Political Islam, Kemalism and the Kurdish issue*, Routledge, 2011

Jongerden, Joost and Ahmet Hamdi Akkaya, 'The Kurdistan Workers Party and the New Left in Turkey: Analysis of the Revolutionary Movement in Turkey Through the PKK's Memorial Text on Haki Karer,' *European Journal of Turkish Studies*, 2012

Kieser, Hans-Lukas, 'Case study: Dersim Massacre 1937-1938,' *Online Encyclopedia of Mass Violence,* 2011

Kılıç, Abdullah and Ayça Örer, 'Devletin Zirvesi Dersim'de,' in: *Radikal*, 20 November 2011

Marcus, Aliza, *Blood and Belief,* New York University Press, 2007

Massicard, Elise, 'The Repression of the Koçgiri Rebellion, 1920-1921,' in: *Online Encyclopedia of Mass Violence*, 2009

Matur, Bejan, *Dağın Ardına Bakmak*, Timaş Yayınları, Istanbul, 2012

McDowall, David, *A Modern History of the Kurds*, I.B. Taurus & Co, New York, 2004

Meiselas, Susan, *Kurdistan: In the Shadow of History*, Random House, New York, 1997

Öcalan, Abdullah, *Prison Writings, The PKK and the Kurdish Question in the 21st Century*, Transmedia Publishing, London 2011

Senol, Nihat Hikmet, *Ape Musa'nın Küçük* Generalleri, Aram Yayınları, Istanbul, 2008

Stekelenburg, Jacqueline van et al, 'Politicized Identity,' in: *The Wiley-Blackwell Encyclopedia of Social and Political Movements,* 2013

Üngör, Uğur Ümit, *The Making of Modern Turkey: Nation and State in Eastern Anatolia 1913-1950*, Oxford University Press, 2011

And a huge number of newspaper articles from the online archives of the Dutch newspapers *De Volkskrant* and *NRC Handelsblad*, and newspapers published in Turkey, including *Özgür Gündem*, *Agos*, *Radikal*, *Milliyet*, *Hürriyet*, *Zaman*, *Vatan*, *Yeni Şafak*, *Sabah*, *Today's Zaman*, *Hürriyet Daily News*, and others.

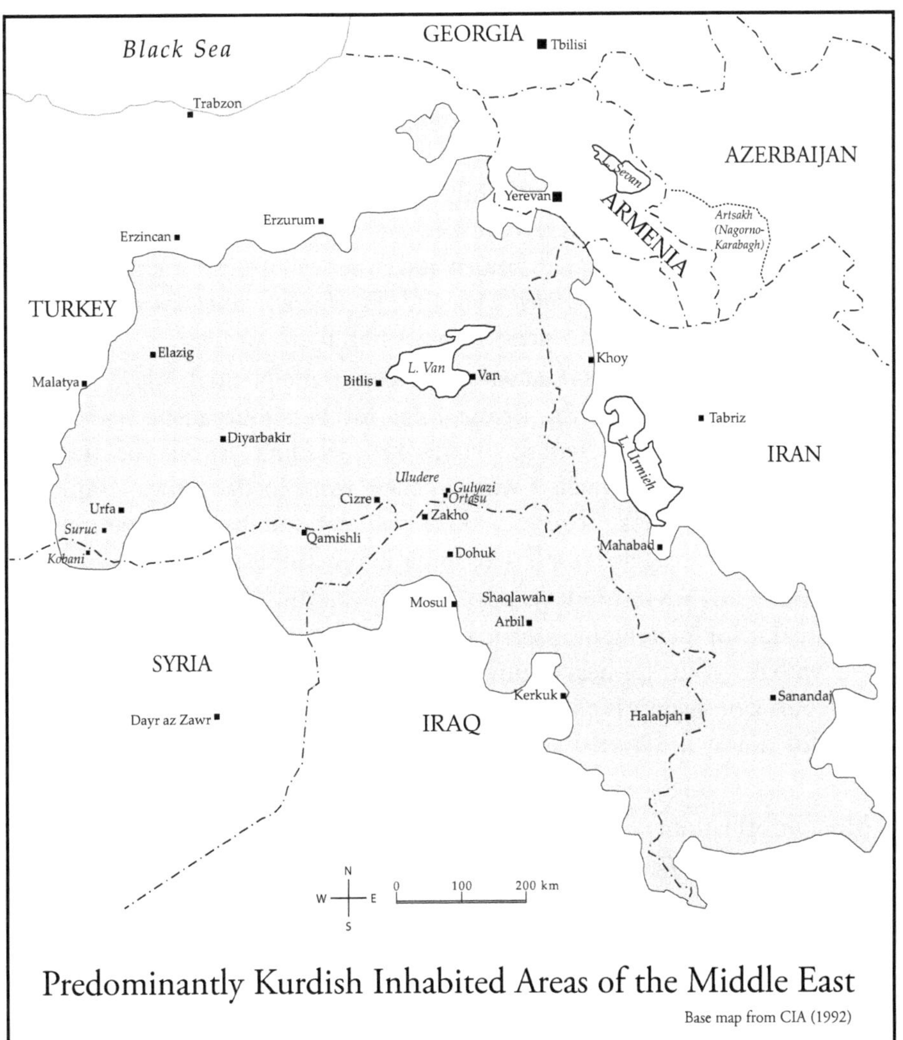

Predominantly Kurdish Inhabited Areas of the Middle East

Base map from CIA (1992)

About the Author

Fréderike Geerdink (1970, Hengelo, Netherlands) has been a journalist for 25 years. Since 2006 she is based in Turkey, and since 2012 she is the only foreign journalist permanently based in Diyarbakir, the biggest Kurdish city in the Southeast of Turkey. She writes and makes radio for a wide range of Dutch, Belgian, British and American media, among which *The Independent*, BBC, *Global Post* and *Al-Monitor*. She has a weekly column on the Turkish independent news portal *diken.com.tr*.

Her book *De jongens zijn dood* was published in the Netherlands in 2014 and was nominated for the Brusse Prize for best journalistic book of 2014. From the jury report: 'Fréderike Geerdink is one of those courageous Dutch journalists who do their work in dangerous conflict zones. (...) Her book became a both political and beautiful personal account of the struggle for self determination in Turkish Kurdistan.'

In January 2015, Geerdink was detained by the Anti Terrorism Police in Diyarbakir for 'making propaganda for a terrorist organisation'. In April, a Diyarbakir court for heavy crimes acquitted her. The state appealed and the court case against her is ongoing. Despite this intimidation, Geerdink decided to stay in Diyarbakir and continue her journalistic work.

More information:
www.twitter.com/fgeerdink
www.kurdishmatters.com
www.journalistinturkey.com
www.beaconreader.com/frederike-geerdink

www.ingramcontent.com/pod-product-compliance
Ingram Content Group UK Ltd.
Pitfield, Milton Keynes, MK11 3LW, UK
UKHW020142250726
13967UKWH00002B/814

9 781909 382190